SEAPLANES ALONG THE INSIDE PASSAGE

The Highs and Lows
of a Modern Bush Pilot

T0160679

GERRY BRUDER

ALASKA
NORTHWEST
BOOKS®

Cover image © 2014 Douglas Peebles / DanitaDelimont.com

Library of Congress Cataloging-in-Publication Data

Bruder, Gerry, 1944- author.
    [Northern flights]
    Seaplanes along the inside passage : the highs and lows of a modern bush pilot / Gerry Bruder.
       pages cm
    Originally published under the title Northern Flights, the adventures of an Alaskan bush pilot by Pruett Publishing, Boulder, Colorado, 1988.
    ISBN 978-0-88240-958-0 (pbk.)
    ISBN 978-0-88240-999-3 (e-book)
    1. Bruder, Gerry, 1944- 2. Air pilots—Alaska—Biography. I. Title.
    TL540.B7447A3 2014
    629.13092—dc23
    [B]
                                2013023868

Published by Alaska Northwest Books®
An imprint of

GRAPHIC ARTS
BOOKS®

P.O. Box 56118
Portland, Oregon 97238-6118
503-254-5591

www.graphicartsbooks.com

CONTENTS

PREFACE

The Sonoran Desert might seem a strange place to find a commercial seaplane pilot, but this arid region attracts me for a couple of reasons. I've spent many dreary winters in coastal Alaska and the Pacific Northwest, and like thousands of other weather-weary snowbirds I head south in the slow season to dry out, to shake off the cold. I also come here to get away from flying after a summer in the cockpit.

Get away, people ask? Isn't flying seaplanes an exciting, colorful way to make a living? Yes—with an asterisk. Although technology has modernized some flight operations in the boondocks, we still transport passengers and cargo to remote lakes, hamlets, and fishing lodges, just like the storied bush pilots of yore. We cruise low enough to spot wildlife and view scenery, and we manipulate the controls by hand rather than by computer. Instead of isolating our passengers behind locked cockpit doors, we fraternize with them as in an automobile. Miles from civilization, we make our own decisions when the unexpected arises.

A passenger observing from the right-hand seat as we land and take off and taxi like a boat will often comment, "You have the most interesting job in the world!"

But here's the asterisk: Just as the desert is a meteorological antithesis of that coastal world up north, the romance of seaplanes has a contrary alter ego. Rain, fog, and gusty winds regularly harass routes and destination. (We hear passengers express envy only in good weather.) Crashes have claimed a score of my fellow pilots—many far more experienced than I at the time. Pressure to complete the mission, long hours, back-to-back flights, missed lunches, mediocre pay, limited career advancement, and troublesome passengers ratchet up the tension. This is the somber side of commercial seaplane flying, its Mr. Hyde personality.

Of course, challenges are inherent, unavoidable ingredients in any adventurous activity. Inevitably, though, the stress drains the spirit and dilutes the romance. Most commercial seaplane pilots move on after a few years, to the airlines or a more lucrative, nonflying profession. Some of us can't seem to stay away. In a fit of disenchantment, I quit just a year after starting my first seaplane job.

6 SEAPLANES ALONG THE INSIDE PASSAGE

Nostalgia soon lured me back. The cycle continued. One burnout took me to the New York metropolitan area for four years (two of them in the heart of Manhattan), as if a radical geographical and cultural change could hush the faraway call of the Sirens. Each new life promised a conventional future. But my work would gradually become meaningless drudgery, my surroundings uninspiring monotony. Like an ex-drinker remembering the euphoria but not the hangover, I would start selectively reminiscing: the roar of an engine in morning mist, mountain goats clinging to cliffs along a fjord, the pungent smell of the sea. . . .

Then, relapse.

Eventually, I stopped resisting and surrendered to a career in seaplanes. To handle burnouts, I took up RVing and embarked on long road trips during the slow off-season. One year my wife and I spent three months traveling around the country, exploring national parks and other touristy places. The Sonoran Desert became a favorite destination, both for its beauty and recreation and for its magical ability to refresh the spirit. Just as the low humidity here sharpens the night heavens, a hike in the desert somehow brings clarity to introspection about goals, values, and choices. The desert was the perfect retreat for the soul of a seaplane pilot.

Our escapes to the desert grew longer. Now I'm semiretired, a snowbird, a summer-only pilot. A modest but adequate financial situation would let me walk away from the cockpit completely. But gazing at the dust devils dancing among the saguaros, thinking about things, I know that even after more than twenty-four-thousand hours of water flying, I'm not yet ready. The Sirens whisper on.

ooooo

A few notes on terminology. Although I use "seaplane" and "floatplane" interchangeably in *Seaplanes along the Inside Passage*, the words are not synonymous. A seaplane is any aircraft designed to operate from the water, while a floatplane is a seaplane with floats, or pontoons. "Flying boat" is a seaplane whose hull provides flotation, like the famous four-engine clippers in Pan American's fleet during the 1930s and '40s. "Amphibian" is an airplane that can operate from both the water and the land; wheels in the floats or the hull are retracted for water phases.

I also use the terms "bush pilot" and "bush flying," even though the Federal Aviation Administration long ago replaced "bush" with the more dignified, regulated-sounding "air taxi." Air services that provide transportation to outlying areas in small aircraft today are indeed more scrutinized and accountable than in earlier decades, and seaplane flying is safer and more efficient. Yet "bush" in an aviation context is still prominent in the informal public lexicon and realistically evokes the colorful side of seaplanes.

Finally, I support liberal positions on current social issues, including full equality for women in pay and opportunities. The female seaplane pilots I've worked with were every bit as capable and reliable as their male counterparts. So use of the traditional editorial "he" in *Seaplanes along the Inside Passage* should not be construed as male chauvinism; it's simply preferable, in my opinion, to a repetitive, clumsy "he/she" or the fashionable but sloppy, grammatically incorrect "they" as a pronoun for a singular subject. I hope readers will recognize the universal, nonsexist intent of "he."

ooooo

For a previous book profiling retired Alaskan bush pilots (*Heroes of the Horizon*), I interviewed twenty-nine subjects. Several told me that burnout had robbed them of all nostalgia for their flying days. I included such comments in the original manuscript, but my editor deleted them, explaining that readers would frown at an old-timer's flying career ending on a down note.

And over the years some of my magazine articles on seaplane flying have brought criticism for telling too much of the inside story. "You're going to scare passengers away and sic the FAA on us," one air service owner lamented, as if public relations should outweigh journalistic candor. Nonetheless, *Seaplanes along the Inside Passage* neither whitewashes nor embellishes, although in places I use pseudonyms to avoid distressing or embarrassing individuals or their survivors. For most of my flying career I kept a detailed journal of events, destinations, and thoughts, and my goal is to present an accurate, frank description of commercial seaplane flying—the highs and the lows, the glamour and the grind. This is also a memoir about how a greenhorn from Connecticut became a veteran bush pilot, and his ongoing love/hate relationship with the business. Some current and former seaplane pilots will have different impressions and experiences to share, but none can deny that bush flying involves extremes of emotion. Often on the same flight . . .

Chapter 1

NO WOLVES IN THE NEWSROOM

Eight hundred feet below, gusts whip around the trailers and corrugated tin buildings of the Cape Pole logging camp and fan out across the harbor in black microbursts, foam spraying off the whitecaps. Twenty-five, maybe thirty knots. I grimace in disgust. Two hours earlier the Cape Pole camp manager had radioed our dispatcher in Ketchikan that the wind was only ten to fifteen knots. "It's not too bad," he reported. "You guys have come out here in worse stuff than this."

Bush residents try to give accurate weather reports. But an observer peering out the window of a warm, dry, camp operations office usually perceives conditions to be more favorable than does a pilot circling overhead within the elements. In addition, when they want transportation, bush residents tend to minimize the weather, aware that once a pilot has flown all the way out from town he'll often grudgingly land in conditions that would have kept him from taking off had he known about them.

Now I face that flying dilemma known as the marginal situation: conditions foul enough to pose serious concerns, yet not quite foul enough to make proceeding downright foolhardy.

Once, twice, three times I circle in the turbulence, squinting through the rain-streaked windshield, assessing, calculating. A green van moves slowly down the causeway below and stops at the top of the ramp by the seaplane dock. Inside, I know, seven passengers and a driver are watching the de Havilland Beaver intently, urging me to land.

Marginal situations have confronted me repeatedly recently. Mid-November is usually a stormy period in southeastern Alaska, and this season Mother Nature obviously has no intention of breaking tradition. Day after day—since forever, it seems—gales have howled in from the adjacent North Pacific, lashing the islands, the forest, the mountains, the communities. Some days none of the company's aircraft have turned a propeller. On others, our usual destinations have been marginally workable.

Cape Pole, by Sumner Strait on the west side of Kosciusko Island ninety miles northwest of my base in Ketchikan, has received no air service for almost a week now. Like most communities in Southeast, as Alaskans call this remote, 500-mile-long archipelago, the camp is accessible only by air or sea. Thus, the cabin behind me is stuffed with overdue mail sacks, cartons of groceries, choker cables, chain-saw blades, cases of beer, boxes of disposable diapers, replacement parts for machinery, and other cargo. In the van below my passengers wait impatiently for a ride to town. Their thoughts focus on shopping in stores or consulting a dentist or just escaping from the boondocks for a few days—not on the hazards of landing a floatplane in a gusty crosswind amid jagged reefs or taking off again with a heavy load.

Of course, I can avoid the hazards by retreating to town and reporting that conditions were clearly unsafe. But avoiding my conscience would be impossible; conditions are not clearly unsafe. I am a bush pilot. My responsibility is to transport people and cargo in the wilderness. Stormy weather is part of the job.

Gritting my teeth, I throttle back, lower the flaps, and line up for a cross-wind approach along the rock-free corridor by the shoreline.

"Ketchikan, Seven-Five Romeo, landing Cape Pole," I announce monotonically into the microphone.

A moment later the dispatcher's distant voice crackles in my headphones: "Roger, Seven-Five Romeo, landing Cape Pole."

Gusts jolt the Beaver like a giant's flicking finger as we descend, and I whip the control wheel left and right continuously to level the wings. I must also alternately jam the throttle forward and yank it back to counter the downdrafts and updrafts that shove the airplane around.

Five hundred feet, three hundred, one hundred. I am still uncommitted; I can still apply climb power and bank away. Remember, my mind warns, you not only have to get down, you have to take off crosswind with some thirteen hundred pounds of additional weight. I hold the Beaver off as long as possible to avoid the rougher water out from the camp and to squeeze a few more seconds for consideration. Then pilings, rocks, and trees loom too close in the windshield, and the option vanishes.

The floats thump onto the waves. The Beaver bounces heavily twice before shuddering off the step, the prop snarling from saltwater spray. As I taxi in, the airplane sways drunkenly in the choppy water.

At the dock I cut the engine, and two rain suit–clad men from the van grab the wing line and strut while I scramble out to tie the float's mooring line to a cleat on the dock.

"Howdy," I mutter. "Beautiful weather."

"Glad to see you!" one of the men answers. Six other people emerge from the van at the top of the ramp, hunching against the driving rain. They pull suitcases, handbags, and a couple of sacks of mail from the vehicle and lug them down the ramp.

With one of the loggers on the float and another on the dock forming a relay line, I hand out item after item until at last the cabin is empty. The men then pass up the baggage and mail sacks, which I cram into the luggage compartment and under and behind the rear, hammock-style row of seats.

"I'll turn you out," the van driver says moments later, when the four men, two women, and child are strapped into their seats. He clutches the tip of the tail's left horizontal stabilizer while I slam the cabin door, untie the line, and climb in through the cockpit door. The nose of the Beaver immediately weather-vanes from the dock in the crosswind, the tail serving as a pivot. I start the engine and the driver releases the tail. As we taxi out, moisture from wet clothing fogs the windshield and all six side windows. I hold my door open for circulation and pass back the roll of paper towels, asking the passengers not to use their hands to wipe away the fog.

"Didn't think we was ever gonna get to town again," comments the man in the right front seat as he rotates a towel across his window. He grins, showing tobacco-stained teeth. Rain droplets glisten on his beard.

Flaps, takeoff position. Prop control, high RPM. Mixture control, full rich. Fuel selector, front tank. Elevator trim, set for an aft center of gravity.

"Everybody have a seat belt?" I ask. A rush of nods and smiles follows.

"Okay, let's go to Ketchikan."

My heart thumping, I pull up the water-rudder retraction handle and push the throttle to the redline at thirty-seven inches of manifold pressure. The idling of the 450-horsepower Pratt & Whitney engine deepens to a roar. As the Beaver lunges into the waves and struggles onto the step with a constant shuddering, a sense of doom engulfs me. The old airplane cannot possibly survive such a pounding with this load. Surely this time I have pushed too much. Transfixed by the waves and adjacent reefs, my mind sees flailing arms in the water by a broken, capsized airplane.

While the waves jolt my buttocks, the wind hammers the airplane from the side, jostling the tail and right wing. I fight back with aileron and rudder, an acrobat swinging a balancing pole on a wiggling tightrope. On and on we thump across the waves.

Then, the vibrating through the airframe begins to diminish, and I sense a lighter feel on the controls. The wings are gathering lift as the Beaver slowly picks up speed. I find myself coaxing the airplane in a whisper:

"Come on, baby, come on, come on, fly!"

The floats are skimming the crests now. At last we stagger into the air. Instantly the crosswind jerks the Beaver sideways, and I must crab some thirty degrees into it to maintain a straight course. Turbulence shakes and rolls the Beaver, but the floatplane plows doggedly upward. When we reach five hundred feet, I turn inland over the clear-cut stumps, scratch, and logging roads of Kosciusko Island, dodging frequent patches of scud. I notice that the logger next to me grips the bottom of his seat. He is no longer grinning. I don't have to turn around to know the other passengers are also holding on.

"Ketchikan, Seven-Five Romeo, Cape Pole inbound."

"Roger, Seven-Five Romeo, Cape Pole for Ketchikan. How is it out there?"

"Windy and rainy."

As it was yesterday, and the day before, as it will undoubtedly be tomorrow and the following day. Suddenly, I realize how weary I am of the gusty wind and the relentless rain and the dirty gray scud racing by just overhead. Weary of marginal situations and the pressure they bring. Weary of the long, long summer days, when I take off for yet another flight while normal people are sitting down to dinner. Weary of floatplanes and wilderness and bush people.

Gone is the sense of romance that compelled me to leave newspaper reporting for bush flying. Like a disillusioned infantryman, I now feel only battle fatigue. Perhaps the time has come to get out. With a degree in journalism and three years' experience on a daily paper, I should be able to find another job. The country has hundreds of newspapers and magazines. I am still young. I can tell prospective editors the adventure is out of my blood and that now I'm ready—no, eager—to resume my career.

My timing for such escape is perfect. Business has slowed considerably in the past few weeks with the stormy autumn weather and the end of seasonal industries like tourism and commercial fishing. I can give notice as soon as we land in Ketchikan and be excused from duty by next week—maybe even the end of this week. Tonight I'll draft a resume and prepare a portfolio of my clippings.

The decision made, I spend the next few minutes thinking about working behind a desk in a white-collar shirt and tie in a warm, dry, secure newsroom. The daydream makes my present world seem even more hostile when I return to it. The Beaver is over Sea Otter Sound now, plodding along at a groundspeed of just seventy knots against the stiff headwind. Below, foaming waves churn the water into a maelstrom that would tear the airplane apart in a forced landing. A mile to the southwest, swells surge rhythmically onto the rocks of little Whale Head Island and explode in huge white sheets that shoot into the air as if trying to slap the base of the overcast.

I can now discern the foggy outline of Heceta Island ahead. As we gradually approach its hills and mountains, the buffeting intensifies. I crossed Heceta through Warm Chuck Inlet on the way out, but a shower now casts an impenetrable curtain of gloom across that shortcut; I will have to follow the shoreline around. When we reach the edge of the shower, thickening rain begins pummeling the windshield, and the cabin darkens as if we've flown into dusk. I descend to three hundred feet, then two hundred, and turn east to parallel the shoreline. Rocky islets, nameless coves, and stands of trees slide by like ghosts a few yards off the right wingtip. I throttle back to low cruise power and extend the flaps to slow down.

"Wipe off your side window," I tell the bearded logger next to me, rubbing my paper towel across the inside of the windshield. But the air vents have long since dispelled the fog on the windows; the misty gray murk outside cannot be lightened with a paper towel.

Near the eastern tip of Heceta, islets begin appearing off the left wingtip. I lean forward against my seat belt, squinting. I have followed this shoreline in similar conditions before, but familiarity doesn't make threading an airplane through a foggy maze of islets at low altitude any more comfortable. A wrong turn, a momentary loss of visibility in a concentrated downpour....

Now the mass of Tuxekan Island materializes ahead. I turn down the channel separating the two islands, then southwest toward Prince of Wales Island. Near a fading pictograph ancient Tlingit Indians painted on a rock wall, a vicious downdraft pops the microphone off its hook on the instrument panel. My right-seat passenger's arms flail in alarm.

Visibility here drops to a quarter mile. I cannot yet pick out Prince of Wales, although I know the 140-mile-long island lies just off the left wing. I descend to fifty feet so I can chop the throttle and land if necessary. But in a few seconds the island dutifully forms in the windshield, and I begin following the Prince of Wales shoreline. Driftwood jumbled at the high-tide line, part of an old skiff, a marten scampering back into the forest, dark little niches, seagulls pecking at a dead salmon, and other vignettes catch the edge of my vision as the Beaver lumbers along the rocky beach.

Not until we reach San Alberto Bay does the visibility return to two or three miles. I increase the power, retract the flaps, and climb back to the base of the clouds. Eight hundred feet is a low cruising altitude for an airplane, even a bush plane; aircraft in the landing pattern at an airport typically maintain a thousand feet. But after twenty minutes of wave-skimming, eight hundred feet seems luxuriously high, a dollar bill to an indigent panhandling for coins.

Suddenly I smell the nauseating odor of vomit and glance behind. Sitting in the middle seat of the rear row, the child, a girl of about ten, is doubled over, her head between her knees. A woman beside her holds her shoulders.

"There's a sick sack in the pocket in back of each seat," I yell, unable to see whether she already has one. "Whoever has the roll of paper towels, please pass it to her." If I am lucky, the girl has anticipated airsickness and prepared for it with an open bag. If not.... Bush flying affords no flight attendants, no catering or clean-up crews. Larger air services employ linemen, or dock hands, to help with chores, but often in this business the pilot loads freight, pumps leakage water from the floats, fuels, empties the ashtrays, polishes the windows, and, whenever necessary, mops up after airsick passengers.

In a newsroom, I won't even have to empty my own wastebasket. "Another forty-five minutes and we'll be in town," I shout over my shoulder to reassure the passengers. Silently, I add the proviso, "if we get through the pass." The Harris

River Valley—"the pass" to Ketchikan pilots—is the normal route across Prince of Wales, which separates Ketchikan and the majority of bush communities in this part of Southeast. It was marginally open on the flight to Cape Pole. I cannot see far enough ahead through the rain and scud to tell whether conditions there have improved or deteriorated, but we'll soon find out.

We rumble past the Tlingit village of Klawock, a mishmash of old dilapidated buildings, new government clapboard ones, a cannery, and fishing boats. Two minutes later we cross the outlet of Klawock Lake. I curse when I see that a wall of rainfog obscures the upper half of the six-mile-long lake, where the Harris River pass begins. We are down to six hundred feet when we reach the lake's head. Too low. I circle, peering into the pass, hoping to spot a hole. Nothing. Wait! Part of a hill seems visible where the pass makes a dogleg, about a half mile in. If so, that's enough visibility to go in and take a look. There will be room by the hill to turn around and fly back out if the valley beyond the dogleg is clobbered with clouds.

I circle again for another look but fail to resight the hill. A third circle: There! The hill, if it is indeed a hill, appears only from an angle by the north side of the lake, a darkish apparition within the misty curtain. An illusion? If I take the bait and find dense fog or heavy rain instead of a hill, we'll be trapped; at six hundred feet the slopes along the upper end of the pass before the dogleg leave too little room in which to turn, and of course there is no place to land in the trees below. I circle one more time. Another marginal situation. No, less than marginal. This is the best pass, but not the only one.

I fly back down the lake and turn south. We bounce past the fishing community of Craig, which occupies a small island connected by a man-made peninsula to Prince of Wales, and then follow the shoreline through a downpour in a fifteen-mile curve into Trocadero Bay. Above the head of the bay, a saddle in a heavily logged ridge leads to Twelvemile Arm on the east side of Prince of Wales, from which Ketchikan is a relatively easy over-water flight. The saddle lies a few hundred feet higher than the Harris River pass, but sometimes it offers better weather.

Not today. Solid clouds hold us relentlessly to three hundred feet. We cannot leave the water, much less climb up the slope to peek over the saddle. There are several other passes to the south, near the Haida Indian village of Hydaburg, but clouds also blockade the valley we would have to cross to reach them. To follow a water route to the Hydaburg area would mean a long, circuitous flight through several clusters of islets and narrow channels close to the open sea, where the wind would be even stronger. If we negotiate that gauntlet and find the southern passes also closed, not enough fuel will remain to return for another look at the Harris River pass. Aviation gas weighs six pounds a gallon; at Ketchikan I pumped just thirty minutes' reserve fuel into the tanks knowing I'd have a heavy takeoff from Cape Pole.

I throttle back to twenty-eight inches of manifold pressure and 1,750 RPM to reduce fuel consumption, then bank 180 degrees and work my way back toward Klawock Lake, calculating. At that power setting the engine burns about twenty-two gallons an hour. The rear and center tanks are empty, while the front one contains no more than twenty gallons. We are about to dig into our safety margin.

"Ketchikan, Seven-Five Romeo."

"Seven-Five Romeo, Ketchikan, go ahead."

"Peggy, we're by Klawock and having some trouble getting through. Has anybody else made it lately, or is anyone on the other side trying?"

"Negative. We're holding due to weather on your side. Keep us advised."

High-frequency radio waves can bend around obstructions and sometimes reach a receiver hundreds of miles away. Thus, the mountains are unable to isolate us from Peggy Acorn's somber voice. I picture the twenty-five-year-old brunette in her tiny dispatching cubicle, sipping a cup of coffee and chatting with one or more pilots but ever aware of who is en route to what destination and when he should be back. We are "her" pilots. She dispatches us into the elements to wilderness places she knows only by name or photo. For that authority she assumes the responsibility for making sure we return safely, or at least are accounted for satisfactorily. Although she can do nothing to help me cross Prince of Wales except relay pertinent reports from other pilots, I know she flies with us vicariously and will not go home until we land safely. We are not totally alone out here.

Before trying the Harris River pass one last time, I decide to continue past Klawock for a quick look at a river valley to the northeast. It leads ultimately to Clarence Strait on the east side of Prince of Wales, where we would have water beneath us the rest of the way home. It's a low-elevation but long, circuitous route; using it is like taking miles of side streets when the interstate is jammed. The visibility in that direction is not encouraging, but we have just enough fuel if things open up right away. Under the circumstances, it's worth a peek.

After six miles we reach Big Salt Lake, and the visibility is getting worse. We cannot afford to probe farther. As I bank for a 180-degree turn, I look for the wreckage of an Air Force EC-47Q—a military version of the famous Douglas DC-3 airliner. There it is, lying like a beached whale in a marsh by the lake, testimony to another pilot's desperate situation. On October 25, 1968, the twin-engine airplane left McChord Air Force Base in Washington State for refueling at Elmendorf Air Force Base in Anchorage. Its ultimate destination on the seventy-five-hundred-mile journey was Southeast Asia, where it would participate in the Vietnam War on reconnaissance missions. But a double-engine failure over Prince of Wales forced the crew to make an emergency landing here. Despite its size, the airplane looks insignificant against the backdrop, even at our low altitude, and its faded olive and beige camouflage paint scheme blends well with the environment. The other passengers undoubtedly don't notice it. I know just where to look.

As we approach the Harris River pass again, a hand taps me on the shoulder. "I can't take this anymore," says the woman in the right seat of the middle row. Homely and overweight, she stares at me with wide-eyed desperation. She holds on to the top of the seat in front of her.

Well, ma'am, I too am feeling tension from the long battle with the weather, and I sympathize with you. But if I could divert to someplace where the wind would kick us less persistently and the rain and fog were less intense, we'd be there now. Unfortunately, southern California is a little beyond our fuel capacity. I could help you relax by not circling so close to the trees, but then we'd have less of a chance of finding a hole in the clouds and we'd have to spend the night out here in the boondocks instead of in town, where there are lots of people and lights and stores. Besides, you've flown in floatplanes before in this country. You ought to know by now that the risk is just something you have to tolerate, like the weather itself. If it's any consolation, I've also known fear. I've been so scared I've pleaded, "Oh dear god! Oh dear god!" repeatedly under my breath, and afterward wouldn't pick up the microphone because my passengers might have noticed the trembling of my hand. Rest assured that I don't want to be crushed and torn by the Beaver's five thousand pounds of metal any more than you do. Like you, I've got a lot to look forward to; I'm going to resume my career in journalism, and I want to do so in one piece. Also rest assured that I've been here before. I know how close to fly to the clouds and trees to make progress or to see if progress is possible and yet avoid that sudden, violent, fiery cessation of flight that pilots and passengers alike experience many times in the mind. Let's try not to consider the fact that several fellow pilots far more seasoned than I experienced such violence in reality.

I force a smile to mask my own tension and turn my head sideways. "Don't worry. This isn't much fun, but I'm not going to fly into any granite clouds, and the turbulence can't hurt a Beaver. When we take you back to camp we'll arrange for some sunshine and blue sky."

The woman smiles weakly and settles acquiescently back in her seat. The front fuel gauge now indicates only enough fuel to reach town, plus about fifteen minutes. That means one more try at the Harris River. If the pass is still impenetrable, we will have to land at Klawock and wait for better conditions—which, according to the Ketchikan Flight Service Station forecast this morning, are two days away. Instead of fire and dungeons, maybe hell is spending eternity trying to cross a stormy Prince of Wales Island in a floatplane.

The darkish apparition deep in the mist of the dogleg still beckons, and the ceiling seems a little higher, maybe seven hundred feet now. Heavy rain wouldn't have stayed in the same spot. I lower the flaps, snuggle as close to the north slope as possible, and enter. For a few moments adrenaline races through my veins as I struggle to see into the wall ahead, wondering whether I have brought us into a foggy cul-de-sac. Downdrafts swirling over the peaks hidden in the clouds above hammer the Beaver, and behind me I hear someone shriek.

Then, the unmistakable outline of a hill forms in front. I breathe deeply. I follow the dogleg around the hill and, still staying to the side for room to turn, glance down the valley. Three-quarters of a mile, maybe a full mile. Okay so far. But the clouds begin sloping toward the surface after a couple of minutes, and when we reach the mouth of the river they intercept the treetops. I curse to myself, bank to turn, and immediately spot salt water through a small hole. We're home. Now we can follow the shoreline at wave-top level the final thirty-five miles to town, if necessary.

But it is not. As if the weather gods have conceded defeat, this side of Prince of Wales shows us a gentler world than we have endured the last hour and a half. Visibility here balloons to ten miles in a mere drizzle from a ceiling of at least fifteen hundred feet. The wind produces only a light chop. In the distance the hills along Kasaan Peninsula look soft and green, scattered puffs of fog clinging like wispy fingers to their slopes. I point the nose on a direct course for town and climb to a thousand feet.

"Ketchikan, Seven-Five Romeo, we're through."

"Roger, Seven-Five Romeo, see you shortly."

Then, over my shoulder, I announce: "Another twenty-five minutes and we'll be on the water."

That good news, along with the conspicuously improved weather, transforms the atmosphere among the passengers. The bearded man in the right front seat lights a cigarette; chatter emanates from the cabin behind. Relieved myself, savoring the thought that soon I will never again have to fly floatplanes in the rain, fog, and wind, I too feel an impulse to talk.

"How much longer is Cape Pole going to operate this fall?" I ask the logger.

"Oh, that kinda depends on the weather," he answers through a mouthful of smoke. "We'll keep going as long as we can, till it snows. Then we'll pack up till spring. Man, that was some ride, huh!"

"Piece of cake."

The exchange fails to develop into a conversation, and he returns to his thoughts. My mind puts me back at a typewriter in a newsroom. Which publications shall I approach first? Free now from the exigencies of weather flying, I ponder that question while absently sightseeing.

No bush pilot tires of studying the country, because even along familiar routes it always shows change, subtle or overt. The lazy stream of yesterday is a rushing, spilling freshet from the rain today. A formerly unremarkable hillside is now scarred with a brand new landslide, uprooted hemlock trees piled at the bottom of the swath. Fall colors seem a little brighter in the bushes along Old Frank's Lake.

And a muskeg meadow near the mouth of Coal Bay now contains several foreign objects.

Blacktail deer. I spot deer on most flights and ordinarily pay little attention to them. Wildlife always thrills passengers, however. These seven have had a rough flight; taking a minute or two to give them a close-up look at the deer will be good public relations. We can spare the fuel.

"There are some deer down there right in the open," I yell over my shoulder. "Anybody want to take a look at them?"

The passengers nod their approval, and one man begins rummaging in a travel bag, presumably for a camera. I throttle back and descend, circling wide to come in low for a close view.

"They'll be on the left side," I call back. "One look's all we'll have before they dart into the forest."

The deer are on the nose now, about a quarter-mile ahead. I count four, clustered in the center of the muskeg by some jack pine. I squint to see whether any have antlers. Then, with a start I realize I am looking not at deer but at wolves.

"Wolves!" the logger next to me exclaims at the same moment, lightly jabbing me on the shoulder.

"Hey, they're wolves!" I tell the rest of the passengers. Those on the far right side of the cabin unfasten their seat belts and crowd with the others by the windows on the left. The wolves, three with dirty brown-and-white coats and the fourth with a grayish black one, stand by what appears to be the carcass of a deer. As we rumble by they look up, tongues hanging out, resembling four big friendly huskies. I circle around again. This time as we approach the muskeg their rumps are disappearing into the sanctuary of the forest. I fly by the spot and bank steeply, hoping to look straight down on them, but the thickly bunched trees have swallowed them.

No matter. The animals have posed for one clear, stirring view. While wolf sightings are routine in the open country of the Alaskan interior, they're uncommon in heavily forested Southeast. So far from the cockpit here, I have spotted hundreds of deer, mountain goats, and black bears, but my previous wolf sightings number just two, each a shadowy glimpse in patchy woods. The cagey, elusive wolf—arch villain of folklore, enigmatic symbol of wilderness, perennial source of controversy between conservationists and ranchers. And, for me, a timely reminder that bush flying is not all hassle and stress, that it brings plenty of delightful rewards, as well.

As I climb and resume a beeline for Ketchikan, I realize I am smiling.

In Ketchikan I arranged for a vacation, and a week later I flew commercially to my home on the East Coast. There I strolled along a mostly deserted, windswept beach on Long Island Sound, pondering my future, wondering if I was really ready for a more conventional lifestyle. Refreshed, I returned to Southeast, determined to continued flying, at least for a while.

After all, there are no wolves to sight in a newsroom.

Chapter 2

THE COCKPIT BECKONS

Someone arriving by sea at Ketchikan, Alaska, usually doesn't notice floatplanes right away. First—if the newcomer is fortunate enough to arrive on a nice day—he admires the scenery: snowcapped, three-thousand-foot Deer Mountain behind town dwarfs everything else and automatically draws the eye. Next the newcomer observes that this community of eleven thousand is long and narrow, like a reclining basketball player. Houses that extend inland seem to cling precariously to steep forested slopes, often with long wooden staircases rather than streets for access. The cluttered waterfront that stretches along the length of the town then attracts the newcomer's attention. It is now, as the vessel draws closer, that he notices the floatplanes mixed among piers, docks, pilings, breakwaters, and every type of boat from skiff to oceangoing trawler.

I had never seen a seaplane before coming to Ketchikan in late 1971 to work as a reporter for the *Ketchikan Daily News*. As the state ferry *Taku* sliced through the waters of Tongass Narrows toward Ketchikan's ferry landing, I counted more than a dozen floatplanes tied up at docks along the waterfront. Several others sat out of the water on wooden ramps. One orange-and-white floatplane was taxiing out for takeoff. Grimacing against the brisk November wind on my face, I watched as the floatplane roared down the Narrows like a speedboat and lifted ponderously into the air, spray trailing from each float. Seagulls in its path flapped wildly to get out of the way.

The reason for so many floatplanes in this part of the world had already become evident. Early that morning I had pulled into the port city of Prince Rupert, British Columbia, ninety miles to the south, after an eight-day drive from my home in Connecticut. All that remained of my journey then was a six-hour ferry voyage up the Inside Passage to southeastern Alaska, the five-hundred-mile-long chain of islands and narrow strip of mainland that extend like a pan-handle from the main bulk of the state.

Exhausted but excited, I had spent much of this final leg out on deck sightseeing. On the mainland and many of the surrounding islands, huge mountains

Juneau, Alaska's capital, lies in the center of Southeast and, like Ketchikan, is accessible only by air or sea. Many residents of Interior Alaska have long objected to Juneau's isolation; statewide referendums in 1960, 1962, and 1974 sought to move the capital to a site more convenient to the population centers of Anchorage and Fairbanks. The 1974 measure passed by a margin of 56.7 percent, and two years later voters selected Willow, sixty miles north of Anchorage, as the new seat. In a 1982 referendum, however, voters decided against authorizing the expenditure of the $2.8 billion planners estimated the move would cost, effectively negating the 1974 action.

rose sharply from the sea to fade into a high overcast. A lush green forest covered every piece of terrain except for scattered muskeg patches and rocky slopes. In places, the trees or cliffs descended right down to the waterline. Where beaches did show, they were strewn with rocks and driftwood.

The pilot of a wheel-equipped airplane would have had trouble finding even an emergency landing site in such a rugged environment. With a seaplane, however, a pilot could casually touch down on the countless coves, bays, inlets, fjords, and other natural "runways" I had noticed. The major, far-flung communities here undoubtedly had airports, but otherwise this majestic archipelago was indeed seaplane country.

Nonetheless, I was unimpressed. A licensed private pilot since my freshman year in college, I had earned my wings as a landlubber, hitchhiking out to the local airport for lessons twice a week. Now I scoffed as the orange-and-white floatplane disappeared around an island with those ugly, cumbersome-looking pontoons hanging down like silver torpedoes. Real airplanes had wheels.

In any event, I was here not for flying but to experience Alaska. The forty-ninth state had long intrigued me, and after graduating with a journalism degree I had written every daily newspaper in the state—all six of them—asking for a job. Only the *Ketchikan Daily News* had offered one. I had been surprised and a bit disappointed to see on a map how far south Ketchikan lay in relation to the rest of the state, at the end of a geographical tail. Alaska to me meant the storybook land of the midnight sun, dogsleds, and Mount McKinley (now renamed Denali). Ketchikan was far removed from all that. It was like wanting to work in New York City and getting a job way out on the southern fringe of Brooklyn instead of in Big Apple Manhattan. At least now I had a foot in Alaska.

Ketchikan may have been an Alaskan footnote, but it lacked not for charm. The narrow, twisty, hilly downtown streets recalled a miniature San Francisco, and some of the sidewalks were built of planks. Creek Street, actually a boardwalk along the banks of Ketchikan Creek, was a former red-light district that once had twenty bordellos. The Frontier Bar had sawdust on the floor. Because of the prodigious rainfall—an average of 162 inches a year—many residents routinely wore brown foot-high rubber boots nicknamed "Ketchikan sneakers." The town's official mascot was the "rainbird," a gangly, Daffy Duck–like cartoon character often depicted standing in a puddle with a sullen expression. There was the Rainbird Bar, Rainbird Drilling, the Rainbird Flyers (a model-airplane club), the Rainbird Flower & Garden Shop, and Rainbird Rubber Stamps. Outside the Ketchikan Visitors Bureau office on the downtown dock stood a humorous, twenty-foot-high rain gauge that made several sage observations, including this one about Deer Mountain: "If you can't see the top, you know it's raining. If you can see the top, you know it's gonna rain." In the 1970s, the chamber of commerce sponsored rain pools in which participants would compete for prizes by estimating the next month's precipitation.

Despite my disdain for seaplanes, I inherited the aviation beat as the only licensed pilot on the newspaper's four-person editorial staff. After a few weeks of popping in at the six air services along the waterfront, I knew most of the town's twenty-five-odd pilots. There was the legendary Ed Todd of Todd's Air Service, who flew in short pants and bare feet in weather that grounded other pilots. Dixie Jewett, Todd's assistant, was the only female commercial pilot in town; according to Todd, she was better than most of the men. I also met Ketchikan Air's Don Ross, who had become a World War II fighter pilot before he was old enough to vote. An avid prospector in his spare time, Ross was credited with making the first floatplane landing on a glacier in the Ketchikan area. Quiet, bespectacled Pete Cessnun, owner of Webber Air, held the distinction of being the second American called for duty after the draft was instituted in 1940; a vegetable clerk in a Kansas City cafeteria at the time, he and fellow employees were gathered around the radio when President Roosevelt read his number. Retired Bud Bodding of the old Ellis Air Lines had the nickname "Father Goose" because he had logged so much time in the twin-engine Grumman Goose amphibian; he had stopped counting at twelve thousand hours fifteen years earlier. Thanks to savvy and keen vision, Webber Air chief pilot Herman Ludwigsen had a knack for finding missing airplanes. One discovery had earned him a $10,000 reward from the victim's family.

A hearty joie de vivre radiated from these and other pilots; before long I began lingering on my rounds after collecting notes and photos to watch them come and go, or to eavesdrop on their chitchat between flights. Some of their anecdotes made me gasp, others made me laugh. Each added another hue to the brightening array of colors on my image of bush flying.

One day Earl Lahmeyer, a tall, studious-looking partner in Ketchikan Air Service, invited me to ride along on a flight to the Tsimshian Indian village of Metlakatla, seventeen miles away on Annette Island. For him it was a routine flight; for me, mesmerizing sensations: the smell of the sea and the screeching of gulls at the dock, the Cessna 185's gentle swaying during taxi, the collage of passing coves, fishing boats, and forested hillsides as we zipped along a few hundred feet above the water. Two days later, stocky, arrogant Carl "Red" Jackson, owner of Revilla Flying Service, also offered me an unoccupied seat on a flight to Metlakatla. Gone now was any lingering prejudice toward floatplanes.

(In the summer of 1973 Jackson and five passengers would die in a fiery crash on Annette Island en route to Metlakatla. A few years later, Lahmeyer would die in a crash in British Columbia after leaving the Rivers Inlet fishing resort.)

Writing my weekly aviation column and making an occasional flight as an observer left me hungry. My own chance to fly floatplanes resulted from a unique newspaper beat. Twice a month, publisher Lew M. Williams Jr. sent two or three staff members to the fishing towns of Wrangell and Petersburg, 80 and 110 miles northwest of Ketchikan, to gather stories and ads for a monthly regional magazine the newspaper published. Because of inconvenient airline and ferry schedules, these trips sometimes took three days, and often the staffers had to leave some work undone to catch the ride home. The flexibility of an air-taxi charter was offset by expense. A rented floatplane, on the other hand, would save both time and money if the paper could supply the pilot.

Since I was already a licensed wheelplane pilot, Williams decided to invest in a seaplane rating for me. Jack Cousins, who had flown for the old Simpson Air in Ketchikan before switching to millwright work at the local pulp mill, offered Ketchikan's only flight instruction and rental floatplane. A fortyish, jovial man, Cousins kept his yellow-and-white Cessna 172 at a marina north of town.

In the air a floatplane handles just like a wheelplane, except that it's a bit slower due to the aerodynamic drag of the floats. On the water, however, a floatplane is subject to the same forces as a boat. Although I had grown up just a few miles from Long Island Sound, I had spent most of my recreational hours on tennis courts, and Cousins discovered several minutes into my first lesson that I knew nothing about boating.

The 172 sat berthed at an angle on a wooden ramp with its tail toward the water. As we conducted a preflight inspection of the airplane, Cousins pointed to the green, slime-like algae that coated the lower part of the ramp, where it met the water.

"Step on that stuff and you'll fall on your ass so fast you won't know what happened," he warned.

For a few moments I remembered. In preparation for getting the airplane off the ramp, we removed the tie-down lines, and Cousins attached a long line to the right rear float strut. Then we pushed and rocked on the bows of the floats. Inch by inch the 172 slid down the ramp on its float keels. Our boots drew closer and closer to the algae. Suddenly, my feet shot out from under me, and I plopped onto the ramp with a splash, my buttocks and legs in the cold water. Cursing, I scrambled to my feet and brushed at my trousers.

The lone survivor in the Carl Jackson crash, Metlakatla resident Paula Anniskett, twenty, had flown to Ketchikan with her fiancé to get a marriage license, and I interviewed her in Ketchikan General Hospital. She told me that on the return flight pilot Carl Jackson had deviated to show the passengers a fishing boat that had gone aground on rocks south of Ketchikan. From there, the shortest route to Metlakatla involved flying over higher terrain on Annette Island, as opposed to the mostly water route of a direct flight. Jackson apparently had trouble getting around fog in the interior of Annette. Anniskett said she was sitting in back with her fiancé—her seat belt unfastened—and suddenly found herself lying on the ground near burning wreckage. "I could hear someone moaning," she said. She spent the night huddled against a tree; in the morning she stumbled her way down through the forest and muskeg to the shoreline, where she got the attention of crew on a passing fishing boat by waving frantically. With her information, searchers quickly located the missing 185.

The accident dampened the mood at the brand-new Ketchikan International Airport on Gravina Island, where, the next day, dedication ceremonies were scheduled along with aerobatics, skydiving, and other festivities. The new facility, just a five-minute ferry ride from Ketchikan across Tongass Narrows, replaced inconvenient twenty-three-mile shuttle flights between town and the old military airport on Annette Island. Years later, the Alaska congressional delegation would lobby unsuccessfully for a bridge to replace the ferries—the infamous "bridge to nowhere."

"Well, now you've been initiated," Cousins said, chuckling.

With a final push we backed the 172 into the water. When momentum had carried it about ten feet from the ramp, Cousins yanked the long line, spinning the airplane around so that the tail now pointed toward us. He then hauled the 172 back in, lifted on the lower rear fuselage, and walked up the ramp a couple of feet until the heels of the floats slid onto the planking.

"There," he said.

The process looked uncomplicated, but on my own I found it an art requiring both finesse and planning. If you yank the long line too lightly, the airplane stops pivoting when it's perpendicular to the ramp. Then you must haul it in sideways and turn it the rest of the way by hand. If the airplane leaves the ramp with insufficient momentum, yanking on the line fails to have a full pivoting effect and instead pulls the machine off to the side, perilously close to a piling or another ramped floatplane. Of course, the wind and current can frustrate the most careful planning.

And always the green algae lurks by the water: step too close while absorbed in maneuvering the airplane around and swoosh—down you go.

Once the floatplane is tailed back up on the ramp, the pilot removes the long turning line, then steps from the ramp onto the left float, walks along it to the cockpit door and climbs in. The passengers do the same on the right side. A floatplane has no brakes. The first time I taxied off the ramp in Cousins's 172 I nearly jammed the toes of the rudder pedals, which activate brakes on most wheel planes, through the floor in an attempt to slow down when a Boston Whaler suddenly zipped across our path.

"In a floatplane," Cousins patiently explained, "you reduce taxiing speed by throttling back. You can do S-turns or circles to wait for a boat to pass. If you're going into the wind, lower the flaps or open the doors to make more surface for the wind to blow against, helping you slow down. If you have to stop, shut off the engine and water friction will do the job. Remember, you're a sailor now."

We taxied around for a few minutes while I got the feel of maneuvering on the water. Then it was time to learn how to dock. I had watched the commercial pilots shut off the engine as they approached the dock. When the left float nudged the bumpers, the pilots casually stepped out and tied up the plane.

"I know how to do it," I told Cousins, hoping to redeem myself for my display of marine ignorance. But I cut the engine too late, and the 172 glided swiftly by the dock before I could clamber out and stop it. I restarted the engine and came around for another try. This time I cut the engine too soon, and we stopped dead in the water some ten feet from the dock. I looked at Cousins sheepishly. "Well," he said, "get the paddle, get out on the float, and paddle us in."

Once I had gained a reasonable degree of basic competence on the water, I graduated to takeoffs and landings. I had thought both would be fairly simple because of the ample "runway" a floatplane pilot has, but my seaplane schooling was teaching me repeatedly that handling an airplane on the water involves more considerations than an observer realizes. While a wheelplane simply charges down the runway, a floatplane has to get "on the step" before it can become airborne—it has to attain enough water speed so that the weight of the airplane is supported by hydrodynamic pressure on the steps, or bottoms, of the floats rather than by the floats' buoyancy, much as a speedboat rides on the step above a certain speed.

First, the wheel is held back for a nose-high attitude so that water pressure will force the bows of the floats out of the water as takeoff power is applied. Then, as speed starts to build, the wheel is eased forward to help the airplane climb from this "plowing" stage onto the step. The airplane accelerates quickly once it is on the step, and the pilot holds the nose at a slightly high attitude until the floats leave the water. Pressure on the control wheel changes throughout the takeoff process; more than any instrument reading or external visual cue, it is the feel of the wheel that the pilot uses as a guide.

In the air, Cousins showed me how to "read" the water for wind direction and velocity by studying various cues: the curvature of the waves, foam sliding off wave crests, and the difference in water conditions between the lee and windward shores of a point or peninsula. Waves breaking on shore with visible foam, he said, indicate too much swell action for a safe beaching. He taught me to circle before landing to scout for driftwood and rocks. I learned to land parallel to swells to avoid the skipping that results from landing across them. I learned to make a very gradual, power-on, nose-up descent to land on glassy water, because depth perception is virtually nil without some disturbance on the surface; one of the most common types of seaplane accidents, Cousins noted, resulted from overestimating the airplane's height above glassy water and descending too quickly. I learned to make turns while taxiing on the step only from upwind to downwind, so that centrifugal force and the wind would cancel each other and minimize the chance of capsizing.

And I learned the art of sailing backward to a dock or beach, a necessary maneuver when a floatplane is upwind of the destination and the wind is too strong to turn out of it. Like a juggler, the pilot manipulates throttle, rudder, ailerons, and flaps to control drift speed and angle. Depending on skill, sailing into a tight spot between boats, pilings, or other floatplanes can be a satisfying accomplishment or an expensive mistake.

Ramping the 172 back at the marina at the end of our session involved lining up with the ramp while compensating for the drift of the current and wind, and then running the airplane onto the planks with power. At first, leery of propelling the airplane over the top of the ramp and into the pilings beyond, I used the throttle too gingerly; the 172 would stop half in and half out of the water. We then had to shut off the engine, push the airplane back into the water, and try again. Eventually I discovered the proper touch.

After ten hours of instruction—all in good weather—I took and passed the practical test (or "checkride") for a seaplane rating with a designated flight examiner for the Federal Aviation Administration.

"Here's your ticket," the man said afterward, handing me the approval form. "But remember: your education in float flying has just begun. This is a license to learn."

His caution was superfluous; while the new rating brought pride, it also gave me the sort of trepidation a newly licensed driver feels when thinking about the local expressway. I had spent enough time listening to commercial pilots talk about their misadventures to realize I was a Southeast aviation cheechako (an Alaskan term for newcomer).

The newspaper now began renting the 172 for me to fly to Wrangell and Petersburg twice a month with a couple of advertising sales people. Sometimes I'd scrub a flight two or three days in a row before Mother Nature provided the fair skies I wanted. Although one of my training sessions had included a familiarization flight to the two communities, I flew with a chart unfolded on my lap and navigated by the easiest routes, whether or not they were the shortest ones. At each stop I refueled, even though the tanks had enough capacity for a round trip with a healthy reserve.

Wrangell was a sleepy town with a population of twenty-five hundred. Originally the site of a Tlingit village, the community sat on the tip of Wrangell Island near the mouth of the Stikine River. While the ad people delivered their spiel to merchants, I visited the city manager for a rundown on official happenings, and then wandered about with my notebook and camera. I deemed one of the most interesting places in town to be at our starting point. Stikine Air Service, Wrangell's only air taxi, was based in a hangar in the city harbor. It was there I tied up the 172.

Chuck Traylor and George Diggs were the co-owners/pilots, and Traylor's wife, Yvonne, ran the office. A talented artist, Yvonne had hung some of her paintings on the walls. The thirty-something Traylor and Diggs offered valuable tips on float flying, but when I tried to take photos of them Diggs repeatedly turned away. I later learned the reason for his camera shyness. On a stormy day in 1968, he lost control of a Cessna 185 while taking off from the tiny fishing hamlet of Point Baker, on the north end of Prince of Wales Island. Diggs managed to struggle out after the airplane struck rocks and began foundering, but he was unable to save a mother and daughter sitting in the back.

Petersburg, off Frederick Sound on the north end of Mitkof Island, had two air taxis, a Scandinavian heritage, and people and seagull populations similar to those of Wrangell. From the Alaska Island Air dock, as from most points in town, the towering, snowcapped Coast Mountains on the mainland across Frederick Sound created a spectacular backdrop. When clouds and showers began obscuring the peaks, I would round up the ad salespeople and take off for home, a skittish settler heading for the fort after seeing smoke signals on the horizon. In a country plagued by fickle weather, an encounter with the bad guys was inevitable.

Raindrops were already splattering on the windshield late one afternoon as we climbed out by the Petersburg waterfront. By the time we reached Behm Canal near Ketchikan, newly formed rain showers surrounded us like anti-aircraft flak. I zigzagged around one after another until we got to the eastern shore of the canal, where an apparent detour turned out to be a cul-de-sac that lured us into the heart of an intense shower. A driving deluge suddenly engulfed and buffeted the little 172, and I gripped the wheel like a lifeline. Visibility blurred myopically through the windshield. I throttled back and descended, my heart booming. Then the sky brightened, the buffeting subsided, and we emerged from the shower, shaken but relieved.

Later, as a full-time air-taxi pilot, flying through rain showers became routine. But perception of adventure is relative; even a flight in sunshine quickens the pulse of someone who has never been up in a small airplane.

Experience gradually bolstered my self-confidence and willingness to venture. Trying more direct overland routes to Wrangell and Petersburg provided fewer emergency landing spots but left us more time for short sightseeing excursions. One of the most memorable was to Le Conte Glacier near Petersburg, which calved turquoise-colored icebergs into Le Conte Bay. Several times we descended to about fifty feet and followed a shoreline for a few miles, viewing a continuous kaleidoscope of marine features: driftwood, seals, sea caves, an occasional derelict boat, kelp beds, and so on.

In the evening, the 172 back on the ramp securely tied down, I reveled in the richness of the day as my fellow workers and I strolled by rows of boat sheds to our car.

During the days or weeks between the Wrangell–Petersburg flights I sat at my desk in the newsroom amid the clacking of manual typewriters and the clicking of the teletype machine, trying not to daydream about flying. But the Sirens of the bush never quieted. They had an ally in a huge, dog-eared map of Southeast thumbtacked on the wall directly across from my desk. I had only to raise my eyes to be distracted by a beckoning world of islands, waterways, and mountains. Returning to my desk from some mission always involved a pause at the map to study details and provocative-sounding place-names: Tombstone Bay, Hidden Inlet, Peril Strait, Escape Point, Cape Decision, Security Cove, Hole-in-the-Wall, Port Protection, Black Bear Lake. . . . Especially when the sun shone through the large picture window up front by the reception counter, concentrating on an interesting story like a Coast Guard rescue took determined self-discipline; a report on an economic-development seminar or last night's city council meeting had no chance at all.

I had once yearned to be an airline or military pilot, but less than 20/20 vision grounded that goal. With no interest in the commuter airlines, which I regarded as ho-hum second string, I settled for a private license and a career outside the cockpit. Now, seaplanes had rekindled a flying goal. As soon as my tenure at the newspaper qualified me for a vacation, I hurried down to Boeing Field in Seattle and took training for a commercial pilot's license. With the certificate carefully laminated and preserved in my wallet and 350 hours of total flight time (including nearly fifty hours of floatplane experience) religiously recorded in my logbook, I approached several air-taxi operators in Ketchikan to ask for a job. Each smiled paternally.

"Fifty hours do not a floatplane pilot make, my son. We need seasoned, well-rounded pilots."

"Okay, I'll fly for free after work and on my days off until I have enough experience to join the payroll."

"Ah, but we have more at stake than pilots' salaries. Our reputation depends on professionalism and a good safety record. Those things come only with experience. Besides, our insurance company demands at least five hundred

> **F**loatplanes in the 1920s and early '30s had no water rudders at all. Pilots gained a little maneuverability on the water by pressing a rudder pedal, which moved the vertical fin (air rudder) on the tail right or left. Wind or the propeller blast hitting the deflected fin then turned the airplane slightly. An opened door also helped by creating a sail-like surface. But taxiing with precision was impossible without water rudders (imagine trying to finesse a car into a tight parking space with the power steering out of commission). When approaching a dock or obstacle, pilots simply shut down the engine and paddled to avoid a collision.

hours total time. Why don't you buy yourself a puddle-jumper, fly the hell out of it for a year, then come back?"

A "puddle-jumper" is any old, small, low-powered, two-seat airplane whose main virtue is economy: Piper Cubs, Taylorcrafts, Cessna 140s, and the like. I learned that the Ketchikan area had just one puddle-jumper for sale, a 1939 Luscombe 8E that sat forlorn and uninsured on a ramp at a windy seaplane moorage on the edge of town. The owner agreed to ride with me on a test flight. I arrived an hour early for a private look-see, but an assessment took just a couple of minutes. At some point, the old-timer's original fabric skin had been replaced with aluminum. Its faded red-and-white paint peeled like eggshell in places, especially on the belly and tail, the areas most susceptible to the sandblasting effects of saltwater spray. There were no flaps and just one water rudder; modern floatplanes had two rudders, one on the heel of each pontoon.

Inside, the controls were sticks instead of wheels, and exposed control cables ran through pulleys on the cabin ceilings and sides. The spartan panel contained the minimum instruments required by FAA regulations. No radio. The two nonadjustable seats had little padding, and although I stood nearly six feet tall, I realized I would need a cushion to see over the panel through the crazed, scratched windshield. Gaps around the doors, the test flight would soon reveal, rendered the cabin's heat control completely ineffective.

But the Luscombe had a current airworthiness certificate and registration, and its ragged, antiquated appearance somehow befitted fantasies of aerial adventure in the bush. The airplane would open up all of southeastern Alaska. No longer restricted to bimonthly flights to Wrangell and Petersburg in the rented Cessna 172, I would have my own magic carpet whenever benign weather and free time coincided. For that luxury I would gladly sacrifice the gilded edges. Luckily, the owner offered generous terms.

For insurance, I contacted a major company that advertised regularly in the pages of aviation publications. We specialize in insuring aircraft, the ads assured. Let us handle all your aviation insurance needs. The ads left out the one exception: floatplanes in Alaska. I appealed to a three-person insurance firm in Ketchikan and managed to secure coverage.

The Luscombe's performance limitations proved to be a perverse silver lining that forced me to become a better pilot. The absence of flaps and the modest 115-horsepower engine made getting airborne challenging with the weight of a passenger and the single water rudder limited maneuvering on the water. Thus I had to develop touch and skills that a more capable airplane would have waived.

Often with a friend from the newspaper, I putt-puttered around the region in the Luscombe, exploring, building flight time, learning the country. On many outings we landed in a lake and fished off the floats beneath steep, forested slopes. When our stomachs began growling, we paddled the Luscombe to shore like a canoe and fried fresh trout for lunch.

We always left Ketchikan with a favorable forecast, but the weatherman provided no guarantees. At a lake on Prince of Wales Island, unexpected fog forced us to overnight in a Forest Service cabin. Our friends back at Ketchikan called authorities when we failed to return as scheduled, and the next morning a huge Coast Guard helicopter from the Annette Island Air Station worked its way through the murky skies to the lake to check on us.

When my logbook finally reached the magic five hundred hours, I again made the rounds of air services to ask for a flying job. This time I got one.

Being the object of a Coast Guard search was a bit ironic, because several times I had ridden as a reporter on Coast Guard helicopters during search missions for others. The most intriguing of these involved a missing Cessna 310 carrying House Majority Leader Hale Boggs and Alaska Congressman Nick Begich. The plane left Anchorage on October 16, 1972, bound for Juneau. Its failure to arrive launched the most intense aerial search in US history and included the use of high-tech military spy planes. When no trace turned up in the first few days, search headquarters asked the Coast Guard Air Station on Annette Island to take a look in lower Southeast. That area lay south of the normal Anchorage–Juneau route, but the thinking was that the pilot might have run into bad weather en route and tried to get around it through the back door.

Southeast's mountains and thick forests had already swallowed many airplanes over the years, and a thorough search there would have required a dozen squadrons. For hours our single helicopter scoured shorelines and valleys, but the only result was a reaffirmation of just how big and sparsely populated Southeast was. The general search ended after thirty-nine days without the slightest clue to the disappearance.

Chapter 3

APPRENTICESHIP

Twenty-four cargo bins lined the walls. Above each was stenciled in black letters the name of a destination: Cape Pole, Port Alice, Craig, Hydaburg, Hyder, Klawock. . . . Some bins were stuffed to the rims with boxes, tires, crates, bundles of newspapers, mail sacks, fishing poles, logging cables, and other cargo, while a few contained just a handful of items. A counter faced the street door and abutted a desk littered with various forms and manifests.

It was March, and this was the freight room, my new work station. It occupied a part of the hangar, with a clapboard wall separating it from the larger portion in which the mechanics worked. The other side of the freight room formed one wall of the building containing the operations office, ticket counter, passengers' waiting room, pilots' lounge, and accounting offices.

Coast Air was the largest of six seaplane air services in Ketchikan, with seven full-time and three part-time pilots, plus an assorted crew of reservationists, dispatchers, mechanics, linemen, and bookkeepers. It operated four Cessna 185s, four de Havilland Beavers, a Grumman Goose, and a Cessna 180. Formerly called Simpson Air, the company was renamed under new ownership after previous owner Russ Simpson was killed in a floatplane crash a few years earlier.

Unlike other pilots in town, ours wore airline-type uniforms, complete with hat, white shirt, black tie, gold epaulets, black shoes, and four gold braids on the jacket sleeves. Other air-taxi people throughout Southeast wisecracked about the absurdity of uniformed bush pilots. After all, the profession involved such messy chores as fueling and oiling planes, handling greasy industrial freight, striding down muddy village streets to fetch a tardy passenger, and stepping into the water at the edge of a lake or cove to beach the aircraft.

But business was robust. The opening the year before of the new Ketchikan Airport on nearby Gravina Island had brought the company a windfall of daily scheduled flights to the fishing communities of Craig, Klawock, and Hydaburg on Prince of Wales Island. Alaska Airlines had used its fleet of twin-engine Grumman Goose amphibians for those runs and also to shuttle airliner

> **B**efore leaving the runway at Annette Island, pilots of the amphibious Gooses sometimes neglected to inform passengers that the landing at Ketchikan would be on the water. When the airplane subsequently touched down on Tongass Narrows, an unenlightened passenger occasionally screamed in terror, believing a crash had occurred.

passengers between the Ketchikan waterfront and the town's old, World War II airport on Annette Island, twenty-three miles away. The new airport, just a five-minute ferry ride across Tongass Narrows, had eliminated the need for the shuttle flights. The Prince of Wales flights alone could not support the Grumman fleet, so Alaska Airlines had decided to sell its Gooses and subcontract the Prince of Wales flights to us.

We had an aggressive advertising campaign, and our airplanes flew from dawn to well into the evening, day after day, except when weather grounded us. The management foresaw continued growth and envisioned expansion into a regional airline. To achieve that goal, the company had to have the right image. Pilots dressed in the traditional checkered shirt, blue jeans, and rubber boots would no longer do.

Before signing on with the company, I too had joked about the uniforms. But now, little higher than a lineman, I regarded them as a status symbol. The right image included professionalism, and green, newly hired pilots like me had to serve an apprenticeship in the freight room so they could learn the day-to-day routine before earning the privilege of donning a uniform. Besides keeping track of freight and mail, my duty was to help the pilots dock, brush the aircraft wings and tails after a snow shower, load and unload the planes, fuel the occasional plane, and perform various maintenance chores.

But the apprenticeship wasn't entirely on the ground. Every two or three days, chief pilot Dwight Gregerson sent me as an observer on a flight that had an empty seat. The forty-five-year-old Gregerson, slender, distinguished-looking, and congenial, admonished me against regarding the flights as breaks from the freight room monotony.

"Get to know the country," he said. "Look at how things are done. Ask the pilots questions. If you don't pay attention now, you'll wish you had when you're on your own out there."

Kirk Thomas, my first teacher at the company, had begun as a common lineman several years earlier. Deciding he'd rather be a pilot, he took flying lessons and, with financial help from the company, earned a commercial pilot's license in the Lower 48. A hardworking Mormon farm boy from Utah with the build of a fullback, Thomas would own an air service in a few years.

Some destinations, such as Craig, Klawock, and Hydaburg, and of course

Wrangell and Petersburg, were familiar from my newspaper runs in the rented 172 and exploratory flights in the Luscombe. But I had never flown to the more obscure hamlets and settlements, nor to the logging camps scattered over the vast upper half of Prince of Wales. And while my newspaper/Luscombe flights had waited for fair weather, air-taxi flights enjoyed no such luxury. As Thomas followed the winding waterways and cut through narrow valleys by thawing ponds under low stratus in the Cessna 185, I tried to do the same with my finger on the chart in my lap.

"It all looks the same from down low," I told him. "I don't see how you can find your way without a map."

Thomas smiled. "I had to use a map for the first few weeks out here. Then it suddenly all just clicked together."

At forty-one, Chuck Collins was one of the oldest line pilots, and the most professional. He had previously flown Grumman Gooses for Alaska Airlines but had been furloughed when the new airport opened. An outgoing, talkative chain-smoker, Collins flew as if he had an FAA inspector on board every flight. He made long approaches and shallow banks and circled each destination before landing to look for obstructions, even at places he had already visited earlier in the day.

With passengers he smiled and catered and never lost patience. At first I assumed his display of caution and courtesy was exaggerated as a model for me, but I discovered that such was his style. In fact, the management periodically chided him for overdoing it, for taking too long to complete flights. But he continued his ways unfazed.

'They can call me a little old lady all they want," Collins told me one day over Prince of Wales. "I consider it a compliment."

Eventually, when his low seniority number finally reached the top of the furloughed-pilot list, Alaska rehired him as a flight engineer on 727 jets.

Al McMannon, by contrast, horsed the 185 around like a fighter pilot. He buzzed a camp or a village before landing as if strafing it to let a passenger know the plane had arrived, and when he banked, it felt like a snap roll. McMannon—tall and solid, with a thick mustache on a somber face—did not fly recklessly; he simply knew he was in a bush plane, not an airliner. Ketchikan-born, he had flown B-25 bombers in the South Pacific with the Army Air Corps. Later he would fly business jets overseas.

There was handsome, arrogant Tom Drake, who, like the famous Wiley Post, had lost an eye but who managed to thread his way through foggy passes more consistently than two-eyed pilots. Chief pilot Gregerson—with fourteen thousand hours of flight time making him one of the most experienced pilots in Southeast—had a maestro's touch that inspired instant confidence and admiration. Prone to occasional temper tantrums in which he yanked off his hat and threw it on the ground, Gregerson charmed his passengers like a master of ceremonies with a natural laugh and tactful banter. Gray-haired Stu Fortuna, a retired air force master sergeant, retained the friendly, disciplined demeanor he had picked up in his first career. Young Will Paulson had transported field-grade officers in Beechcraft King Airs over the jungles of Vietnam as a US Army pilot. Before moving to Ketchikan he had flown floatplanes for an air service in Seattle. Each pilot had a different style, with me as well as with a bush plane.

Collins took a few minutes at each stop to give me a quick walking tour of the camp or village, occasionally pausing to drop into an office for an introduction with the local manager or agent. Drake, who had an insatiable appetite, circled each camp to point out the location of the cookhouse and provided a commentary on its culinary virtues: "Norma bakes the best cookies in southeast Alaska; treat her like a queen when she flies to town."

A couple of pilots kept up a steady monologue of operational caveats: "Stay away from the west shoreline when you land because the water there is riddled with rocks . . . There's no water to land in for six miles if you try to save time by flying through the notch in the mountain over there . . . Don't fly anywhere near that goddamn cliff in a strong southeast wind, 'cause the downdrafts will shake your fillings out."

And a couple, preoccupied with their own thoughts, seemed oblivious to my presence and rarely uttered a word.

After two weeks, Gregerson began sending me out in the little Cessna 180 to make an occasional freight run when benign weather prevailed and the regular flights were unable to handle the accumulation in the bins. I also began making weekly contract-mail flights. One run went up west Behm Canal to a cabin in Deep Bay, the settlement of Loring, a logging camp in Neets Bay, and the fishing resorts at Bell Island and Yes Bay. A second run stopped at the Haida village of Kasaan in Kasaan Bay, an old cannery in Steamboat Bay on Noyes Island, and the fishing hamlet at Meyers Chuck, while the third went to the old mining town of Hyder at the head of Portland Canal by the British Columbian border.

Assistant Manager Art Byron, a retired naval aviator who had served a tour in the stormy Aleutian Islands, rode in the right-hand seat to introduce me to the mail runs. A stocky man with graying, curly hair and narrow, hooded eyes, Byron usually opened the facilities in the morning and locked them up at night, after the rest of us had gone home.

On the familiarization flight to Hyder, over the sweeping wilderness of the Coast Mountains still buried in winter white, I suddenly noticed he was sleeping. How long had his eyes been closed? I had thought his silence over the last few minutes signaled affirmation of my navigation. The endless valleys and peaks around us looked alike to me, and I debated waking him. Then I decided that no one could miss a landmark as conspicuous as seventy-mile-long Portland Canal on a sunny day. For more visibility, I climbed until the altimeter read almost nine thousand feet. Sure enough, a few minutes later Portland Canal appeared on the horizon. Now a gradual descent over the canal, keeping the power up to avoid a change in engine noise that might awaken Byron. I'd show him I could do the job unsupervised. Two settlements were evident at the head of the canal—Hyder and its neighbor, tiny Stewart, British Columbia. I glanced at my slumbering copilot again and again, hoping he would remain asleep until I landed. What better demonstration of my ability than this?

The Hyder seaplane dock was conspicuous at the end of a long causeway three miles ahead. Slowly, slowly, I eased back the throttle as the airplane lost altitude, paying little attention to the magnificent scenery lining the canal. The wind was calm, the water flat. Plenty of time to grease the 180 on smoothly. A notch of flaps. Keep the nose up, don't fly into the glassy water. A second notch of flaps. A third. Power back a hair, nose up, hold it there, hold it. I felt a slight swooshing as the float keels touched the water. Ah, Arthur, no need to ride with *me* anymore!

Byron's eyes finally opened as we taxied toward the dock.

"Next time," he said gruffly, "don't waste time and fuel climbing all the way to nine thousand. Five thousand is plenty high enough to get across safely."

Alone on the freight and mail flights, surrounded by grandeur and fair skies, I basked in the glory of being aloft in my new career. Sometimes I slapped the empty seat on my right as enthusiasm overflowed. Like Santa Claus delivering letters, magazines, mail-order merchandise, and other bush treasures, I found welcome at each stop.

The old salmon cannery at Steamboat Bay on Noyes Island, at the edge of the open ocean, had not operated for a quarter century, but the owner, New England Fish Company, maintained the buildings as a supply station for fishing vessels during the summer. The rest of the year, a solitary caretaker looked after things. Charlie Waters had a radio to call in his needs to the New England Fish Company office in town, which would have the order filled and delivered to our freight room. But he had trouble receiving messages: Waters was almost deaf.

Each Wednesday I deposited his mail and cargo in a large wooden box on an anchored float behind the cannery complex and picked up his outgoing mail there. Waters couldn't hear the airplane come in, but he checked the box periodically during the day if the weather appeared flyable.

Although Steamboat Bay was almost a mile long, swells rolling in from the Gulf of Esquibel typically left a floatplane pilot only a few hundred yards in which to work. Land too far out, and you bounced in the swells as if on a trampoline, subjecting the airplane to a terrible pounding; land too late, and you risked skimming off the water and up onto the pebbly beach at the head of the bay, as one of our pilots had done. Sometimes the swells extended all the way to the beach, rendering a landing unsafe. Like so many destinations in Southeast, Steamboat Bay presented floatplane pilots a one-way-in, one-way-out situation with steep forested slopes on three sides.

The third week, swells kept me from landing two days in a row. The swells had diminished a little when I tried again that Friday, so this time I held my breath and plopped down. But how to contact Waters? I wasn't sure he would be expecting me, and my load included some groceries that might spoil if uncollected. I taxied in circles in front of the cannery, checking the old red buildings and docks for a sign of him each time the windshield swung through the complex. Only the seagulls moved about.

Finally, I decided to drop off his mail and freight in the box on the float, then taxi over to one of the docks, tie up, and try to find him on foot. As I was unloading, the putt-putt-putt of a motor suddenly joined the screeching of the gulls and the slapping of the water against the cannery pilings. A moment later, a long wooden skiff slid into view from behind a building and headed for the float

"LOOKED FOR YOU THE PAST COUPLE OF DAYS," Waters yelled, smiling, his stringy white hair awry. I caught the boat and wrapped a line he handed me around a cleat. "I WAS PAINTING UP TO THE HOUSE AND SAW YOU CIRCLING." I noticed splotches of white paint on his halibut jacket. "NICE DAY."

"I tried to get in Wednesday and Thursday, but the swells . . ."

"I'M DEAF," he interrupted, shaking his head, still smiling. "CAN'T HEAR YOU." I handed him the mail sack and boxes of food, which he stacked on the bottom of the skiff. "YOU'RE THAT NEW FELLOW, AIN'T YOU?" I smiled and nodded my head. Waters caressed the stubble of his beard and scrutinized the upper slopes, which disappeared into gray stratus. "GONNA BE A WET SUMMER. BUT GOOD FISHING."

About eighty-three miles east-northeast, next to the mainland where Behm Canal looped by the north end of Revillagigedo Island, another facility also attracted fishermen. But while the old Steamboat Bay cannery served the blue-jean-clad, free-spirited men and women who fished for a living on commercial trollers and seiners, Bell Island Hot Springs Resort catered to board chairmen, bank presidents, and other such VIPs who fished for pleasure—some of whom arrived on their own or company yachts. When I began delivering mail and supplies there, patches of snow still lay in the muskeg meadows that broke the forest on the island, and the resort's opening was a few weeks away.

Nestled in a small cove flanked by steep, lush slopes, the resort defied circling unless I climbed to about fifteen hundred feet, which the clouds often did not permit. Instead, I buzzed by in front of the resort before landing and hoped owner Jim Dykes would hear the engine. If the fortyish, mustachioed Canadian national was not standing on the dock when I taxied in, I piled the freight on the dock and carried the mail sack up a long boardwalk that paralleled a stream on one side and hugged a slope on the other. I would find Dykes, his wife, and several workmen in one of the cabins or the generator shed or the lodge, painting this, installing that.

The resort's facilities included an anomaly in the Alaskan wilderness—a swimming pool, heated by water piped from a nearby natural hot spring. The Dykeses usually invited me to take a dip in the steaming pool. Being on a schedule, I'd settle instead for a fistful of cookies in the lodge before hurrying on my way.

Elderly Hal and Gertrude Clifford lived more modestly in Deep Bay, an unremarkable body of water near the mouth of west Behm Canal. Hal, seventy-seven, was a retired Alaska Fish and Game Department employee who now shuffled about on a cane. The two had been married to each other for fifty-five years. Each week I carried their mail sack and whatever freight they had ordered by radio up the beach slope to the porch of their cabin.

"Won't you stay for a cup of coffee?" they would ask. Impatient to get on with my run, I declined the first three weeks. By the fourth week, however, I had begun to feel guilty about rejecting the hospitality of the kindly old couple in their isolated retirement. Besides, I reminded myself, landlubber freight-room tasks awaited me for the rest of the day as soon as I returned to town. I could spare ten minutes.

Inside, the cabin illuminated only by light cascading through Visqueen-covered windows, I sat in a springy armchair while Gertrude placed a pot of water on the wood-burning stove. Hal worked his way around furniture and piles of magazines to a bookcase, where he pulled out a photo album.

"I was a Fish and Game agent," he told me for the third time in four weeks as he shuffled back to my chair. While Hal provided commentary, I turned page after page of fading, often poorly focused snapshots—many cocked against the backing—showing various outdoor scenes of people and wildlife.

"Here you are, honey," Gertrude finally announced, handing me a mug of coffee.

Forty-five minutes had passed when I lifted back into the air, a sense of dereliction stirring in my conscience. The 180's radio was in the maintenance shop for repairs, so I was unable to notify the dispatcher of the delay. I hurried through the rest of my stops. Back in Ketchikan, chief pilot Gregerson strode up to me while I was tying up the airplane.

"Run into some trouble?" he asked. "You're an hour late. We were about to send someone out to look for you."

I was only a little more than a half-hour overdue, but I didn't argue the point. I confessed my visit with the Cliffords and mumbled something about public relations.

Gregerson shook his head. "We don't have time to dillydally with the customers. This is a business, not a social club. You pull this crap this summer and you'll screw up the whole schedule."

Humbled, I retreated to my station in the freight room, wondering if there would be a summer for me at the company. But when Gregerson sent me out on another freight flight two days later, I knew I was forgiven.

Now that I handled the controls periodically, checking in freight and toiling at dock tasks with the teenage "ramp rats," as the linemen were called, seemed intolerably dull. I ached constantly to be airborne. Each time a delivery truck pulled up outside the freight room's street door, I crossed my fingers; if a huge order came in, the regular flights might be unable to handle it all and I would get to transport the balance in the 180. But too often the freight disappeared in the cavernous baggage compartments of our larger 185s, Beavers, and Goose.

I learned to keep an eye on the accumulation in the bins and to tug Gregerson on the sleeve when it reached a level that would fill a 180. Sometimes the strategy worked. Even so, I averaged only four or five flights a week, while the line pilots sometimes logged that many a day. I would watch them land in Tongass Narrows out front, taxi in, unload their passengers, load up for another flight, and—after ducking behind the line shed to relieve themselves in the water—taxi right back out. Helping Gregerson load baggage into the Goose for a flight one day, I casually asked when I might be elevated to passenger-carrying line status.

"When we think you're ready," he answered, reaching for another bag. And just what constitutes readiness, Mr. Chief Pilot? What tests must I pass, what homage must I pay, what gauntlet must I run?

"Be patient," Collins told me. "Work hard and smile a lot. They like you; I haven't heard any criticism. They just want to break you in slowly. It's standard operating procedure for an unseasoned pilot around here."

To speed up the process, I resorted to subterfuge. Quiet Judy Ball had joined the company as a reservationist the same week I began work in the freight room. Perhaps she felt a sympathetic kinship because we were both new; perhaps I represented a psychological replacement for her son, who had been reported missing in action in Vietnam a few years earlier. Whatever her motive, she became an ally in my campaign to join the full-time pilots on the line.

Several times a week a party would phone or radio a request for an immediate charter when no pilots were available. Sitting behind the counter in the waiting room across from the dispatcher's cubicle, Ball would eavesdrop on the discussion between the dispatcher and a member of management about how to handle the situation: Should Paulson be diverted on his way back from Hydaburg to pick the party up? No, that would make him late for that charter with the bankers to Wrangell, and we can't have that. Well, maybe the Naha Bay charter could be postponed for a couple of hours to squeeze in the new charter. No, those Naha-bound people came all the way from Georgia and their flight has already been postponed once. Could Drake make an extra stop on his logging camp run to pick up the party? No, he already had a full load.

While the dispatcher wrinkled her brow and the management representative scratched his head, Ball would slip out from the counter and walk into the freight office to alert me. A minute later I would saunter through the waiting room with a smile, lingering by the dispatcher's cubicle if necessary until I was noticed.

"Hi. Busy day?"

None of my timely appearances produced a direct result, but they might have been indirectly effective through repetitive suggestion. On a late April Thursday morning in my sixth week of apprenticeship, Gregerson walked up to me in the freight room, where I was placing destination stickers on a newly delivered load of groceries.

"Two passengers got bumped off the ten o'clock flight to Craig," he said. "I want you to take them there." Before I could utter a flustered reply, he added, "Your uniform is hanging up in the pilot's lounge. You'd better hurry: you've got to take off in fifteen minutes."

I tried to look nonchalant in the starched uniform as I strode from the building onto the dock a few minutes later, but I grinned self-consciously when several pilots chatting by the seaplane elevator saw me and catcalled.

Though I had flown passengers routinely many times in private aircraft, the realization that now I was being paid to transport people who themselves had paid for the service tempered my elation with a somber sense of responsibility. Like a brand-new father cradling his infant, I carried my first two commercial passengers gingerly. I cruised at an unnecessarily high altitude. I circled for a second look at a light shower I would have flown into unhesitatingly if alone with freight. I made an excessively conservative approach at Craig and landed a quarter mile out from the seaplane dock.

I adhered to the same regimen with other passengers over the next few weeks (for the time being I was restricted to fairly uncomplicated destinations in good weather), and such circumspection cost extra minutes that occasionally made me late for the following flight. But no complaints resulted; I was in a honeymoon period. The company expected me to tread cautiously, to deport myself with humility and conservatism. A fledgling who keeps pace with seasoned pilots is guilty of recklessness, for by definition seasoning takes experience. To compensate for my lower efficiency, the dispatcher calculated a greater margin into my flight times when scheduling subsequent flights for me.

Ironically, some passengers for whom flying was a finger-crossing, white-knuckle ordeal felt so secure with my conservatism that forever afterward they loyally requested me as their pilot—even though I eventually adopted the same shortcuts in routes and methods that had accelerated their pulses with other, far more experienced pilots.

Most of our aircraft spent the night tied down on the upper dock, and we warmed up the engines there in the morning. The rumbling of the Goose's and Beavers' Pratt & Whitney engines and the snarling of the Cessnas' Continentals electrified me with excitement in the crisp dawn air. With a little imagination I envisioned a squadron of Hellcats warming up on the deck of an aircraft carrier before a launching.

When the engines were ready for work, pinging with heat, we pushed the aircraft one by one on a dolly across the planking to the seaplane elevator for lowering to the sea-level dock. Carts of freight and baggage also rode on the elevator. Below, we emptied the carts into the baggage compartments of the airplanes, unraveled the fuel hoses, and fetched cans of oil from the line shed, all the while bantering with the linemen and each other.

"Hey, you want to trade flights?"

"What for?"

"Mary Simpson's on my airplane. The old bag has a crush on me."

"Anybody get the weather for Cape Pole?"

"Yeah, it's pretty good; the camp said two thousand feet and five miles, light wind."

"And you believed them?"

"Goddamn it. Someone must have puked in Nine-Four Golf yesterday. It stinks in here."

"That's just your breath ricocheting off the walls."

"Okay, go get my people, Kevin."

Lineman Kevin scrambled up the ramp, and a minute later a small group of passengers filed slowly down, gripping the railing.

Often three or four planes taxied out at the same time, as if in formation. After takeoff a couple would continue up Tongass Narrows, bound for Craig or the logging camps on the north end of Prince of Wales. Another—Hydaburg the destination—peeled off to the west over Gravina Island, while a fourth turned north up Ward Cove for points on Behm Canal or the mainland.

Still on honeymoon, I stayed behind to sip coffee and pace about the waiting room if fog or wind plagued the morning.

"I think I can handle it, Dwight. It doesn't really look that bad."

"We'll decide what you can handle," Gregerson would answer.

One weather-bound morning, I had lots of company in the waiting room. I stepped around several suitcases and shopping bags to the coffee urn and poured myself another cup, then returned to the big picture window that overlooked the dock and waterfront. Through the rain-streaked glass I resumed staring in fascination at the scene outside. Huge, foaming waves and swells raged up Tongass Narrows, spray driving a hundred feet or more from the crests. Every few seconds a sheet of horizontal rain whipped by, lashing and rattling the window. The floatplanes on the dock jiggled constantly in the forty-knot wind, tugging against their tie-down lines as if trying to escape. Even the big Goose danced a bit. The tonal pitch of the wind moved up and down the scale in moans and whistles with the gusts.

It was late May, and the Season, spelled with a capital "S" in the Alaskan air-taxi business, was upon us. For the next four months, travel demands would stay at peak level. Even a few hours of weather delays now caused backlogs that took a couple of days of extra hustling to clean up. This was the second full day of no flying due to an intense low-pressure system that had swept in from the North

Pacific with high winds and heavy rain. Behind me, the waiting room was jammed with people and luggage bound for villages or camps. Some passengers had been trying since the previous morning to fly home to their families, their dogs, their chores, their livelihoods. A few had taken a state ferry to destinations that were close to home (some ferry runs had been cancelled due to rough seas). Those for whom flying was the only alternative to swimming had idled away the hours shopping in the stores, or drinking in the bars, or sleeping in the waiting room.

The National Weather Service station on Annette Island had predicted diminishing winds for this morning, prompting many absentee passengers to return hopefully to the waiting room. But weather in Southeast is even more fickle than elsewhere. The wind had instead increased. Now, as I glanced about the room, frustration was evident in the taut faces. There was little talking. Most people dozed or read or stared vacantly. Even the children and babies stayed sullenly silent.

Behind the reservations counter, Judy Ball read a paperback, pausing occasionally to answer the telephone and solemnly report that no, the weather still had not improved. The dispatcher's cubicle was empty; no need for Peggy Acorn at the moment. She was probably sipping coffee elsewhere in the building or downtown on errands.

A blast of air suddenly tousled my hair as the door next to the picture window opened and fellow pilot Tom Drake stepped in, pushing hard against the door to close it. Hunched inside a dripping rain suit with hood, he shook his head and wiped the rain off his face.

"Checking the tie-down lines," he muttered. "Christ, I'm getting sick of this crap." We walked upstairs to the pilots' lounge, where the other pilots and the linemen were playing ping-pong, darts, or cards, or reading *Playboy* from a stack of the magazines.

"Two more refugees," somebody said as we entered. "Relax while you can."

Early in the afternoon the wind finally dropped to a steady twenty knots in the Narrows, and radio reports from Prince of Wales indicated conditions were improving there, too. Gregerson took off in a Beaver with a couple of hardy passengers and a load of freight to investigate.

"It's breezy but workable," his voice crackled over the radio in the dispatcher's cubicle fifteen minutes later. "Let's get going!"

Engines throbbing. Telephones ringing. Pilots and linemen scrambling about loading carts and pushing dolly-supported airplanes. Passengers stretching, gathering hand luggage, and standing in line at the restroom. Fuel hoses snaking across the lower dock. Suitcases, shopping bags, and mail sacks being stuffed into baggage compartments. Yells. Epithets. Passengers crowding the ramp. In the bustle someone forgot or ignored my status as a fair-weather honeymooner, and I found myself taxiing out with a full load of passengers and gear for Craig and Klawock.

An hour and a half later I taxied in, weary from the tension of battling turbulence and rain but gratified that I had completed the flight without incident. Now for a cup of coffee inside and a few congratulatory words from the management for having eased the burden, for having, at a time of severe backlog, accepted without hesitation a mission in weather above and beyond my level of experience.

A lineman stood by to help dock my 185. As I stepped out I noticed a cart full of suitcases next to him.

"You've got to go right back out to Craig with another load," he said. "And I think you've got one more flight after that."

Thereafter, my metamorphosis from a fledgling to a real line pilot apparently complete in the eyes of the company, I flew to all destinations in all conditions suitable for the more senior pilots. Along with that privilege came equal responsibilities; unreasonably long flight times or en route itinerary changes without notifying the dispatcher now brought reproof.

The honeymoon was over.

But not so my education, most of which continued spontaneously. Other pilots could offer tips about places and techniques, of course. Yet the bush seemed to be a world of extenuating circumstances and unpredictable situations that forced me to improvise, to learn by trial and error as I went along. No helper stood on a beach as I taxied in to point out rocks lurking just below the surface. No radar controller was stationed in a mountain pass to advise me whether it was wiser to fly over or under a certain cloud layer. No weather briefer waited in a gusty fjord to report areas of wind shear. No fancy, multibutton computer was installed in the instrument panel to calculate how long I could try a detour and still have enough fuel to retreat.

I flew by the seat of my pants, and sometimes I got spanked.

One day my itinerary called for stops at the logging camps of Port Alice and Naukati, in that order. But visibility-reducing rain and a five-hundred-foot ceiling forced me to fly so low that I could not relate the surrounding terrain to my chart. I weaved along shorelines, through waterways, and around forested islands in the direction of Port Alice for almost two hours before finally accepting the fact that I was hopelessly lost. I was about to land, admit the situation to my passengers, and wait for an improvement in the weather when suddenly a camp appeared out of the rain a mile ahead. I squinted. Naukati! Immensely grateful to have my bearings although fifteen miles off course, I immediately throttled back, set up an approach, and landed.

"I thought you said we were going to Port Alice first," one of the passengers for that camp complained as we taxied in.

"We were," I lied. "But on the way I remembered there was a Port Alice mail sack at Naukati that another pilot dropped off by mistake, so I thought I'd stop here first and pick it up."

A perfect excuse. I'd have to collect an outbound mail sack at Naukati anyway, and we had a Port Alice mail sack on board; no one would know that the sack I ultimately unloaded at Port Alice was not the one I had picked up at Naukati. Of course, the passenger bound for Naukati was delighted with the change in plans.

Airborne again a few minutes later with the two Port Alice passengers and two Naukati residents going to town, I managed to work my way around to the north side of Heceta Island. Now I had only to follow the shoreline to Port Alice. I had visited the camp on observation flights with other pilots and had flown there on my own several times. But local landmarks that had become familiar at higher altitudes took on perplexing features in the rain from a perspective of five hundred feet. An islet surrounded by sentry-like boulders appeared prominent as I flew by. Had I noticed it on previous trips to Port Alice? Was I really on the north side of Heceta?

Up ahead, the shoreline broke at the mouth of a major indentation.

I relaxed. Port Alice, after all. I turned the corner there, began a slow descent by logged-off slopes, and peered into the rain for the camp. But instead of a community of trailers and logging vehicles a couple of miles away, the windshield suddenly filled with a log raft and the empty head of a cove. What the hell? No room to turn. I yanked off the power, lowered the flaps, and landed. The airplane fell off the step about twenty-five yards from the log raft.

When my heart dropped from my throat back into my chest, I realized we were in a similar-looking, uninhabited cove Port Alice used for storage of log rafts about five miles east of the camp. This time I could think of no excuse.

"Guess I made a wrong turn. Sorry about that," I said to my passengers as I taxied around to take off from the cove. All longtime loggers, they settled back into their seats, glaring at me.

The chief pilot of a rival air service in Ketchikan required new pilots to cruise at five hundred feet everywhere, even in perfect weather, for the first few months so they could recognize landmarks when visibility or ceiling forced them to fly that low or lower. It was wise strategy; new pilots who routinely flew high for the easier navigation of a broader perspective tended to suffer some confusion in bad weather in the relatively unfamiliar shoreline world.

Chapter 4

OF PASSENGERS AND PLACES

I knew nothing about logging before moving to Ketchikan. Now, after several months of flying floatplanes commercially to logging camps and chatting with loggers both in the air and on the ground, my vocabulary blossomed with new terms: "I hear your bullbuck had to stop a fight between a couple of choker setters over a pair of corks during hoothowling last night."

But the conversations also extended beyond life within the camps and woods. With one cheek bulging from a chaw of chewing tobacco, the loggers offered their opinion on which team would win the National League pennant, the best caliber for deer hunting, why the Russians could not be trusted, and other matters.

Many were fascinated with the airplane and asked about the function of this control or that instrument.

On one issue the loggers were in unanimous agreement. Environmental groups such as the Sierra Club had successfully sued in federal courts to prevent logging in some of the more scenic or ecologically sensitive areas. And the groups' lobbying had spurred the Forest Service into imposing additional restrictions on logging practices. Pointing out that timber is a renewable resource and that logging boosts Southeast's economy, the camp people continually blasted "those goddamn environmentalists."

In Ketchikan, where a pulp mill was the town's largest employer, many car bumpers displayed anti-environmentalist stickers. "Let the bastards freeze in the dark" was a favorite.

Although I realized logging provided considerable business for the company, I frowned at the ugly clear-cuts that had denuded thousands of acres on Prince of Wales and some other islands. (The thick Southeast forest defied large-scale selective cutting, so virtually all trees were removed within areas designated for logging.) I supported efforts to preserve untouched parts of Southeast and surreptitiously joined the Tongass Conservation Society, whose members enjoyed the popularity of Christians in the Roman Empire. One TCS president was fired from his air-taxi dispatching job because of notoriety over his association with the organization; he complained to the *Ketchikan Daily News,* which published an article, and the Associated Press and *The Wall Street Journal* ultimately picked up the story.

I was no martyr, however, so among the camp people I diplomatically kept my mouth shut when the conversation got around to "those goddamn environmentalists."

Like loggers, commercial fishermen wore beards and suspenders and chewed tobacco. But the fishermen radiated a subtle sort of bush civility absent among the Paul Bunyans. While the logger's words often grated with redneck prejudice, the fisherman's echoed quiet philosophy. The logger cussed the flies and the devil's club in the forest; the fisherman spoke of the smell and the lilt of the sea. The logger's face reflected the hard lines of a seasoned infantryman, the fisherman's the weathered features of a farmer.

I kept a camera loaded with color film by my seat and welcomed flights to fishing boats for the photogenic scenery at the destinations. But while the stark clear-cuts, muddy roads, and aluminum trailers of a logging camp at least stayed in the same place, the fisherman's peripatetic home was often hard to find, a speck in a world of islands and waterways.

"We're in the second bight on the south side of Ingraham Bay—you can't miss us," a skipper would radio to the dispatcher, neglecting to mention that adjacent islets hid his seiner from a lateral view and that the pilot would have to be almost directly overhead to spot it. During special fishing openings in specific locations, several dozen gillnetters might be clustered in a cove. The *Stephanie* is white with black trim? Fine, except that an airplane cannot circle low enough in the steeply sloped cove to pick out names, and there must be six or seven white gillnetters with black trim in the crowd. With fishermen moving about performing chores on most decks, waving arms are inconspicuous. Finally, with a sigh, you land, taxi amid the vessels, shut off the engine, step out on the float, and cup your hands at crewmen on a random boat:

"Where's the *Stephanie?*"

Sometimes finding the right boat was the easy part. Logging camps offered secure bumper-equipped seaplane docks in relatively sheltered waters, but a fishing boat anchored frequently in places no one had ever flown to, places with ocean swells and unmarked reefs. Not all obstructions were visible from the air. I learned to scout my proposed landing stretch for kelp patches, which often grow around marine rocks, and for the little whirlpool disturbances that reveal a slightly submerged rock or reef.

When the airplane arrived, a larger boat usually dispatched a skiff to deliver or pick up the passenger and his duffel bag, and I simply shut off the engine and waited for it to pull up alongside. Lowering a skiff was inconvenient for a smaller boat such as a troller, however. Instead, I taxied at slow idle toward the stern or the lowest point along a side, turning off the engine to drift the last few yards. I tossed the mooring lines on the floats to the outstretched hands of the crew, and they tied off the airplane—nice and tight, thank you, so the wind won't swing a wing into the vessel. My passenger climbed up to the deck or, if outbound, stepped down to the float. Then, the lines untied, I let the plane drift away or paddled it backward until I had maneuvering room to fire up and return to the air.

Once on board, both loggers and fishermen had flown enough to became able right-seat copilots. Fit and agile, accustomed to working outdoors at potentially hazardous tasks, they hesitated not a second to unfasten their seat belts, open the door, and lean out to help me watch for rocks as we taxied to a beach to wait out the fog. If the location of a dock and the direction of the wind required coming in on the right side of the airplane, they clambered out to tie up. Under those conditions with a right-seat tourist or other passenger unschooled in the ropes, so to speak, I had to scramble out my side and duck-waddle across the forward spreader bar connecting the floats to reach the dock—sometimes bashing my head against the hot exhaust stack, sometimes slipping on oil that had dripped from the engine. Often the wind or current drifted the plane away from the dock before I could reach it. Then I had to pull the paddle from its sheath on the float and paddle in.

Most veteran fishermen, and some loggers, knew the waterways better than I. In low visibility, their presence was more valuable than a radar set: "No, no, don't turn yet; the inlet's still another half mile ahead, after that next point."

As the spring days lengthened into summer, other passengers came in endless variety: contractors, tourists, students, clergymen, state troopers, sportsmen, writers, Forest Service workers, backpackers. . . . Many chatted above the engine roar about their activities and goals as we droned through the sky, and I felt no envy of airline pilots, who had little interaction with their passengers.

Business professionals and executives from the Lower 48, who flew occasionally to bush communities for insurance, investment, or other purposes, seemed to emit a critical air that increased the pressure. Looking incongruous with their suits and slick grooming, they sat quietly, sullenly, and I imagined them disdainfully comparing the bush plane—and its pilot—with their usual business-jet environment. In reality, they may have been tired from long hours of multistop airline travel, or apprehensive about riding on a floatplane, perhaps their first such experience. Still, I felt less on stage with nonchalant bush folk in grungy jeans and shirttails. These frequent travelers considered a floatplane as simply an aerial taxicab, and they understood that bumpy air, or circling to look at weather ahead, or changing altitude as visibility went up or down, did not signal an incompetent pilot.

Village women flying to town to give birth, or back home afterward, brought out a paternalistic inclination in me. Gone then was a sense of obligation to the company to complete the trip quickly, to get back to town for my next assignment. Instead, I would fly extra carefully and take detours to find smoother air. When the flight scheduling coincidentally made me the pilot both ways for the same woman, we established an unspoken bond; I was special to her in the same sense that the delivering doctor would always be special. She and her infant were special to me because of the responsibility I had felt, because I had been a minor participant in a solemn event in their lives. I might not remember—or never have noted—their names, but ever afterward, when they traveled on my airplane, the mothers and I smiled at each other as if we shared a secret.

I also felt a kinship with members of the clergy, who traveled often by air to minister in the camps and villages. We shared an admiration for the grandeur and variety of the scenery, although their appreciation was spiritual and mine was romantic. If weather and time cooperated, I sometimes detoured a few miles so they could view an area I thought was especially beautiful.

"How can anyone deny Creation when they look at something like that?" a young, curly-haired Baptist minister shouted above the engine as he swept his hand at a cliff with a cascading waterfall one day. "How can anyone say that just happened by chance?"

Reluctant to play the devil's advocate, I opted against pointing out the geological fact that the features around us had been carved by the sluggish ramblings of glaciers in the last ice age, billions of years after formation of the earth. When bad weather blocked the scenery, the clergymen still sat calmly and confidently, rarely displaying concern. Although intellectually I realized that the piety of my passengers exacted no special treatment from the laws of physics, I somehow felt more comfortable in inclement conditions with a minister at my side.

"I thought I could expect sunshine with *you* on board," I quipped to the same minister on one rainy flight.

He chuckled and glanced out his window at the rain and clouds. "Well, my car had a lot of dust on it today."

Four Roman Catholic priests from California, who spent a week at Essowah Lake on Dall Island and caught not a single fish, philosophically suggested afterward that the Creator had not meant life to be removed from such a beautiful spot.

Many lay passengers reacted less magnanimously to fishing disappointments or other problems. During periods of unflyable fog or wind, the waiting room inevitably contained at least one person—often a bush resident who ought to have known better—who blamed the company for the delay. The reservationist and dispatcher served as the most convenient scapegoats, but the impatient passenger would berate a pilot, a lineman, or a mechanic if one of them dared walk by.

"Well, I'm gonna fly with somebody else!" the passenger eventually would announce, striding out the door. Sometimes he found a heroic pilot at another air service. More often the passenger returned in a few minutes, still irritated but subdued after discovering that pilots elsewhere were also holding for weather.

Occasionally, flights aborted due to weather brought tears to passengers. A pilot might tell himself that the fog ahead was unsafe, that in turning back he was fulfilling his legal and moral obligations to protect his passengers. But those facts could not always allay the anguish he felt when a young native girl on her way home for summer vacation began to cry because the pilot aborted the flight.

For some passengers, the problem was *not* turning back in adverse weather. When a pilot banked sharply while straining to get through a foggy pass, he could not afford distractions like a sudden scream from a frightened passenger. Fear was contagious; soon the airplane seemed to smell of it.

Fear could also be unreasonable. A young schoolteacher at Hydaburg absolutely refused to fly except in sunny, calm air—an infrequent combination in Southeast, even in summer. One week she cancelled her reservation to fly to town three times in a row because clouds moved in or a breeze picked up. Yet she was a spunky outdoors person who owned a skiff with a small outboard and spent much of her spare time exploring in it. In Alaska more people drown than die in airplanes.

Another young woman, a resident of Metlakatla, would not get in a float-plane unless the pilot promised to fly low and slow. We tried to explain to her that an emergency at low altitude gave the pilot less time to react than one at a higher altitude, and that like a bicycle, a slow-moving airplane was less controllable than a fast-moving one. Nonetheless, she remained adamant, and we humored her as much as possible.

Some of the most anxious passengers were Lower 48 tourists visiting Alaska for the first time. Accustomed to airliners, which cruised miles above the peaks, some cowered after takeoff in a floatplane. "Do you *always* fly this close to the mountains?" they asked reproachfully, eyeing modest hills a safe quarter mile away. Others thought that because the airplane was equipped with floats, it should be flown only over water for safety—not realizing that a floatplane could no more land safely on really rough water than a wheelplane could land safely on a rocky field.

I found that smiling at nervous passengers often reassured them, even if I secretly felt more like praying. I tried to remember to turn around and smile at everyone in general on each flight lest their fear go undetected behind a mask of confidence.

Fear, especially when allied with a stomach unaccustomed to bumpy air, occasionally resulted in airsickness. We placed airsickness bags conspicuously in the pockets behind each seat, and frequent passengers routinely opened one up to hold in their laps for their children. The bags also served other purposes. On one flight I noticed a stirring behind me and looked over my shoulder. A boy was peeing into an airsickness bag his mother held open for him. More than once a tobacco-chewing logger or fisherman used a bag as a spittoon.

Each pilot in the company had a different tolerance level for passengers' peccadilloes. At one extreme, chief pilot Gregerson, who threw his hat on the ground when angry at company people, never lost his patience with passengers, regardless of how late, drunk, or obnoxious they might be. At the other end, one of our pilots was quick to exchange curses or even threats with passengers who riled him.

Like the majority, my tolerance ranged in between. When a tardy passenger finally hurried down the ramp and scrambled into the cabin to join those who had shown up on time, I smiled politely at him but withheld a greeting. When someone in the airplane lit a cigarette (remember the days when people smoked everywhere?), I refrained from criticism or grimaces but jerked open the air vent. When a garrulous passenger talked on and on in my ear while I tried to concentrate on flying in bad weather, I grunted once in a while to acknowledge him but offered no other encouragement.

For drunks, however, I had no compromise.

In many Alaskan communities you could buy a drink or a bottle as late as 5 A.M. 365 days a year. Alaskans habitually took advantage of that liberty at a higher per capita rate than residents of any other state. They drank to alleviate loneliness, to unwind in town after weeks in the bush, to celebrate the state's easygoing atmosphere. The problem was particularly prevalent among the state's Native Americans, who were struggling with cultural upheaval and who, some people believed, had a genetic predisposition to alcohol abuse anyway.

The FAA prohibited a commercial pilot from knowingly transporting a drunken passenger. But in Alaska, solvent passengers could find a bush plane as easily as they could a drink, and if one outfit turned a drunk away, another would gladly accept his money—and perhaps inherit his future business. Thus, our criterion was not whether a passenger could stagger to the airplane unassisted (we helped him if he could not), but whether he was reasonably orderly. Like squalls, drunks were simply part of the job.

Given the choice, I would always have chosen the squalls. The drunk crawled into the airplane in slow motion, further delaying an already late flight. He fumbled with his seat belt like a child with shoelaces until finally you reached over and fastened it for him. If he sat up front (I allowed him to do so only if the other passengers were more soused), he poked playfully at the controls while you taxied. "Come on, letch get goin'," he would mumble. After takeoff he lit one butt after another and ignored the ashtray at his side. He babbled relentlessly in your face with whiskey-soaked breath and for emphasis jostled your arm with his elbow. When the unintelligible monologue eventually ceased and he began to squirm and cross his legs, you knew what was coming next:

"Hey, partner, I jush can't hold out no more."

You were tempted to let him pee in his pants, but you would have to do the postflight scrubbing. So, you landed on the nearest lake or waterway, shut down the engine, and opened the door. He crawled out and tinkled off the float.

While I chuckled at kids relieving themselves in airsickness bags, I refused to trust drunks with the same privilege.

A certain type of passenger never got drunk or airsick, never filled the cockpit with smoke, never caused the slightest trouble, yet was always unwelcome. The first corpse I carried was a heavy, middle-aged mechanic I had flown to Craig the day before. While working on a project, he collapsed and died. He was in a black body bag when I returned in a Cessna 185 to take him back to town. Rigor mortis had not yet set in, and the village constable and I groaned as we struggled to lift the body into the cabin. It sagged into each cranny we dragged and pushed it over, as if reluctant to go any further into the airplane. After takeoff I glanced over my shoulder at the bag, trying to associate the contents with the breathing, moving man I had carried the day before. I kept the engine controls at climb power after leveling off and reached Ketchikan in what may have been record time.

Some corpses had entered rigor mortis days before they traveled with me and emitted a stench despite the local mortician's injections of formaldehyde. No odor, not even of vomit or feces, destroyed an appetite more readily than that of death.

Injured and sick passengers also prompted me to cruise with high power settings, unless turbulent air caused bumps that aggravated their discomfort. Sometimes I was unable to minimize the bumps by throttling back or changing altitude or course, and I winced vicariously with the victim at each jolt.

My constant nightmare with passengers en route to the hospital was that weather would delay or prevent me from getting them to town in time for medical help. Somehow, like the Old Testament parting of the Red Sea, bad weather always moderated enough for us to push on through.

One commercial fisherman who had smashed his leg on his troller was so apologetic about the blood that dripped from his dressing onto the cabin floor during the flight that he offered me a ten-dollar bill to pay for the cleanup job. I refused it.

Ironically, the passengers who caused the most stress for me in my first months as a bush pilot were not business professionals or drunks or corpses or the injured, but fellow pilots. Employee benefits included free travel on our aircraft, and occasionally I dropped a peer and his family or girlfriend at a lake for an outing. Although pilots who ride along as passengers observe an unwritten code to avoid overt criticism of the left-seat occupant's performance, they cannot help covertly judging his every action, and with a deadheader on board, I felt the self-consciousness of a speaker addressing an auditorium of orators.

Non-pilot passengers generally assess a pilot's competence by the smoothness of his landing, although pilots riding as passengers realize that preflight planning, engine management, weather savvy, and other factors are also important yardsticks. Still, the landing is one of the most evident skills a pilot can display to a peer. Somehow, the presence of a pilot on board my airplane always seemed to activate wind gusts that caused a bouncy landing. The fellow pilot understood, of course, but no doubt silently reveled in a bit of schadenfreude. That phenomenon also applied on landing where one or more pilots from another air service stood watching from the dock. The severity of the arrival depended on both the esteem the spectator(s) commanded in my opinion and the number of them: the greater my eagerness to impress, and the larger the audience, the harder I bounced.

Like passengers, charters now also came in endless variety. I flew a free-lance photographer to the mainland on a balmy afternoon and circled repeatedly while he snapped the shutter again and again and again to capture just the right scenes for a magazine feature on Alaskan fjords.

I took a man who had grown up at the Mary Light Station on Mary Island back to the now-automated station, where he wandered along the grounds and beaches reliving forty-year-old memories.

A cartographer on a mapping mission had me climb to ten thousand feet, an altitude so foreign to our usual scud-running routes that I felt light-headed there.

A state Fish and Game Department agent rode with me to count mountain goats on the mainland and check the degree of winter mortality among the animals.

I flew a retired plumber around the perimeter of Revillagigedo Island, Ketchikan's island. He had lived in the town all his life but had never gone on a tour of the island, which measured fifty-three by thirty-two miles. "I didn't realize how big it is," he commented to me afterward.

The purpose of some charters was to transport things rather than people. When the bank in the Tsimshian village of Metlakatla ran low on cash, I flew a sealed bag containing $20,000 in bills to the community. With the seats removed in a de Havilland Beaver, I took a load of mattresses to the Yes Bay Lodge and three fifty-five-gallon drums of kerosene to a surveying camp in Wilson Arm. I ferried a dozen buckets of abalone from a boat in Cordova Bay to Ketchikan and hauled almost a thousand pounds of textbooks to the one-room school at the Neets Bay logging camp.

A black bear that persisted in raiding garbage cans in a hillside neighbor-hood in Ketchikan eventually earned a tranquilizer dart from a Fish and Game Department gun. A van delivered the drugged bear, all four legs bound together, to our dock, and after much sweating and cursing, six of us finally got the 250-pound animal into the Beaver I was flying that day. Three agents rode along to administer another tranquilizer in case the bruin awoke prematurely and to help unload it on a Prince of Wales beach.

Most days brought each of us at least one charter along with the scheduled flights to the villages and camps. Charters held the anticipation and excitement of mail call. They often took us to places we had never visited, and they could develop suddenly with the ring of a reservationist's phone or the crackle of the dispatcher's radio: "My brother is sick up at Point Baker; can you take me there right away?" Thus, we arrived at work in the morning never knowing where the day's charters would send us, or what adventures they might bring.

Some charters involved standby time, in which we waited at the destination while the passengers went about their business. For many pilots, standby time brought an opportunity to nap in the cockpit or read a few more chapters in an interesting paperback. At a logging camp, pilots on standby typically proceeded directly to the cookhouse, off-limits to loggers except during mealtimes but always open without charge to pilots. Pastry, freshly baked pies, sandwiches, cookies, fruit, salads, soda pop—the cookhouse was a glutton's delight on standby, especially when a busy schedule had allowed no time for lunch.

Camp cooks were aware of the risks inherent in bush flying. They realized pilots were their source of mail and supplies, their connection with civilization. So, in both pity and gratitude, they invariably mothered us. Some were almost annoying in their insistence to thrust additional food at us after we had sated ourselves, but we dared not be rude, not to a cook.

At a village or town, a pilot on standby could wander about with his camera to explore, browsing in the shops, pausing to chat with residents, warding off the local dogs' sallies.

No standby destination was more magnetic to me than Hyder, the old mining town in the extreme eastern edge of Southeast eighty miles away. The glaciers, fjords, cliffs and other en-route scenery alone made a visit memorable— when weather permitted a direct flight across the mainland mountains; otherwise we had to follow a circuitous water route that doubled the flight time. But it was Hyder's Old West frontier atmosphere that I found especially fascinating.

Situated deep in the mainland, its only connection with the sea the seventy-mile-long Portland Canal, the town had a population of up to five hundred during its boom years in the 1920s. But mining petered out, and now pilings jutted like tree stumps from a tidal flat where most of the false-fronted buildings once stood. The surviving buildings lay on dry land near the mouth of the Salmon River beneath towering, snowcapped cliffs and peaks—terrain so steep that in late spring and early summer, a waiting pilot had an excellent chance of witnessing an avalanche. A distant rumbling, like the prolonged thundering of a battery of cannon. You scan the high slopes and cliffs for a moment. There! A wall of snow tumbles down a rock face, leaving a trail of frozen clouds.

Although a sign festooned across the unpaved main street proclaimed "Friendliest Ghost Town in Alaska," the unincorporated community was home to eighty to a hundred residents (the population fluctuated). Many of them qualified as eccentric individualists for whom Hyder seemed the last stop, a sanctuary where at last they could enjoy relief from society's constant frowns. Resident Tom Taggart, a bearded, bespectacled iconoclast who expressed his distrust for most institutions in frequent, vitriolic letters to the editor of the *Ketchikan Daily News*, made state history one year when he became the first candidate to run for a seat in the House of Representatives as an indigent. Taggart apparently had few supporters in Hyder and failed to win there, or in any other precinct in the state.

At night the population swelled when Canadians from Hyder's only neighbor, Stewart, British Columbia (population two thousand), two and a half miles to the north, crossed the border to take advantage of Alaska's liberal liquor laws and the town's lack of law enforcement. The walls in the oldest of Hyder's two bars, the Glacier Inn, were plastered with hundreds of dollars in autographed paper currency of several nationalities. Look closely and you could find a few bullet holes in the walls, too: partying in Hyder was often unrestrained. So was squabbling.

On one flight to Hyder, my passenger was a young, somber Alaska state trooper who sat in the right front seat of the 185 with a warrant for the arrest of a Hyder man who had blockaded a mining road at the border. The Canadians had declared the suspect an "undesirable" and denied him the use of the road, so he had parked his truck across it. The US Department of Transportation office in Hyder had contacted the troopers. A state Department of Highways worker met us at the head of the causeway that led to the seaplane dock, and he fidgeted with excitement.

"Boy, we're glad you're here," he said to the trooper, shaking his head. "There's just been a shooting in town; one man's dead and the other's wounded, off in the woods."

He drove us into town, where the trooper pieced together the story, unrelated to the road-blocking incident, from residents milling about on the street. Thomas Williams allegedly had been trying to saw down a fence on a disputed right-of-way between his property and that of neighbor Richard James Shields. Shields didn't approve, and both men pulled guns. Williams took several slugs in the chest and was dead on arrival at the Stewart hospital, while Shields was hit in the neck. The trooper called for help, and an hour later a Grumman Goose arrived with more troopers. Shields, who survived his injuries, surrendered peacefully. Troopers initially charged him with first-degree murder but let him go a few weeks later when the investigation failed to determine just who had shot first.

One of the newly arrived troopers took over the case of the man who had blocked the road and, after arresting him, found he was carrying a handgun. The suspect rode back to Ketchikan in handcuffs in my 185 with that trooper.

In some way each charter to Hyder proved memorable. Descending over Portland Canal one August day, my passenger and I noticed that the typical turquoise water of the canal became increasingly caramel-colored as we approached the town.

"I bet Summit Lake has gone out!" exclaimed my passenger, who was returning to her home in the community after visiting her husband, an immigration officer assigned to Boundary, Alaska. Sometime between late summer and early fall every year, she explained, the melting of the Salmon Glacier about fifteen miles above Hyder allowed the adjacent Summit Lake to drain suddenly into the Salmon River. The massive influx of water swept mud off the banks and for a few hours discolored the canal.

A few minutes later, when we reached Hyder, the sight of a torrent pouring out the mouth of the river confirmed that the lake had indeed "gone out." I dropped my passenger at the seaplane dock, then took off and flew up the river to investigate. The normally tranquil river had gone berserk. Water raged downstream with uprooted trees and angry waves, flooding the paralleling mining road in places, licking at it in others. At the base of the glacier an explosion of water spewed continuously out of a huge tunnel.

I clicked the shutter of my camera until the film-advance lever would move no further, then turned toward Ketchikan, rich with the serendipitous good fortune of having witnessed a phenomenon that occurred at an unpredictable moment just once a year.

Hyder was no ghost town, despite its greeting sign, but some destinations had better qualifications. The Southeast forest was quick to reclaim neglected development. Many erstwhile mining communities, abandoned when the market for minerals declined before World War II, had since been absorbed by nature, with little to indicate their locations from the air save stands of second-growth timber.

Pilings protruding from the water and shore usually constituted the only conspicuous remnants of former salmon canneries. Among the second-growth trees at a village that Indians abandoned with the arrival of Caucasians, you might find rotting clan poles and ground depressions where homes once stood. Most old camps, canneries, and villages lay undisturbed for months or years at a time, more from their remoteness than the fact that state and federal laws officially protected them from the scavenging of artifacts. Exploring was okay as long as you left the site undisturbed.

But the need to baby the airplane often frustrated exploring at such saltwater places. With the tide ranging up to twenty-five feet and changing about every six hours, a beached floatplane could easily go adrift on an incoming tide—or aground on an outgoing one.

The dispatcher tried to schedule charters to tide-sensitive destinations like sloughs so that the airplane would arrive when the water was creeping up the gravel and mud instead of going the other way. Unfortunately, such timing often conflicted with the customer's schedule. Sometimes bad weather delayed takeoffs while the tide kept to its rigid timetable.

Arrive an hour late, and the bottom might look distressingly close on the taxi in. If rocks guard the area, you stand on the bow of the float and paddle the final fifty feet around slightly submerged boulders, using the paddle blade to ward off those that suddenly appear in front, hoping you'll remember how to retrace the course on the way out.

"Chop-chop!" you tell the sport fishermen at the beach as they hand you their soggy, muddy gear. The plane loaded, you start to paddle back out. But the relentless tide has dropped the water level a few more inches. And the airplane rides a lot lower now under the weight of eight hundred additional pounds. The float keels no longer clear rocks they skimmed over a few minutes earlier.

Desperately you paddle around the new obstacles to a rock-free area, then scurry in and start the engine. Sandbars nudge the keels and mud tugs at the water rudders as you struggle toward freedom. Half throttle pulls the plane through some of the stickier places. In others, the floats simply stop. Cursing, you jump out and with the paddle push the plane backward to try a different route. The remaining channels form a confusing maze as the receding tide chokes off one after another. Then, at one dead end you find the retreat too narrow, too shallow. You're stuck.

In minutes mud banks and puddles surround the aircraft in agonizing contrast to the deep water that sparkles tantalizingly a quarter mile away.

Three pairs of eyes stare at you solemnly. "Well," you finally announce, sticking your head in the cabin, "we might as well hike back to the beach and build a fire until the tide comes in."

You step off the float to lead the way. Instantly you sink to your knees in quivering, stinking mud. You pull yourself back up on the float, brushing the muck from your trousers with your hand.

If you and your passengers are lucky, there will be a few magazines in the seatback pockets.

Even on an incoming tide, wading a dozen feet or more was often necessary where a shallow slope grounded the floats offshore. Smart pilots kept hip waders in the airplane for such occasions. I found them too bulky and preferred simply to slip off my boots and roll up my pants.

Charters to saltwater beaches could be challenging in other ways. When I had to pick up a party another pilot had dropped off, that pilot or the dispatcher would tap the spot on a chart before I departed. But on-scene features the chart excluded, such as reefs uncovered at low tide, could complicate pinpointing the spot. If I failed to sight my passengers after circling a few times, I throttled back, lowered the flaps, and flew slowly along the shoreline a few feet above the water. Sometimes even then I saw only windfall, tree trunks, and rocks. A second pass. A third.

Then, like a double image that suddenly becomes discernible in an optical illusion, people were standing on the beach, waving jackets, and I wondered why I hadn't noticed them immediately.

Parties whose occupation or recreation often took them to undeveloped bush sites—survey crews, hunters, Fish and Game agents—had learned how insignificant people look to a pilot against the wilderness. They spread some conspicuous, brightly colored blanket or garment in an open spot near the pickup point.

By contrast, inexperienced bush travelers like "outsiders," the name many Alaskans reserved for nonresidents, frequently lacked the sense even to come out of the woods when they heard the airplane. Assuming the pilot knew exactly where to land, they instead stayed at the campsite packing gear and cleaning up. Eventually, the sound of the airplane roaring repeatedly by alerted them to the pilot's problem, and they hurried out to the beach to wave arms and yell.

A pilot could not hear yelling from the cockpit while the engine was running, of course. But yelling was effective when, as a last resort, he landed in the area of the proposed pickup, shut off the engine, climbed onto one of the wings, and scanned the shoreline.

"Heyyyy, over hereeee!" a voice would echo across the water.

In rugged areas with narrow beaches, like fjords, passengers who had wandered off to explore might become stranded at high tide hundreds of yards from the pickup point. Even after a pilot found the party, winds and swells could keep him from landing. All you could do then was rock the wings in a farewell gesture and hope the people had enough food and dry clothes to last until conditions improved.

Freshwater lake charters seemed sweetly uncomplicated compared with saltwater operations—more shelter from the wind, fewer rocks to taxi into, and no tide. Lakes could be inviting for other reasons, too. . . .

Chapter 5

BURNING OUT

Manzanita Lake lay on the eastern side of Revillagigedo Island near Behm Canal, along the route a pilot would logically follow back to town after dropping off two kayakers in Walker Cove. Thus over Manzanita one sunny afternoon, I noticed a Beaver tucked into a little bight on the southern shore of the lake. Staring to see if I could identify it, I recognized the color scheme as our own. I was bewildered. I had the habit of studying the schedule each day and monitoring the company frequency en route to keep track of who was flying where.

Besides myself, I thought the only other pilot currently east of Ketchikan was Jack Newport, a curly-haired, overweight high school teacher from Oregon who came north after graduation each year to fly for us during the Season. Newport had had supplies to deliver to a group of Ketchikan men who were building a cabin on a river on the mainland, but as far as I knew his itinerary included no stops on the return trip.

Had he encountered engine trouble? I throttled back and descended to about eight hundred feet. I could see no sign of Newport or anyone else on the narrow, tree-lined beach as my Cessna 185 flew by. Well, I had a flight to Craig as soon as I returned; I'd tell the dispatcher about his unscheduled stop, and if anyone began considering him overdue, the company would know where he was.

I crossed the southern shore and headed toward town over the muskeg and groves of trees that separated Manzanita from Ella Lake.

But suppose Newport was sick? He might have landed because of an attack of appendicitis or other medical problem. I banked 180 degrees and, two minutes later, touched down on Manzanita. After beaching the 185, I stepped out, walked over to the Beaver, and climbed up on the right float to peer inside. The door was propped open.

Newport was sprawled on the middle row of seats, his mouth ajar, his left arm dangling by the floor, his potbelly rising and falling rhythmically with his breathing. "Jack! Hey, Jack! Are you okay?" I shook his shoulder.

His eyes opened to stare at me for a long moment. Then they glanced about the cabin for another moment. Fully awake now, he sat up quickly as if I had kicked him. "What are you doing here?" he growled, moving toward the door. I stepped off the float, and he followed. "I saw your Beaver here and thought you might be sick or something."

Newport shook his head, strode to the tail, and pushed the plane off the beach into the water. "No, no, no, I'm fine."

"Then what were you doing here?"

He climbed into the cockpit. "What do you think I was doing, painting my toenails? I was taking a nap." The propeller spun and the 450-horsepower engine rumbled into life. He stuck his head out the window as he taxied away and yelled, "Hey, nobody has to know about this except you and me, okay?"

Newport undoubtedly was not the only floatplane pilot who had succumbed to the combination of long working days, warm, lazy weather, and an empty airplane. In recent weeks I had often had to open the cockpit air vents and direct the flow on my face to keep from nodding off. We were now in the middle of summer, the heart of the Season, and bush flying had become a test of endurance.

During my first several months at the company, the ringing of the alarm clock each morning had brought immediate spiritual intoxication. Unless the weather was bad, I dressed with the impatient excitement of a boy about to go exploring on his grandfather's farm. Where would I fly that day, I'd wonder. What interesting people would I meet, what wildlife would I spot, what adventures would I have? Days off were endless hours of fretting over the charters I was missing.

My enthusiasm persisted well after the other, more experienced pilots had begun their seasonal griping about long hours and back-to-back flights. But now, in midsummer, the frenetic pace had finally caught up with me, too. The alarm clock these days usually brought a groan and a willingness to sell my soul to the devil for another half hour of sleep. The anticipation returned once I was up, showered, shaved, and fed, and it flew with me most of the day.

But it waned again in late afternoon or early evening. By then I was saturated with flying. I was exhausted physically from manhandling freight and jumping in and out of the airplane, and exhausted emotionally from the challenge of the bush. I wanted to go home, to have dinner, to visit friends, to do errands. Surfeit drowns any joy. Yet the job left little time for other interests. Whether the company, or any other Alaskan air taxi, could survive the lean winter months depended on the Season's profits. No operator was going to turn away business because a pilot was on a lunch break. The pilot could darn well take the flight and munch on a sandwich in the cockpit.

Although we were limited by FAA regulation to eight hours in the air in any twenty-four-hour period, often it took twelve or fourteen hours to accumulate that much flight time. Most destinations in southeastern Alaska lay within a hundred miles of base, and many flights involved four or more stops coming and going. Such time-consuming aspects of the job as loading and unloading freight and passengers, taxiing, docking, fueling, and perhaps pumping water out of a leaky pontoon didn't count as flight time.

The FAA also restricted pilots to a maximum of fourteen hours on the job in any single day. Such limits were arbitrary. Some pilots could exceed them and still function efficiently. For most of us, efficiency and judgment deteriorated before maxing out on either flight or duty time. Late in the day, homeward bound, we tended to push through weather that would have caused us to circle and perhaps seek a detour in the morning, when we were fresh and unconcerned about getting stuck in some chilly, uninhabited spot overnight. We were more amenable to taking off with an overload on the last flight of the day, because dealing with excess luggage or cargo at the dock or beach then would have delayed the glorious moment when we could finally shuffle toward home.

Although we regularly chided the FAA for imposing excessively conservative rules in other areas of our business, most of us would have voted for shorter legal caps on flight and duty times. Since our pay depended on flight time, we applauded the eight-hour allowance only on payday.

Each pilot was responsible for keeping track of his own hours. For months I felt guilty when I told the dispatcher, "I can't take another flight or I'll be over my limit," despite my obligation to so inform her. Still grateful to the company for opening the door for me, still eager to impress, I felt duty-bound to continue hustling as long as the sun remained above the horizon. Bob Reeve, Noel Wien, Harold Gillam, and other famous pioneer Alaskan bush pilots rarely paid attention to the clock in the less regulated era of the 1920s, '30s, and '40s. Many reportedly flew up to two hundred hours a month during the Season. Who was I to complain about a mere eight hours a day?

But I could not stifle a curse when, taxiing up to the dock in Ketchikan after what I hoped was my last landing of the day, I saw a lineman waiting for me with a fuel hose and a pile of baggage. Another flight. Minutes later I was back into the air with the late-afternoon sun glaring through the windshield and the engine roar aggravating the ringing in my ears—back out once more while landlubbers were ordering dessert at a restaurant or holding hands in line at the Coliseum movie theater in town.

At home at last, I took a shower and fixed the easiest dinner possible. Even if I had the energy for socializing, the hour was often too late. So I collapsed into bed. Sleep came instantly, like passing out after a night on the town. And, almost as quickly, it seemed, came the shattering noise of the alarm clock.

Each pilot had two scheduled days off a week, two precious days in which to sleep forever and attend to overdue chores like laundry and bills. In practice, we typically had to settle for one, because business would overflow and the company would run out of duty pilots. "You'll be home again in three hours," the dispatcher would say. Never mind that a single flight might force a pilot to cancel a prearranged recreational outing that would have occupied the whole day. Most of us acquiesced. It was, after all, only one flight, and to refuse once we picked up the phone seemed disloyal, uncooperative. We had fewer qualms about just not answering the phone.

During my first Season, the grumbling actually prompted an attempt among some of the company pilots to unionize—a radical action in a traditionally conservative profession. A union representative from Anchorage flew down to Ketchikan several times to provide guidance during after-work meetings, and friction between the pilots and management flared occasionally into fist-shaking, threatening incidents. After initial hesitation, I joined the organizational effort, the last pilot to do so. But my misgivings continued.

Long hours, working on days off, pressure to get the job done—were not these the customary working conditions of the trade? Wouldn't the great pioneer bush pilots have shaken their heads in disgust at our flirting with a union? Perhaps because we wore airline-type uniforms we felt we were entitled to airline-type benefits.

Yet bush pilots no longer flew rickety, underpowered airplanes built of wood and fabric. Pilots and their craft now had to meet and maintain fairly rigid standards imposed by the FAA and insurance companies. In fact, the term "bush pilot" had been officially defunct since 1958, when Congress passed the Federal Aviation Act and the FAA coined the term "air taxi" to represent updated standards of small-airplane charter pilots. Bus drivers, truck drivers, ambulance drivers, train engineers, ship captains, and airline pilots also bore the responsibility of adhering to strict rules and standards, and all had unions. Why not seaplane pilots? Should we continue accepting long hours, working on days off, and other unpleasant aspects of our livelihood just because our predecessors had?

In the end, the unionization campaign fizzled with the involuntary departure of the ringleaders.

I noted that members of management themselves stayed on the job ten, twelve, fourteen hours a day during the Season, as did the reservationists, the dispatcher, the mechanics, and the linemen. Like us, they too wore scowls by the end of the day.

Only reservationist Jeannie Hansen maintained a constantly cheerful attitude. Her boyfriend worked at the Yes Bay fishing resort up Behm Canal, and the two planned to leave soon on a grand adventure: a three-hundred-mile kayaking camping odyssey from Ketchikan to Skagway. Sometimes in the operations room the slight brunette would adjust her glasses, smile, and gaze wistfully out the window while the rest of us chattered around her.

Gradually I found ways to make the most efficient use of my nonflying time. Letters could be written between flights. Socks for the morning could be hand-washed during the evening shower. But what to do about exercise? I was much too tired to jog after work, and jogging on my two days off a week, if I wasn't called in to fly on them, failed to satisfy my aerobics-starved body.

One morning, flying by a logging camp on Tuxekan Island, I spotted someone running along a lonely stretch of road below. I grimaced in envy for a moment. Then an idea flashed in my mind. Several times a week I got a charter with standby time; why not use that time (which might last for hours) for running instead of casually exploring or indulging at the local cookhouse? Camps and some villages offered miles of unpaved roads. I could shower in a bunkhouse or public facility.

Thereafter I stowed my running gear in the baggage compartment of the airplane and, whenever I had at least an hour's standby time at a destination, slipped into a private place to change as soon as I moored the plane.

I quickly discovered running in the bush provided an unexpected benefit. Long accustomed to sightseeing from the cockpit, I could now enjoy the country from a ground perspective. As my shoes kicked up dust on dry days and splashed through puddles on wet ones, I saw rock striations, the network of roots in an overturned tree trunk, and other details not normally noticeable from an airplane. Free from the engine noise, I listened to the rushing of a stream, the croaking of a raven (an eerie sound in fog), and the rustling of the wind in the trees. And I savored the smells: the coniferous fragrance of the forest, the pungent odor of a tidal flat, the rubbery sweetness of skunk cabbage. Sometimes my sudden appearance around a corner startled a grazing deer. Once I nearly ran into a black bear cub.

The areas I flew over every day now seemed animated, like a photo transformed into a film clip. Such intimacy with nature, along with the exercise and the hypnotic cadence of my pace, both relaxed and refreshed me. Afterward, the rest of the day always seemed to have fewer frustrations.

Too soon, these therapeutic breaks ended. Dripping with sweat one day, I returned to find my passenger, a heavy-equipment salesman, pacing by the airplane. "Where have you been?" he snapped, glancing at his watch. "I've been waiting over an hour."

"You said you'd need a couple of hours."

"Well, the person I had to see wasn't there. I could have called on a customer over at the Shoe Inlet camp, but by the time we'd get there now it'd be too late. My whole day's wasted."

I apologized, but back in town he complained to the dispatcher anyway. The word came down to all pilots: no more leaving the vicinity of the airplane on standby. Stay available in case the passengers change their plans.

Except when on standby, we seldom had time to poke around the many hamlets, camps, and outposts on our regular itineraries. With subsequent flights looming on the schedule, often already late because of weather detours, we usually taxied in, dropped passengers off or picked them up, then taxied right back out like harried New York commuters. In the air, we passed other isolated, interesting-looking pockets of present or former habitation like old canneries that were rarely on the schedule and which we were thus even less likely to explore. And of course everywhere we flew, in the mountains, along rocky shorelines, across meadow-strewn valleys, were unnamed, uninhabited, and inaccessible (at least by float-plane) geographical features and areas that we could visit only with our eyes, which we did continuously. Pilots gazed out the window as much as passengers, for fascination with the country was one of the appeals of bush flying.

Toward the end of the day, though, we tended to ignore the scenery and stare straight ahead in a fatigue-induced semi-trance. The country no longer mattered. Only getting home.

In such a state one evening, I hurried from Wrangell to Klawock to pick up three passengers. It was the last flight of another long day. Hunger gnawed at my stomach, and my buttocks ached from six hours in the seat of a 185. The weather was benign with a high overcast and good visibility. There was nothing in partic-ular to grab my attention. No reason to study the beaches on Brownson Island or the waters of Ernest Sound below. Instead, I flew along with my eyes fixed on the horizon and my mind in suspension.

Two days later I walked into the operations room after a flight to check on my next trip. I glanced at dispatcher Acorn in her cubicle and opened my mouth to ask about it. The words faltered. Her eyes were red, and tears streaked her cheeks. The corners of her mouth turned down, taut. Assistant manager Byron stood by her side, comforting her like a kindly grandfather.

"What happened?" I asked.

Acorn wiped her nose with a handkerchief. "An overturned kayak was found with the bodies of a man and a woman," she answered through sniffles.

I thought immediately of reservationist Jeannie Hansen and her boy-friend, who had left on their Skagway adventure two days earlier.

Byron filled in the details. A fishing boat had discovered the kayak in Ernest Sound with the boyfriend's body tangled in the rigging of a makeshift sail. The crew had called the Coast Guard, and a forty-foot utility boat from Base Ketchikan had rushed to the scene. After a search, the vessel had found Jeannie Hansen's body washed up on the shore of Brownson Island.

Residents of the Meyers Chuck fishing village reported the two had stopped there before entering Ernest Sound and that the kayak appeared to be overloaded with camping gear. Residents also noticed that the kayak looked unstable with the crudely rigged sail. Apparently swells in the sound had cap-sized the kayak. Friends had already identified the bodies.

"What time did the accident happen?" I asked.

Byron shrugged. "Nobody knows for sure. Sometime the day before yes-terday after they left Meyers Chuck. Those poor kids. They were so excited."

Over coffee at an adjacent restaurant, I tried to shake off the image, but it hovered around me like a mythological harpy: a woman clinging to an overturned kayak with one hand and waving for help with the other while my Cessna 185 floatplane flew blithely by.

That flight had taken place in the evening. Hansen and the boyfriend were probably already dead. Certainly they were. The boyfriend, caught in the rigging under water, would have quickly drowned. Hansen probably couldn't swim and also drowned, or died from exposure after a short struggle. And if one or both of them had still been alive when I flew by, an upside-down kayak would have looked just like an inconspicuous log from the air. Few pilots would have noticed a miniscule head and waving hand in the cluttered wilderness of water and forest even if they had happened to glance at the right spot at the right instant.

Rationalization helped only a little. When company employees took up a collection for the Jeannie Hansen Memorial Fund, established by Hansen's alma mater, Peninsula College in Port Angeles, Washington, I donated a twenty-dollar bill. Each time I flew by Brownson Island thereafter, a shadow fell across my spirit, and I would wonder again about flailing hands below, there or anywhere.

Chapter 6

WINTER

The days seemed endless but the weeks sped by. Soon it was August, and then September. The students who had come north to work at whatever odd jobs they could find returned to college with their memories and calloused hands. The last cruise ship of the Season blared its horn and sailed back down the Inside Passage to Vancouver, Seattle, or San Francisco. Loggers and fishermen spent more time in the bars. And bush pilots began going home earlier.

Now sunset rather than flight- or duty-time limits determined the end of the day. When we griped, the subject was usually the autumn gales. Although the volume of business gradually decreased, the nature of it stayed much the same with regular daily flights to bush communities. On the recreational charter side, however, sportsmen put away their fishing gear and came to us with guns. Their most frequent quarry was the agile mountain goat on the mainland, where we would land on high-elevation freshwater lakes. Chief pilot Gregerson advised me that I was still too inexperienced for mountain goat charters and would continue to make the less challenging saltwater trips. But whether he relented without notifying me or the dispatcher forgot about the restriction, I was occasionally assigned a goat charter anyway.

With their sheer cliffs and steep, rocky valleys, the Coast Mountains created a natural sanctuary for goats. Rare were the hunters who ventured the long, arduous, precarious climb necessary to reach goat country from sea level. Yet access by aircraft presented its own problems. State law prohibited the use of a helicopter for hunting, and most of the lakes in the high country where goats lived were too small for a seaplane. In marginal weather, getting to the lakes we could work meant climbing over and around a labyrinth of cloud layers and showers—then threading our way back through on the descent.

Unless the hunters requested a specific lake, we first scouted the ridges and slopes to locate a band of goats, which resembled little tufts of snow against the rocks, then looked for a suitable lake within reasonable stalking distance. In considering lakes, we had to think not only of getting the hunters in safely, but also of getting them back out a few days later with the added weight of goat meat; a heavily loaded seaplane needed much more room for takeoff than for landing.

While the hunters fidgeted with excitement in the cabin, I'd circle a potential lake several times, juggling its size, the gusts, the clouds, the probable load at pickup time, and the obstacles to clear on climbout. A pilot entering rainfog over a waterway in the islands could usually turn around if the visibility ahead looked too low, but here the terrain left little room for maneuvering. Many mountain lakes lay tucked in cirques, bowls surrounded on three sides by near-vertical walls, and there we faced a one-way-in, one-way-out situation, usually via the notch over the outflow waterfall, the lowest point. On approach to the confined deck of an aircraft carrier, a pilot could peel away at the last second to try again; a seaplane pilot who crossed through that notch was committed to land, even if he realized the lake was more challenging than it had appeared. Sometimes, still unsure after circling, I'd shake my head and tell the hunters, "Too small, fellows. Let's find another lake." There, the mental juggling began anew. The process left my mouth dry and my armpits wet.

Similar deliberations went on while fueling in town for the pickup, because at six pounds a gallon the fuel load was critical: too much and the airplane might not get off a mountain lake in time to miss the shoreline rocks; too little and the tanks might run dry on the way home. On a sunny day, a pilot could simply calculate distance and fuel consumption and add a few extra gallons as a safety reserve. A cloudy, showery day, a more typical condition, complicated the process, for you could never be sure how much detouring would be necessary to reach the destination lake, or whether the hunters had scored and the extra weight of the quarry would require ferrying the hunters out in two loads—that is, take off with one hunter and gear, deposit them on a beach at a larger body of water, return to the lake for the rest of the load, then pick up the first hunter and finally head for town. If a pilot fueled for weather problems that never materialized and thus arrived at the lake with excess fuel, a common remedy was to drain or pump out a few gallons. Environmentalists would have been aghast at the notion of raw fuel polluting a pristine mountain lake, but of course safety always trumped all other concerns.

Like a race car driver tearing around an oval track, sensing the shifting line between max speed and lose of control, a bush pilot had to know his airplane's performance capabilities precisely. Especially here. Taking off from a small mountain lake, you had to know within a few pounds how much weight the airplane could carry for this elevation, temperature, wind, and takeoff length. You had to feel in the seat of your pants if the momentum was sufficient as it plowed onto the step. As the other side of the lake drew closer and closer, you had to decide within seconds whether to keep going or yank back the throttle. (Without brakes, a last-second abort could necessitate vigorous fishtailing with the rudders to slow down before smashing into the rocks.)

If the load was too heavy for a straight-ahead takeoff on a bowl-shaped lake and lateral space permitted, a pilot might make a circular takeoff around the perimeter. One circuit, perhaps two, building speed. The airplane finally lumbers off. The pilot keeps the circle going as the craft slowly spirals up, around and around, past the cliffs and rocky slides. When he's gained enough altitude, he levels out and exits by the notch.

Some mountain lakes were long enough for a takeoff in either direction. The upper end typically fronted steep terrain; take off that way and you'd have to make a turn on the climb. The other way, you could climb straight out over the mouth. Most pilots would prefer to take off toward the mouth, but several factors might dictate an uplake takeoff. Convenience—if the hunters' camp was located near the mouth, a takeoff toward the upper end would avoid a long taxi to position for a downlake takeoff. Wind—a strong flow from the upper end would mean taking off upwind in that direction; airplanes need more runway length and are less controllable going downwind on takeoff. (But, depending on the nature of the wind, taking off upwind toward higher terrain could pose the possibility of dangerous downdrafts.) And visibility—if clouds had moved in around the mouth, a pilot might want to take off toward the upper end and gain some altitude to better assess conditions at the mouth.

Dwelling about all this would keep me tossing and turning half the night if I was scheduled for a goat-hunting charter the next day.

Hunters had a lot to think about, too, even before setting up camp at a lake. "If something happens to you on your way back, how will they know where we are?" a hunter asked one day as I was about to depart. It was a legitimate question when the drop-off lake was not predetermined. The mountains blocked most radio transmissions. In the unlikely event a pilot died before informing the dispatcher of a group's location, searchers might need days to find the right lake. (In a related situation, one air service in Ketchikan forgot to return for two hunters at Reflection Lake; somehow, the pickup was never entered on the schedule. Eventually, realizing they had been abandoned, the desperate men hiked down to salt water, built a raft, and made their way to the fishing resort at Bell Island.)

Cliffs and sheer terrain stymied some hunters in their efforts to get within rifle range of the goats, or to retrieve an animal they might have shot. Storms could keep them huddling in their tents, unable to go after the game they might have traveled thousands of miles to hunt. Low visibility and ceilings could also force them to spend extra days on the mountain while we waited for a break to sneak in. Occasionally, a seaplane company had to call the one helicopter air service in town when bad weather lingered too long; able to inch along, hover, and land and take off vertically, a chopper could handle conditions that kept a seaplane at the dock. Many hunters climbed back into the airplane for the return leg cold, wet, and skunked, down to their final rations, their clothing reeking from campfire smoke.

One of my passengers returned in a body bag. I landed in a lake to pick up two local hunters, but only one waited on the beach. He told me his buddy had broken his neck in a fall the previous day while descending a slope after shooting a goat. He cried in the airplane on the flight back to Ketchikan. There were more tears on the dock, because the wife and the widow were standing there to greet their men. State troopers flew out in a helicopter and retrieved the body the next day.

The snow line gradually lowered in the mountains. Soon the lakes were frozen, and even the goats abandoned the windy crags, taking shelter in the timbered areas far below. Now I confronted a new, more insidious menace.

While winter keeps a firm, season-long grip on the Coast Mountains, as it does on most of Alaska, it slips in and out of the archipelago like an indecisive invader. The prevailing oceanic air currents that bring Southeast its notorious rainfall also keep it mild. "The banana belt," interior Alaskans contemptuously dub the region. Even in January, precipitation in Southeast is more likely to fall as rain than snow at sea level. When snow does accumulate in the lower elevations, it turns to slush and puddles in a few days. Some low-level, freshwater lakes there stay open all year, and even in cold snaps the temperature seldom drops below the teens. At the same moment that much of interior Alaska is shivering in bitter, subzero cold, Ketchikan might be dripping in midforties rain.

"The weather here's the same all year long; there's just more of it in winter," a fisherman once commented to me with little exaggeration. Thus, while pilots farther north had switched from floats to skis weeks earlier, we kept on splashing down at most of the same places we had served in summer.

The company had cut back to four pilots now. Still the junior member, I had been retained because several of the more experienced ones had left to spend the winter in other pursuits. During informal chats, the remaining three counseled me about winter flying. "Watch out for snow," one said. "Spend as much time looking over your shoulder as you do straight ahead," warned another.

But to me, winter seemed little more than a nuisance. The rain was harder, the wind stronger, the clouds thicker. It took longer to get from Point A to Point B, and there were more aborted flights. In return, the short daylight hours let us leave work at 4:30 P.M. or even earlier, like normal people. Winter wasn't so bad.

One morning, rain had fallen from a cold, heavy overcast for hours. Now as I flew down Clarence Strait with a Ketchikan-bound couple from the Tlingit village of Kake, the rain began turning into brief sheets of sleet. The stratus seemed to be spitting at us, defying us to continue. I had flown through sleet often in the past few weeks, never with difficulty. But the sky looked bloated, and coming from it this precipitation brought a vague apprehension.

Had I been paying attention to the outside-air temperature gauge, I would have noticed—the information came afterward from the Ketchikan Flight Service Station—that the temperature had fallen eight degrees in the past four hours, and the apprehension would have become justifiable. The Tlingit woman may have sensed the same foreboding, for now she paused in the monologue she had harangued her husband with since takeoff. Uncomfortable with the sudden human silence in the airplane, I looked over my shoulder at the passengers, sitting together in the middle seats.

"You folks going to stay in town long?"

"Till the money runs out," the woman answered. The husband laughed, and both turned to stare out their respective windows. Out the windshield, the world had grown smaller. Points and bights along both sides of the strait several miles in front were disappearing in what had become continuous sleet. I angled the 185 toward the Cleveland Peninsula side of the strait until about a hundred yards separated the shoreline from the left wingtip. Now I could keep land in sight in case the visibility continued to drop.

It did. The sleet thickened, and the Kasaan Peninsula side of the strait four miles off the right wingtip faded away. On our side, the hills and slopes above six hundred feet also vanished in the wet, murky slop. I pushed the wheel forward to stay under the clouds and banked toward the shoreline another few yards. The microphone was clipped to a hook on the lower part of the instrument panel. I reached for it to check conditions in Ketchikan, then noticed again the black rectangular hole in the upper panel, reminding me that this airplane's radio lay on some avionics workbench down in Seattle for repairs.

If I had been able to communicate with the dispatcher, the Ketchikan Flight Service Station, or other pilots in the area, about weather conditions ahead I would have turned 180 degrees and spent the night with my passengers at Meyers Chuck, the nearest settlement to our position.

Snowflakes now mingled with the sleet—big, thick, flakes the size of quarters. More and more of them. I throttled back to slow cruise power and pulled the flap lever between the two front seats to the first notch, lowering the flaps ten degrees. Thus far in this, my first winter, little snow had fallen to sea level in the southern part of Southeast. The flurries that had fluttered over my routes had not affected visibility much.

But in this stuff I could see only about a mile. Would it get much worse?

I glanced over my shoulder to look at the weather behind us and stared into the taut faces of the Tlingit couple. Beyond them, out the rear side windows, visibility remained better. Town was but a twenty-minute flight from here over an easy water route. Cleveland Peninsula offered a fairly straight shoreline uninterrupted by dead-end bays and coves I might inadvertently enter. I could hug the beach and keep flying straight ahead, holding the same course at the end of the peninsula across Behm Canal, until the outer neighborhoods of Ketchikan appeared. If the visibility deteriorated too much, I reasoned, I could simply go back the way we had come, back into the sleet and then the rain, and seek another way home from there.

But the faltering visibility seemed to have stabilized at about three-quarters of a mile, maybe higher. The altimeter read a reasonably comfortable five hundred feet. I had flown in similar conditions in rainfog. This snow was a little grayer, a little thicker looking, that's all. I pushed nervously on.

Ship Island, actually a small, mostly barren islet, slid by off the right side. A few minutes later we passed False Island, a point with an isthmus submerged in the higher tides. Familiar, friendly faces in the gloom. The next landmark would be a tiny bight, and then. . . .

I shifted my attention from my memory to the shoreline. The snow had suddenly intensified, and, just as suddenly, the shoreline became a vague, ghostly, barely visible outline. I immediately descended to a few feet above the water and turned toward the shore to keep it in sight, but we were already just a couple of wingspans away and the extra yards made no difference. I pulled the throttle back and jerked the flap lever up to twenty degrees. Slowing down further made no difference, either; the shoreline, so close now I could have hit it by throwing the useless microphone out the window, continued to fade in and out of obscurity.

The swells by the rocky beach looked huge and ugly—too big to land safely in, or even crash-land in. Nor was turning around an option now. I could not, of course, execute a 180 toward the shore; we were below the treetops. And the right window showed absolutely no features beyond, just a gray wall. To turn away from the shore, to lose my precious hold on what was left in the world to grope blindly through the snow, hoping to end up back on the shoreline heading in the opposite direction. . . .

Firewalling the throttle and trying to climb through the snow on instruments would also constitute suicide. Besides the fact that this 185, like most bush planes, lacked the gyros, navigational radios, and other equipment necessary for instrument flying, my own instrument skills were woefully rusty. (Air-taxi pilots were required to have an instrument rating, but maintaining proficiency in instrument procedures was necessary only if the job involved instrument flying.) Had a sandy beach been available, I would have chopped the throttle and crashed on it. But the shore, when I could see it at all, showed only rocks and reefs and swells crashing over them.

Panic welled inside as I realized there was no escape, that I could only founder helplessly on. I made no attempt to reassure the passengers with white-lie downplaying of our situation. On the edge of my seat, my nose almost touching the windshield, I moved my head constantly across the Plexiglas, as if by shifting my eyes a few inches I could gain a bit of visibility. The snow now was so thick it seemed solid; clumps of it stuck to the windshield for a moment before the relative wind and propeller blast slid them up or off to the side. The airplane began to mush, and without looking—I dared not spare a second for a glance—I knew snow was accumulating on the leading edges of the wings, slowly robbing the aircraft of lift. I added a little power and the mushing ceased.

With forward visibility virtually nil, I concentrated on the shoreline out the side window. Here and there I saw a bight, a reef, a jumble of driftwood, just enough to keep the wings level. A new danger suddenly occurred to me. We were probably approaching Caamano Point, the lower end of Cleveland Peninsula. Between it and Point Higgins on Revillagigedo Island (the Ketchikan side) was the mouth of Behm Canal. How could I cross its six and a half miles of open water without a land reference? With no forward visibility, how could I avoid flying right into Point Higgins, or wherever we ended up on the other side, if we reached the other side?

I decided instead to turn north at Caamano Point and follow the Behm Canal shoreline to keep land in sight, hoping the snow would let up. I had never followed that shoreline in poor visibility, although I remembered from casual observation that it was indented with many coves and bays, all of which ended in rocks and trees. Yet I had no other option; perhaps one of the coves or bays would provide water calm enough to plop down in before I flew into the rocks and trees.

The faint image of a Coast Guard navigational beacon appeared for a moment out the side window and faded into the snow. Caamano Point lay just ahead. I stared for the point, cautioning myself not to turn prematurely. But on and on ran the ghostly parade of rocks and driftwood like fuzzy scenes viewed with severely myopic eyes. Where was the point?

The shoreline faded again and I strained to pick it up. Seconds passed.

Suddenly I realized we were surrounded by shrouds of snow on all sides. The point had slipped by unnoticed in the snow. New adrenaline exploding into my stomach, I started to turn in panic but leveled the wings immediately, realizing the opportunity was gone. Trying to pick up the Behm Canal shoreline now, after the 185 had traveled away from land, would entail a steep bank: we'd surely catch a wingtip this close to the water. And in such limited visibility, how could I find the shoreline and turn to parallel it before crashing into it? I considered an emergency landing, but the water was too rough, certain disaster.

The very waves that denied us sanctuary, however, became a lifeline, for the turmoil below created enough definition to distinguish the water from the snow; I was able to maintain a sense of balance by looking down out my side window. For awhile—was it seconds, minutes?—I focused solely on my tenuous view of the water, as I had the shoreline earlier. If the snow thickened to the point of zero-zero visibility, or the waves smoothed out, robbing us of the lifeline definition, I'd lose the water and likely crash soon after. At times the waves practically disappeared in a concentrated curtain of snow, sending another tingling rush of adrenaline through my body. Then the snow lightened just enough to bring the waves dimly back into view.

Desperate situations induce extreme measures of last resort. An animal caught in a snare will chew off its foot to escape. Some starving members of the Donner party reportedly engaged in cannibalism. And I, never religious, never a believer in divine intervention, started praying. Whether that inconsistency resulted from a subconscious cultural indoctrination or something else, I cannot say. But I had occasionally found myself praying before in the cockpit, and over the coming years I would again.

I had planned to cross Behm Canal anyway, of course, though not like this. Like a fool who had blundered into a near-dark warehouse to grope for a light switch somewhere on a distant wall, I ached to see the other side. An imaginary extension of the Cleveland Peninsula shoreline, I knew, would lead to the vicinity of Point Higgins and, around the corner, Ketchikan down Tongass Narrows. I flicked my eyes up to the compass, then back down to the water. East-southeast. At least we were still pointed in the right direction. How much longer? How much farther?

It occurred to me afterward that simple arithmetic would have provided the answers: plodding along with the flaps down at a groundspeed of about sixty knots, the airplane was traveling a mile a minute, so we'd traverse the six-and-a-half-mile-wide canal in six and a half minutes. But such dead-reckoning would have required a time check when we started over the canal, and even if I had thought to glance at the cockpit clock then, I might have been too stressed for ongoing time-speed-distance calculations.

Another question was just where on the other side we'd end up. East-southeast was only a general direction without correction for wind. In these conditions I was unable to tell whether we were drifting right or left of that imaginary extension of Cleveland Peninsula. The wind had been on the nose earlier, along the shoreline. It might have changed out here in the open. In the snow the turbulent, foaming waves muddled any clues about wind angle. On a couple of previous flights, I had crossed open water in reduced visibility dutifully holding a compass heading and been confused when land finally appeared ahead, or out one side. The lay of things failed to match what I had expected to see. Where were we, I had wondered? The opened chart on my lap had failed to help with an orientation because not enough landmarks were visible. When you don't know where you are, you don't know whether to turn right or left or, if the airplane is entering some channel, whether to keep going straight. In each case, I explored this way and that and eventually recognized our position.

Then I had had several miles of visibility. Now, with almost nothing. . . . Trying to find Ketchikan from Prince of Wales Island in fog, one of our pilots had flown across Clarence Strait and right into a bay on Gravina Island, south of course. Unable to turn because of a nearby shoreline on each side, he made a quick landing but not in time to stop before contacting the beach at the head of the bay; his Beaver skidded up onto the pebbles and driftwood, fortunately without causing injuries. Another pilot, flying commercially for a logging company, had had a similar emergency up on Baranof Island after a foggy crossing of Chatham Strait. Suddenly realizing he was inside a cove or bay, with no time to turn or slow for a normal landing, he slammed the Cessna 206 onto the water; both pontoons tore off, and the rest of the airplane shot up onto the beach. Again, no injuries.

I fretted about our own encounter with land on the other side of Behm Canal. I could only hope I would see the trees or reefs looming ahead out the windshield in time to maneuver safely. On impulse I flicked on the landing lights, thinking they might improve forward visibility. The lights merely intensified the snow, and I turned them off.

Perhaps due to an illusion caused by changing swell patterns of the open canal, I soon got the impression we were drifting too far north, although the compass still showed an east-southeast course, about 120 degrees. As if to compensate for that impression, the airplane began to drift right to a south-southeast course, 150 degrees or so. Pilots learn in flight training to trust their instruments rather than their instincts, and I kept correcting back to 120 degrees. But the airplane—guided no doubt by my subconscious motor input—insisted on drifting to the right, continually requiring correction. The contest of wills brought on a mixture off claustrophobia and vertigo. I began to doubt land existed across the canal, or anywhere. We had entered a Twilight Zone where the whole world was snow and water; we'd fly on like this forever. Already it seemed we had been over the canal for an hour, though the actual elapsed time could not have been more than several minutes.

A light flashed ahead. Seconds later it flashed again. Then a rocky islet with a lighthouse suddenly slipped by in the snow off the right wing, close but not alarmingly so. Guard Island! A once-manned, now automated Coast Guard light station, Guard Island, I knew, lay a half mile off Vallenar Point near the mouth of Tongass Narrows. Like all Ketchikan seaplane pilots, I practically worshipped Guard Island, for it served as the principal landmark for seaplanes crossing Clarence Strait from Prince of Wales Island in low visibility. How many times I had welcomed the sight of that blinking light after a low-visibility crossing. Now, from a different direction, Guard Island had again shown me the way home, a fortuitous Saint Bernard.

Relief overwhelmed me. "We're almost there!" I yelled over my shoulder to the two passengers.

From the corner of my eye I noticed a hand clutch the top of the empty seat next to me as one of my passengers leaned forward to look out the windshield. At first I planned to land as soon as possible in the typically calmer water of the channel ahead, but moments later as we entered it, visibility improved a bit, so instead I flew on. Now I could make out the shoreline on the Gravina Island side of the channel, and then buildings and marinas on the Revillagigedo Island side. We passed the Ketchikan Airport, and ahead I could see the town's waterfront.

The trembling started while we taxied toward the company dock. My entire body quivered as if with delirium tremens, and I noticed my mouth was so dry I could scarcely move my tongue. Feeling the need to make some comment to the Kake couple, I turned around.

"Well, I think we're here," I croaked.

Both passengers smiled wearily. "How did you see through that?" the woman asked. "I didn't see nothing."

The company was astonished at our appearance. The snow had moved in from the southeast hours earlier and no one had flown in or out of Ketchikan since. The airport was closed and schools were letting out early. The company assumed I had landed somewhere to wait for an improvement. No, I assured everyone, the fact that I had returned did not mean the weather was now flyable to the northwest. I had had enough visibility to sneak in, I lied, and decided to come home while I could, lest the snow last several days.

There was no reprimand from the company, no phone call from the FAA for having flown through the airport control zone without a clearance while the weather was below minimums (the specialists at the flight service station, we later learned, had heard an airplane fly by but were unable to see its registration number because of the snow). External criticism was unnecessary, anyway; self-reproach said it all. The traumatic flight was to have a lasting influence on my future flying standards and habits.

As if to punctuate the lessons with an exclamation mark, a Beaver floatplane from Juneau crashed in snow on Chichagof Island a month later. The pilot and sole occupant, who was killed, apparently was following a shoreline at very low altitude and flew into trees at the mouth of a stream. Not long afterward a float-equipped Turbo Beaver disappeared in snow on a flight from Tenakee Springs to Juneau. Searchers found a crumpled pontoon in Chatham Strait, and weeks later remains of the pilot washed ashore on an islet up in Lynn Canal. Nothing was ever found of the rest of the plane or the four passengers.

Like a hiker leery of distant rumbling after an ordeal in a violent thunderstorm, I tread gingerly for weeks. Sleet and flurries had me grinding my teeth and thinking about aborting the mission. I turned around often in simple rain if the visibility slipped below a couple of miles. Gradually relaxing, I rediscovered that rain and fog, unlike snow, change slowly enough to allow a pilot time to consider and reconsider the situation. I developed the habit of regularly monitoring the outside-air temperature gauge on rainy days and formulating some early escape plan when the needle approached the low thirties.

Snow had more to teach me. I learned, for instance, that it did not always develop insidiously from rain. On days when moist, cold air blew in from the southwest, snow came in clearly defined squalls: intense, dark cells with areas of good visibility, often sunshine, in between. Snow squalls brought not only zero visibility but vicious gusts of thirty knots or higher, and I needed no warning from the other pilots to stay away from them. Although I could see squalls easily, avoiding them proved more difficult.

They had a tendency to sneak into an area, like bullies suddenly stepping out from behind garbage cans in an alley. Again and again I'd take off from a camp or village to return to town, flabbergasted to find a squall threatening the route, which had been clear just ten minutes earlier. Pushed by strong winds, a squall could sweep across an airplane's path before the pilot could skirt it. Or it might simply move off in another direction. If fog was a German shepherd that barred its fangs, giving you a chance to back off, a snow squall was an unpredictable pit bull that might let you pass or just as readily attack.

Sometimes I chose to land en route rather than try to evade snow that began engulfing us. I'd taxi in circles for awhile. If the snow seemed to be taking its time moving through, I would shut down the engine and let the airplane drift. The passengers and I would chat, shivering as the cabin heat dissipated. Once or twice I beached the airplane so we could climb out, stretch, throw snowballs at each other, or otherwise divert ourselves while we waited.

A typical snow cell passed within an hour, lifting its curtain of gloom to startle and delight us with a soft white world instead of the familiar green of the forest. Takeoff, however, had to await sweeping the blanket of snow from the airplane. Each company plane carried a whisk broom with which to clean the floor of the day's accumulation of dirt, cigarette butts, sick-sack envelopes, and other debris, and the broom worked well for snow removal. But climbing up on the slippery wings with little to hang on to could be treacherous, especially if the airplane was drifting rather than at a beach.

If the snow was dry, a pilot could avoid that chore by allowing the powder to blow off during the takeoff. But such laziness was risky. One morning a shower forced me to land in the West Arm of Cholmondeley Sound on a flight from Hydaburg to Ketchikan. The snow seemed dry, and when the sky brightened twenty minutes later, I decided I could simply warm up the engine and take off. But we roared down the arm for nearly a mile before the 185 finally left the water, and then the airplane climbed as if it were hauling a thousand-pound overload. Obviously, part of the snow had not blown off. The remainder was altering the delicate aerodynamic design of the wings enough to rob them of much of their lift. Well, I told myself, the rest of the snow would come off momentarily, and the airplane would promptly regain its performance.

Again I was wrong. Although I held climb power all the way to town, the 185 never attained more than ninety knots of airspeed. At the dock I climbed onto the cowling to look at the wings. Five or six foot-wide sections of snow, worn smooth by air friction, still clung to the aluminum.

Later, I realized that if the snow had blown completely off one wing but not the other, the resulting aerodynamic imbalance might have caused control problems.

As winter deepened, getting rid of the night's blanket of snow, ice, or frost became a frequent preflight chore. If the morning temperature was above freezing, we placed each airplane on the elevator, lowered it until the wings were below us, and blasted the surfaces with water from a hose. But in subfreezing air such action would quickly result in a coat of ice. Instead, we resorted to muscle power with scrapers, brooms, and ropes. The ropes we draped over a wing and pulled alternately on each end to rub off the accumulation. Sometimes we needed an hour of work in the predawn chill to get the fleet ready for the first departures.

And sometimes, minutes after we finished cleaning the airplanes, a shower of snow or freezing rain moved through and replaced the accumulation, forcing us to repeat the process.

At smaller outfits with no seaplane elevator, ice and snow also meant problems in getting passengers and cargo down a slick ramp, especially at low tide, when the ramp pointed at a steep angle. We cheated; we simply used the elevator.

Cold mornings likewise caused tough engine starting. Since an engine that had sat in the elements all night needed prodigious priming to awaken, the possibility of fire loomed. The de Havilland Beavers' radial engines were especially hard to start when very cold, and they were prone to backfiring and igniting excess raw fuel that dripped out from priming. In case a fire spread while the pilot tried to start a Beaver engine, we stationed a second pilot or lineman with an extinguisher a few feet away.

These irritations were intermittent. As in spring, summer, and fall, many mornings in winter brought mere rain or drizzle, with temperatures in the high thirties or low forties. Different irritations arrived every few weeks, when the usual mild oceanic air currents retreated before a high-pressure system over Canada. Then the sky cleared, the temperature dropped into the teens, and vicious northeast winds roared down the mainland valleys to shoot across the waterways in black microbursts that often created waterspouts. The temperature differential between the air and the water was enough so that fog-like vapor wafted from the warmer water. Such a period—without a cloud in the sky—brought thorny operating conditions.

We stamped our feet and wiped our gloves across our noses while loading the aircraft in the uncommon cold, which the wind aggravated to chill factors well below zero. We screamed for someone to turn off the fuel pump master switch when, having filled a tank, we released the lever on the hose nozzle and the frozen plunger failed to pop out, allowing fuel to gush over the wing, the fuselage, the dock. Even on short flights, jarring turbulence justified climbing to six thousand or seven thousand feet to get into smoother air above the peaks. At those altitudes the outside-air temperature gauge read fifteen or twenty below; even with the cabin heat turned up to maximum, we saw our breath in the cockpit.

Destinations protected from the prevailing southeast wind became unworkable in swells driven by the northeast wind during one of these clear winter spells. Freezing spray accumulated on the tail and floats with each takeoff, the weight on the tail requiring full forward elevator trim if the payload had a rearward center of gravity. Water rudders froze in the retracted position, forcing us to shut down the engine after landing and crawl carefully along the icy float to kick them free so we could steer.

To encourage an operable water rudder system in a cold snap, we cycled the rudders up and down several times after takeoff. Sometimes they jammed up anyway. A surer remedy was simply to fly with the rudders down, but even then the water rudder cables themselves sometimes froze, rendering the rudders useless.

When we could steer after landing, we sometimes found sheltered coves and harbors that had freshwater runoffs to be clogged with ice. The pontoons could serve as icebreakers if the ice was fairly thin, although cutting a swath made a terrible crunching and scraping noise.

The sole virtue of a clear, cold spell was the chance to gaze at the panorama of snowcapped mountains and hills so often hidden behind the persistent winter murk. But scenery had its limits as compensation for fighting the chill, the northeast gusts, and the ice. After a few days of a cold snap we almost cheered when the temperature finally climbed back into the thirties, the wind switched around to the prevailing southeast, and the rain returned. Once again the docks glistened, and the forested slopes wore their rich green verdure and poetic misty shrouds. Even the gulls approved, swooping and screeching with their old frenzy.

Besides the short working hours, winter brought a few other advantages: like the virtual absence of tourists. While visitors generated substantial revenue for the company and other businesses around Alaska in the Season, they created hassles for pilots. Sedentary and overweight, tourists were often unable to struggle into the airplane without a push or a pull. Then they needed help adjusting and fastening their seat belts. In the air they badgered the pilot with inane but serious questions ("Can you show us an igloo?") and complained like spoiled children because of turbulence or rain that hid scenery. On summer days when several cruise ships lay anchored in port, some of us were stuck with tourists on sightseeing flights from morning to evening.

But not in winter. Then almost all passengers were resident Southeasterners, who neither needed nor expected pampering.

For most company employees, the seasonal slowdown of winter offered a chance for a long vacation. Our inter-airline agreements permitted us to travel on the major carriers at greatly reduced fares; in some cases only the tax applied, putting southern California, Hawaii, and even Tahiti within financial means. I flew throughout the winter. When battle fatigue finally prompted me to get away, I had more than a vacation in mind.

Chapter 7

ESCAPE ATTEMPT

For the third time I tore the copy paper out of the typewriter, crumpled it in my fist, and threw it in the wastebasket at the side of my desk. I sighed and glanced about the newsroom. Managing editor Clinton Andrews was studying me, his elbows on his desk and his hands folded together under his jaw. When our eyes met he lowered his to a clutter of envelopes, manuscripts, and memos in front of him.

It was July and I was in my fourth month as a reporter for the *Anchorage Daily Times*. In March I had contracted a severe case of disenchantment with bush flying. The last few weeks of winter had brought unusually bad flying weather, and almost daily bouts with snow or gales had left me exhausted physically and emotionally. When the weather finally moderated with the approach of spring, the specter of another Season brought no joy. Once again I faced a long, frenetic summer with little time for socializing, hiking, fishing, and other activities I enjoyed. Life had more to offer than flying floatplanes, I told myself. What future did bush flying hold for me, anyway? Rungs to climb on a career ladder, promotions to strive toward? At thirty, some journalists had become department editors, while I was still flying drunks and greasy freight through the rain in the boondocks. If I remained a bush pilot, I would still be flying drunks and greasy freight when I turned forty—assuming the law of averages hadn't sent me into a foggy slope by then. A few bush pilots advanced by becoming air service owners, but not on flight pay and bank loans. Each had capital from other sources. I didn't.

Like an adventurer who had backpacked abroad after graduation, I had tasted a year of color and excitement in the sky. But overindulgence in it had produced a hangover. The party was over. Time to come back to earth and move on.

Resumes and writing samples to newspapers in Seattle and Anchorage had resulted in an interview with Andrews of the *Times*, Alaska's largest paper. Yet now, after more than three months in the newsroom in Anchorage, disenchantment again tormented me. Day after day I sat at my desk typing stories of importance to Anchorage but which, increasingly, meant yawns to me: faulty engineering in a new office building, overcrowding in local jails, traffic jams on area highways. Once or twice a day I varied the routine by walking over to the courthouse to peruse legal documents; I had the court beat as well as general-news assignments.

My present project concerned reaction to expanded benefits the Ninth Alaska Legislature had voted for the state's workman's compensation insurance program. But my mind refused to bring order to the facts, figures, and quotes scribbled in my notebook. Instead, it wandered seven hundred miles southeast and wondered if the rotting totem pole by the beach at the abandoned village of Old Kasaan was still standing. It worried about the health of the elderly Cliffords in their cabin in Deep Bay, and smelled Martha Fosse's freshly baked cinnamon rolls in the cookhouse at the Port Alice logging camp. Efforts to concentrate on increased insurance premiums were interrupted by images of seiners pursing their nets in a quiet inlet. The clacking of other typewriters in the newsroom faded before the throbbing of a half dozen engines in the dawn air as pilots and linemen pulled carts of freight, mail, and baggage to the seaplane elevator.

Other interference came from daydreams of snowcapped mountains, shimmering waterways, and forested islands, for only in my imagination did I see such scenery now. My desk was in a windowless corner, and the *Times* building sat in the heart of downtown Anchorage amid a jungle of concrete. At home, my seedy, partially furnished, ground-floor apartment looked onto a house-lined street in front and a scrap-littered lot in back. Even those views had taken weeks to find.

The ongoing construction of the eight-hundred-mile-long trans-Alaska pipeline, connecting the oil-rich North Slope with the port of Valdez, had turned Anchorage into a boomtown. Every month thousands of job hunters, entrepreneurs, prostitutes, and dreamers flooded the city, already the state's largest community and home to half its residents. The housing market had become a rat race. Our paper had run a story about a one-room apartment—without plumbing—that had rented for $500 (in 1975 money) a month in Fairbanks, which was also booming because of the pipeline. Every afternoon before publication, dozens of apartment-hunting newcomers crowded the *Times* lobby with a fistful of coins. They grabbed a paper as soon as the circulation people placed a stack on the counter from the pressroom, then slapped down twenty-five cents and rushed for the nearest pay phone while tearing the paper open to the classifieds. By the time I got off work and made the rounds, each vacancy had been rented and unsuccessful contenders stood in a group outside, commiserating.

A *Times* employee who used his position to gain an economic advantage over the public faced dismissal if caught. But I was living in the basement of a fellow reporter's house and my dog was living in a kennel. One morning I strolled into the production room, sneaked a look at that day's classified pasteups hours before publication, and memorized the phone number of a suitable new listing.

Back in the newsroom, I called the landlord. Then I drove to the address and gave him a deposit.

At last I was able to retrieve my dog from the kennel.

Feeling Andrews's eyes on me again, I forced enough concentration to type a couple of sentences. During the job interview I had assured the managing editor after his questions that, yes, I had indeed "gotten flying out of my system" and was quite "willing to give up Southeast for life in the city." But Andrews, a bespectacled, easygoing, veteran newspaperman with a southern drawl, had no doubt seen the look of homesickness on the faces of new reporters before; I doubted that my self-conscious efforts to emit enthusiasm fooled him.

I had already ceased trying to fool myself. Trouble was, the Season was half over and operators had hired all the pilots they needed weeks earlier. One evening I had called the owner of Coast Air, my old company, ostensibly to say hi but actually to get a feeling for pilot needs. The company had a full crew. So did the other air services I subsequently called in Ketchikan. And, I assumed, so did other air services around the state. So now I was grounded in a city, typing boring articles.

The buzzer on my phone sounded, and I picked up the receiver. Static on the line. Long distance.

"Hi, this is Paul Breed of Flair Air in Klawock. Heard by the grapevine that you might be interested in coming back to Southeast to fly. We're so damn busy here that neither Kirk nor I can take a day off. We could sure use an extra pilot."

As a reporter in Ketchikan I had interviewed Paul Breed when he was commander of the Coast Guard air station on Annette Island and again, after his retirement, when he started an air taxi at Klawock on Prince of Wales Island. As a pilot I had often chatted with the tall, gaunt, forty-five-year-old Coast Guard Academy graduate when we met at the same places in the bush.

I had flown to Klawock many times, but when I arrived there to work for Breed later that week, the sleepy Tlingit village looked smaller than I remembered. With just four hundred residents, a couple of stores, a salmon cannery, a sawmill, and no paved roads, Klawock seemed an odd place for an air taxi. But Breed had wanted his own air service in southern Southeast, and Ketchikan already had six outfits. No air service was based on Prince of Wales, one hundred forty miles long and forty miles wide, the third largest island in the country (behind Kodiak and Hawaii). Since many flights originating in Ketchikan went to the island, Breed reasoned that establishing his business in some community there would prove profitable for him and convenient for the island's twenty-five hundred residents.

He decided on Klawock as a logical base for his Flair Air, an acronym for fishing, logging, aviation, industry, and recreation. The village lay about fifty-five miles northwest of Ketchikan on the west coast of Prince of Wales roughly at the island's midpoint along the north/south axis. An old, twenty-four-mile logging road wound along the Harris River from Klawock to the tiny settlement of Hollis on the east side of the island. Since Hollis was the terminus for the ferry that made several runs to Ketchikan each week, Klawock had a convenient surface link with town.

Klawock also had a surface link with Prince of Wale's largest shopping center; the road extended from Klawock six miles to quaint little Craig, a mostly Caucasian fishing village set on an islet connected by a short causeway to Prince of Wales. With seven hundred residents, it featured a handful of grocery and general stores, a couple of restaurants, two bars, a bank, a hotel, a cold-storage plant, and a lively atmosphere. Why not base Flair Air there? Due to exposure, Craig often was unworkable in southeasterly gales while at the same moment Klawock, sheltered behind several islets, might have a breeze of just ten knots.

Flair Air, at the bottom of the foot ramp in the Klawock boat harbor, consisted of a small office cluttered with files, magazines, and paperwork, a seaplane ramp, a fuel-storage tank, and two de Havilland Beaver floatplanes. Until two days before my arrival, the outfit also had a Cessna 185 on amphibious floats. On that day Breed, harried by a tight schedule and delayed by a Grumman Widgeon ahead of him in the takeoff sequence at the Ketchikan Airport, had flown all the way back to Klawock without retracting the landing gear.

"I knew something was wrong because the cruise speed was low," he admitted, "but 1 was tired and thinking about the next flight, and it just didn't occur to me that the gear might still be extended."

As soon as he touched down in the Klawock harbor, the sudden deceleration caused by the drag of the gear flipped the 185. Neither Breed nor his three passengers suffered injuries beyond bumps and bruises, but of course all got wet during the evacuation. A witness hurried out in a skiff to pick them up. (Ironically, the Widgeon, which had headed in the other direction from Ketchikan, also crashed and sank.)

The accident was an acute embarrassment for Breed, the first blemish on an illustrious, twenty-year, fourteen-thousand-hour military flying career. In between two tours of duty at the Kodiak Air Station on Kodiak Island in Alaska, he had served as the commander of the Coast Guard's VIP unit, which was responsible for flying cabinet-level officers and other top-rank personnel all over the world. Several times Breed himself flew the Coast Guard commandant to Europe in jets. His last assignment was as commander of the Annette Air Station near Ketchikan.

Breed's three tours in Alaska included many hazardous search and rescue flights. Even as a commander, he frequently assigned himself to a mission, performing dramatic helicopter rescues of crews aboard foundering fishing vessels, sometimes at night in stormy seas. In 1967, during his second tour at Kodiak, the Air Force selected him as the person who had made the greatest contributions to search and rescue missions in Alaska for the year.

His new air service was a family operation, typical of the ma-and-pa outfits across Alaska. The first year Breed did all the flying and maintenance himself, sometimes working sixteen hours a day. "This is the only job I've ever had which consumes all my energy," he told me. His wife, Betty, served as dispatcher, reservationist, and bookkeeper. An attractive woman four years older than her husband, she chain-smoked Kools and wore her hair in a pony tail. Paul Junior, eleven, a precocious youngster who attended school in Craig, earned his allowance by pumping leakage out of the pontoons, keeping the windshields clean, and performing other tasks. Eventually, Breed hired a Klawock woman part-time to "give Betty some time off so she could run the family." Later, he lured pilot Kirk Thomas from Coast Air in Ketchikan to help with the flying. The Breeds had a house by a lagoon near the village.

Thomas and his wife, Pam, lived with their infant son in a rented house in Craig. Pam often worked in the company office.

Although I had been hired as a pilot, the small size of the outfit imposed some nonflying duties on me, as it did on all of us. When Betty wanted to go home for an hour or use the portable latrine outside the office, and I had no immediate flight on the schedule, I moved behind the counter to answer the phone, log reservations, dispatch for Thomas or Breed, and accept payments from customers. I also handled payments in the field, working from a fifty-dollar bankroll for cash transactions. (In Ketchikan, the office people had collected fares.) I gave passengers courtesy rides in the van and picked up supplies in Craig. Such involvement gave me a homey sense of belonging and a deeper interest in the operation's success than I had experienced in Ketchikan. And I felt more comfortable in jeans and a casual shirt than a formal uniform.

One frustration for all of us came from the Klawock phone system. The gremlins that occupied the system were experts. They often gave both our lines a busy signal when neither was in use, thwarting efforts by potential customers to contact us. Or the gremlins deactivated the ringer on our phone so that we were unaware when callers were on the other end. When they allowed callers to reach us, the gremlins frequently interjected so much static on the line that both parties had to yell to communicate, even if the other party was as close as Craig. The Breeds had a phone extension in their home to accommodate persistent customers who finally managed to get through after the office had closed. Again and again Breed complained to the phone company, and he took out an ad in the *Ketchikan Daily News* to apologize to customers for the trouble they had in contacting us. Eventually the phone company installed new equipment, and the gremlins went elsewhere.

Many of the places I flew to now were also served by the air services in Ketchikan. But our location in Klawock often gave us an advantage over the Ketchikan outfits. When the passes across the island were shrouded in fog, but the weather was otherwise workable, we inherited some flights that originated and ended on our side and which the Ketchikan pilots were unable to make. We also attracted many island residents who wanted to get to town as early in the morning as possible; we didn't have to dispatch an airplane from Ketchikan to pick them up.

The hours were as long as they had been in Ketchikan, but my greater responsibility in the operation made them more meaningful. Breed assured that Thomas and I each got two days off a week; never once were we called in to work an extra day. While he sometimes ranted at his family to vent frustration, he rarely uttered a word of reproach to either of us. He realized different pilots have different levels of skills and standards. In a small outfit, idiosyncrasies quickly become apparent. I usually needed a few more minutes to complete a multistop flight than Thomas or Breed, probably because I was less experienced than they. On particularly frantic days Betty might fuss, but Breed did not. He was satisfied that I brought the airplanes back without incident, that I got the job done, and that passengers had no complaints. Perhaps he also remembered the lesson he had learned about haste with the 185 amphibian.

Only once did Breed let me know he disagreed with the way I had handled a problem. I took off one morning to pick up a Ketchikan radio/television manager and his party from Black Bear Lake, just ten miles east of Klawock. The lake sat in a mountain bowl surrounded by sheer slopes and jagged peaks, with a fairly narrow gap at the mouth as the only way in or out. When I arrived, clouds swirled around the gap. I circled a few times, occasionally spotting the lake through holes. The lake itself looked open, so I radioed the office that I was going in.

After landing and loading my passengers and their gear, however, I realized I could no longer tell, from my position on the lake, whether holes still remained in the clouds at the gap. I would have to be in the air to have the proper angle to check conditions there. A heavy load would make the airplane less maneuverable in case I had to make a sudden, sharp turn. I explained the situation to the passengers, unloaded them and the gear, took off and squeezed out of the lake along one side of the gap. Back at Klawock, I told Breed we would have to wait for better weather to retrieve the party safely.

"Don't you think it was kind of dumb to go into the lake if you couldn't get back out with the people?" he snapped. He shook his head in disgust and strode out of the office. That afternoon, when the sun had burned away some of the clouds, he brought out the Black Bear Lake passengers himself. He ignored me until late the following day, when he suddenly began bantering as if the incident had never happened.

Despite whatever problems the day had brought, Breed almost always said "thank you" to Thomas and me as we left for home. When we quit in early evening, the Breeds occasionally invited us to dinner at their home or the Prince of Wales Lodge down the road. While the local Klawock residents were cordial—

they had adopted Betty into the Frog Clan—they kept to themselves, and we did not socialize with them.

I had rented an A-frame cabin in a stand of woods near the road to Hollis, about a mile and a half from Klawock. When I walked through the village to my cabin in the evening, only the dogs were outside to notice me, to bark at my squeaky boots or sniff at the salmon scales on my trousers. From the lighted, ramshackle houses scattered along the hill that bordered the unpaved main street came the sound of quiet voices or music.

Since Klawock was officially dry, area people wanting to unwind went to nearby Craig. Once a temporary camp for Indians gathering fish eggs on adjacent Fish Egg Island, Craig had two of the island's four public bars. There, fishermen and loggers gathered, still in their work clothes, to escape the labor and frustrations of the sea or woods. On weekend nights the jumble of voices and bursts of laughter in the smoky bars became progressively more boisterous. Not wanting to compound the challenges of bush flying with a hangover, I was content to sip soda pops there on nights when I felt a need to be around merrymaking. In the airplane the following morning, the sight of some passengers rubbing their bloodshot eyes and thrusting their pallid faces into the stream from the air vents reinforced my teetotaling ways.

After hectic Anchorage, Prince of Wales seemed a refuge in both environment and mind. When I was Klawock-bound without passengers on the last flight of the day, I sometimes throttled back to better absorb the spell that turned the archipelago into soft purple on a clear evening at dusk.

I realized that Flair Air's need for a third pilot was seasonal only and that in the fall I'd be out of a job, but for the time being I was willing to live one day at a time, to leave the future alone. There were moments of regret. On difficult days when rain and fog backed up the schedule, fomenting grumbles and scowls, I wondered if I had been too hasty in leaving the *Anchorage Daily Times*. Four months was a scant period in which to acclimate to a new journalism situation, I mused. And Anchorage's troublesome boomtown turmoil would have subsided with completion of the pipeline in a couple of years. A commercial seaplane pilot could always find at least a summer job, but lots of job-hunting journalists were driving taxicabs. Maybe I should have stuck it out at the *Times* for twelve months to see if my attitude changed.

Then, a day or two later, the skies would clear and the mountains, islands, and waterways would sparkle in the sunshine. Flying in short sleeves, I'd see killer whales frolicking in the waves and bears lumbering along streams and bald eagles soaring over the forest. People would smile and joke. And the good fortune to be a bush pilot would justify any sacrifices.

The transience of life and opportunities was underscored in early September when Betty, just forty-nine, suffered a near-fatal heart attack.

Too soon, the Season ebbed and business dwindled. At the end of October

I moved back to Ketchikan, expecting to hang out until air services resumed hiring in the spring. But five weeks later my old outfit there offered me a flying job. Now called Tyee Airlines, it had recently undergone a change in ownership, and a personnel shuffle had left the pilot roster short. The reorganized company was smaller and leaner. Gone were the uniforms; pilots now wore typical bush garb.

When Betty died suddenly after another heart attack, Breed himself moved to Ketchikan, bought controlling interest in a different air service, and merged Flair Air with it. Competition eventually forced him out, and he resettled in California.

While pilots played musical chairs and air services underwent periodic turnovers, some things stayed constant. The ocean continued to sweep a Pandora's box of clouds and moisture into the region. And the forest and the mountains remained as unyielding to the aircraft of one outfit as another.

Chapter 8

PRESSURE POINTS

Scattered puffs of scud hung in the Harris River Valley like ragged balloons, the only remnants of heavy rainfog that had blocked this and other routes across Prince of Wales Island all morning. Now, in early afternoon, the rain had stopped and the associated fog had lifted into overcast. Beneath it, visibility was good all the way to where the pass took a sharp dogleg.

During my observation flights as an apprentice, each of my mentors had cautioned me that thick clouds often bottlenecked in the dogleg portion of this pass during precipitation. Several years earlier, a Beaver had crashed into trees there after the pilot, flying alone with cargo, lost visibility in bad weather. Remarkably, he suffered few injuries, and after extracting himself from the wreckage he swung the mail sacks over his shoulder and hiked out.

When moisture was evident in the air I routinely hugged the outside slope before entering the dogleg to check conditions there and gain maneuvering room for turning around, if necessary. Sometimes I had indeed found the dogleg to be blocked by thick fog. But more often it contained just a mist or isolated scud I could squeeze around.

My gradually maturing weather savvy now activated an alarm somewhere inside my brain: Recent rain. Lingering scud. Watch out for dogleg.

An alarm cannot prevent danger, however, only warn of it. I chose not to listen. The morning weather delay had backed up the schedule. In addition to the five people on board my Beaver who were impatient to reach Craig on the west side of the island, a family of three inbound passengers waited there hoping to sail on the ferry *Malaspina*, due to leave Ketchikan for Seattle in just over an hour. It was winter again, and short days meant less time to probe the weather, to squeeze in the business. Swinging wide at the dogleg would cost an extra thirty seconds.

So, like a racecar driver cutting corners on turns, I barreled headlong into the dogleg—and met a wall of fog.

The curtain stretched from slope to slope and apparently from surface to ceiling. It offered no holes, not even a light spot. Yet I was too low to turn, and the stratus immediately above prevented a climb. No water lay below for a hasty landing, only the forest and a narrow, winding road. Now the racecar had become a locomotive committed to rails; I could only continue on.

Terror gripped me in my helplessness. I throttled back, lowered the flaps, and shoved the nose toward the treetops, hoping for some space there beneath the fog, although none was evident. If the fog indeed lay on the trees, I would have to decide instantly whether to crash-land wherever I could, or plunge into the cloud to grope blindly through the rest of the pass to Klawock Lake on the other side.

People like to think that confronted by imminent, unavoidable, violent death or injury, they will face it with teeth clenched and head held high. Stoicism can be elusive. I gripped the wheel like a vise and began chanting, "Oh god, oh god!"

Suddenly, at about fifty feet above the forest, I discovered a narrow, clear space between the trees and the fog, a corridor that had been undetectable from an angle above. Klawock Lake appeared a mile ahead at the end of the dogleg. It was the glimpse of the lobby when the sluggish doors of a crowded, claustrophobic elevator finally creaked open.

Over the lake in open air again, I climbed back to my original altitude, my mouth like paste. How loud had been my pathetic plea? Had my passengers heard? At the seaplane dock at Craig, they stepped out of the cabin with no sign of strain on their faces. A couple of them smiled at me. Obviously, they hadn't realized how close they had come to obliteration. Apparently they had regarded our sudden descent in the dogleg as a routine maneuver, though perhaps a bit roughly handled. The pilot, they presumed, knew the corridor was there.

After takeoff with the three inbound passengers, I turned south to try an alternate pass from Trocadero Bay to Twelvemile Arm. It was wide open. As the Beaver rumbled along toward Ketchikan, I sat grim-faced, numbed, angry at myself for having been so reckless. I had surrendered caution to pressure and had nearly killed myself and five innocent people in the process. The thought of death in the fog resurrected images of a recent grim experience.

Months earlier a thirty-six-year-old pilot for another air service in Ketchikan and four of his six Forest Service passengers had died when their Beaver crashed in fog on climb out from the Thorne Bay logging camp on the east side of Prince of Wales. Approaching the camp shortly after the accident on a charter of my own, I noticed a flotilla of boats racing down the bay. "I wonder what's going on," I said to the loggers on board. At the seaplane dock we learned about the crash; the boats were hurrying to the scene to help. We watched solemnly as a rescue helicopter arrived and dangled a stretcher over the wooded knoll where the crash occurred, the rapid *whomp-whomp-whomp* of its rotor blades puncturing the air.

The less injured of the two survivors had already been taken to the camp infirmary. After he received initial aid, an official asked me to fly him to town for hospitalization. Still in shock, with caked blood embedded in his beard and tangled hair, and blood-soaked bandages on his face, the twenty-nine-year-old man stared blankly at his feet on the flight to Ketchikan. In short, halting sentences, he told me that the floats had grazed the treetops before a wing struck a tree. One moment he was looking out the window at the fog and the next he was lying in the brush outside the wreckage, he said. I radioed the company, and an ambulance with its red light flashing was parked on the upper dock when we landed.

I returned immediately to Thorne Bay to resume my charter. As I entered the bay I flew over the crash site and spotted the crumpled wreck by the knoll, about a hundred yards from the beach. One wing had separated and lay nearby. Loggers had already cut a swath through the woods to the site.

Like motorists driving more cautiously after passing the accordion-like remains of a head-on collision, the rest of us had tiptoed about the skies for the next few days as if a crash were contagious. And for weeks afterward, the tragedy had cast a pall of gloom over the Ketchikan flying community.

How close I had come this afternoon to replenishing that gloom. A hand tapped me on the shoulder. "Pilot, are we going to get there in time?" one of the passengers yelled. "The ferry's due to leave in a half hour."

"I'll do my best."

I could only speculate whether pressure had compelled my fallen peer at Thorne Bay to dilute his own caution, despite his far greater experience. He would not have heard overt pressure. No air service owner was going to take a pilot aside, put a hand on his shoulder, and say, "Joe, this is a really important charter. You've got to get there come hell or high water." But like palpable prejudice in small Bible Belt towns, tacit pressure to complete flights pervaded every air service in the bush.

Fortunate was the pilot who turned around because of impenetrable fog or gale-force winds. He got a free pass. The weather was indisputably unworkable, and he had no choice. Everyone understood. Air service owners had little use for a pilot who *never* turned around; that sort would inevitably kill himself and his passengers and destroy an expensive airplane. A single crash could bankrupt an air service with lawsuits, bad publicity, and a spike in insurance premiums that were already exorbitant.

On the other hand a pilot who turned around in marginal conditions, when he did have a choice, faced a gauntlet of subtle recriminations that could only jack up the pressure next time. The first would come from his passengers after he announced, "Sorry, folks, the weather's no good, we'll have to go back to town." Some passengers accepted a turn-around magnanimously, but many grumbled and pursed their lips in disappointment and disgust. Occasionally one even started crying. There was no isolating cockpit door in a floatplane to block a

In a 1980 special study on air-taxi accidents in Alaska, the National Transportation Safety Board (NTSB) concluded that pressure played a major role. Between 1974 and 1978, the data period for the study, the rate of fatal air-taxi accidents in Alaska per 100,000 hours flown was double (2.57 versus 1.11) and the nonfatal rate almost five times (15.2 versus 3.29) that of the rest of the country. "In Alaska, the study said, "it is not uncommon for pilots to fly in extremely bad weather—stories abound about pilots who have been involved in numerous accidents and have survived. These pilots have become near-legends and are spoken of almost reverently by some young pilots, especially those who have arrived only recently in Alaska. Taking chances is considered a part of flying in Alaska by many Alaskans—not just the pilots, but also the passengers. Passengers affected by the 'bush syndrome' demand to fly even in hazardous weather conditions, and if one pilot or operator will not fly, the passengers will go to another operator. . . . The 'bush syndrome' goes beyond the realm of poor judgment compounded by pressures and into the area of unreasonable risk-taking."

The NTSB found that pilot error was more often an accident factor or cause in Alaska than in other states: 86 percent compared with 72 percent. The report also noted that "The Southeast, in which the flying involves significant float operations, also has a substantial portion of the state's accidents."

Another agency taking note of Alaska's air-taxi accident record was the National Institute for Occupational Safety and Health, which reported in 1999 that professional pilots in the state faced an 11 percent chance of dying over a thirty-year career, versus 2.5 percent for professional pilots in other states.

pilot's view of such reactions, or to block his ears from the cajoling: "Aw, hell, this ain't nothing. I've flown with ol' Joe in stuff a lot worse than this! Let's keep going."

Next his alter ego began nagging: The weather wasn't really that bad. You should have tried harder. Maybe you could have gotten through by skimming the treetops in the valley or taking the shoreline all the way around. The company hired you to fly airplanes to wherever the customers want to go, not to burn up a lot of fuel for nothing. Being resourceful is part of the job. The famous pioneer bush pilots would have found a way.

Back in town, the pilot saw the disgruntlement in the dispatcher's face as she studied the schedule behind her desk. "Well," she told the passengers you led into the office for rebooking, "we're really busy today. We won't be able to try again with you until four o'clock." Perhaps a couple of the passengers said forget it, we can't wait that long, we'll try another outfit down the street.

The linemen also made faces. They had hauled three hundred pounds of catalogs, mail sacks, food cartons, and other cargo from the freight room to the seaplane dock for your flight. Now they have to take it all back.

The company owner tried to act nonchalant. "Found the pass closed, huh? Well, maybe it'll be better this afternoon." But nonchalance didn't compensate for the lost revenue on the flight or pay for overhead like fuel and engine wear and tear. You knew that the owner, walking away hands in pockets, was filing the turnaround in his mind alongside previous turnarounds and the records of other pilots.

On particularly hectic days, owners trying to keep the company afloat and dispatchers trying to keep the schedule flowing could not always restrain their frustration when a pilot announced that he wasn't able to get through: "Well, we'll have to get somebody who can," one might snap, or, "Well, *Joe* got through!" No matter that Joe might have enjoyed the good timing to arrive when the route was between rainfog showers. Or maybe the weather was the same as when you tried and he emerged on the other side with trembling hands and cotton mouth. What counted is that he got through. You didn't. People remembered.

In late summer 1978, after one of his pilots came back from a turnaround because of fog, an air service owner in Ketchikan took over command of the Grumman Goose. "I'll make the damn trip myself," he was overheard muttering. Later that day, a passing fishing boat came upon airplane debris and a body floating on the surface of Sumner Strait near the Goose's destination at Labouchere Bay. The skipper radioed another nearby boat, which had to use its radar to locate the scene in the fog. Searchers eventually collected three more bodies, but deep water at the site prevented recovery of the other eight victims or the wreckage. (The twin-engine amphibian contained one passenger more than the legal limit.)

Peers rarely criticized a fellow pilot for a turnaround or refusal to carry an overload, especially if the pilot was still relatively new. But a pilot's performance determined his reputation and his credibility. A weather report from a gutsy pilot who turned around would persuade others bound in that direction to hold back for a couple of hours, while an identical report from a hesitant pilot after an abort would be tactfully dismissed. In the latter case, someone might say, "conditions change fast around here, so we'll send out Joe right away to check for an improvement."

Joe takes off. Forty minutes later the radio crackles in the operations room, where the rest of the flight crew has gathered, drinking coffee, waiting. "It's pretty spooky in the scud and drizzle," he reports, "but it's workable down around three hundred. It's a couple of miles in most spots. I'm making it." Everyone scrambles.

Soon, you reach the vicinity from which Joe issued his assessment. You judge the ceiling to be two hundred feet and the visibility closer to one mile.

A t least five other air service owners in Ketchikan had fatal seaplane crashes between the late 1960s and the mid-1990s. One might assume that these owners spent too much time in the office and grew rusty at bush flying, but in fact all were proficient. A pilot typically logs thousands of hours over many years before becoming an owner, and he then continues day-to-day flying alongside his hired hands. But financial pressure to complete flights often compels owners to take extra risks, for an aborted mission affects them directly.

Conditions might have deteriorated a bit, or maybe Joe simply has a different perception, the way one person will describe a paint job as maroon and another will say red. In any event, you don't want to push on in such low weather. But Joe's making it.

Unless a federal inspector was in town poking around, operators and pilots ignored most official rules governing weather, loads, and other flight considerations. Instead, the criterion was what could be done safely. And common sense. A pilot could cruise along just as well beneath a four-hundred-foot ceiling as the five-hundred-foot limit. If the airplane could get off the water with a two-hundred-pound overload, good enough. And as long as the babbling, drooling drunk could stagger to the airplane, he was welcome aboard despite the regulation banning transportation of obviously inebriated passengers. Because if you refused to carry him, he'd take his money elsewhere.

Although a paycheck was not contingent on completed flights, a pilot with a history of turnarounds experienced job insecurity. If pay was by salary, he might return after a vacation to find his services were no longer needed—and that the pilot roster included a brand-new name. If pay was by the flight hour, he might spend more and more time sipping coffee in the operations office while the dispatcher assigned flights to comrades with less seniority but fewer turnarounds.

Realizing all this, pilots pushed themselves and their airplanes, flying a line with pressure on one side and disaster on the other. Whether they survived depended on the width of that line.

I dutifully carried the overloads and the drunks, and I managed to slog through fog and drizzle as successfully as most pilots. In snow, however, I was a thrown horseman who had not yet climbed all the way back into the saddle. Still haunted by the traumatizing ordeal in snow down Cleveland Peninsula and across Behm Canal the previous winter, I continued to step back whenever the beast reared. Most of the winter was mild, with only scattered days of cold, icy, snowy weather.

Then came March. Like a retreating lion turning to roar before disappearing into the brush, winter now unleashed snow squalls that swept through the region almost daily in thick, dark cells spewing gusty southwest winds. They seemed to stalk my routes relentlessly. Everyone had to detour, knock on multiple doors, and land along the way to wait. While other pilots eventually struggled through on most of their flights, though, I limped back to town on many of mine, shuffling into the operations room with taut lips and oily skin. One afternoon late in the month, company part-owner Terry Wills called me into his office and closed the door. Wills was one of the most popular pilots in town for his flying expertise and amiable personality. He fidgeted a moment after we sat. "This is the hardest thing I've ever had to do," he said, frowning, "but I'm going to have to let you go." The office, a windowless, converted storeroom, suddenly felt overly warm. Wills said I was "too scared," and that both pilots and passengers had commented on my trepidation.

Shocked, dismayed, I admitted snow was a nemesis but pointed out that I had otherwise held my own. "It's almost April," I pleaded. "The snow season is about over. You're going to need all the pilots you can find for the summer ahead. Let me stay on till fall, and then I'll leave before the snow starts up again."

Wills consented to the compromise, perhaps in empathy over aviation-related stress. When he owned a previous, now-defunct air service in Ketchikan, he had had to deal with the crash of two of his airplanes. In one accident, the pilot stalled a Beaver after takeoff from the Deweyville logging camp on Prince of Wales Island, killing himself and all six passengers. Ever afterward, he lived with daily apprehension about another tragedy. Now, chronic financial worries plagued him. Soon, suffering from hypertension, he would get out of commercial aviation altogether.

Before dark I took a quick walk on a path in the woods, deeply chagrined. Fired! Although Wills hadn't stated so, the reprieve seemed conditional on future performance. I was on a quasi probation. Unless I redeemed myself over the next few weeks, I might not even make it to fall. Now the pressure was suffocating. The lion was finally inside the brush, but predators just as deadly prowled on. I'd have to slay each one.

In the first week of April, an Alaska Airlines 727 slid off the end of the runway at Ketchikan International Airport and caught fire after a botched approach in snow. Rescuers had to use crowbars to free the trapped cockpit crew, but only one passenger died. The accident reminded me that even the big boys, with their fancy instrumentation and intensive training and helping hands in the cockpit, were not immune to the consequences of pushing too hard. It reminded me that I was no half-god Hercules trying to perform an onerous Twelve Labors.

Still, the pressure. . . .

In midspring I was assigned to fly two fishermen up to Sitka, the old Russian capital of Alaska on the outside coast of Baranof Island. A lucrative, two-day herring fishery would begin in that area at eight o'clock the next morning, and the men had to catch a four A.M. sailing of a seiner. Fog had grounded Alaska

Airlines' flights throughout Southeast, and the ferry to Sitka was not scheduled to leave Ketchikan until a day after the fishery ended. A floatplane charter was their last hope.

Rainfog plagued our flight right from takeoff, forcing me to grope my way around islets and up channels and shorelines. Sitka was reporting fair conditions, so I had hoped that the weather would improve by the time we got to the Chatham Strait area. Perhaps we'd even be able to climb high there and take a direct route to Sitka over the mountains on Baranof. But as we approached the Cape Decision lighthouse on the southern end of Kuiu Island, I saw that Chatham Strait beyond looked gray and dingy. The water, rainfog, and ceiling were all the same color. Now we would have to cross more than twenty miles of open water at low altitude out of sight of land and follow the shoreline to Sitka around Cape Ommaney, on the southern end of Baranof.

The long open-water stretch across the strait between Cape Decision and Cape Ommaney was uncomfortable even in good weather; the swells were usually too deep for a safe emergency landing, and the water was too cold to survive in for more than a few minutes. Miss Cape Ommaney in low visibility by navigating too far south and the next landfall would be the continent of Asia. Cape Decision seemed aptly named.

Normally, I would have decided to turn around under these conditions. Not now. Not on probation.

The fisherman in the right front seat must have sensed my tension. He leaned toward me. "Sure appreciate your flying us out," he yelled. "The next two days have got to pay the bills till we go after salmon this summer."

"Well," I yelled back, "the strait's a little marginal, but I'll take a look." Off the right side, the white lighthouse at Cape Decision slipped by in the rain, swells exploding against its rocky base. Moments later, the 185 crossed the eastern edge of the strait. With no land in sight ahead and the horizon blending into the rain and water, visibility seemed much lower. I descended to about two hundred feet. Every few seconds I twisted my head for a glimpse of the receding Kuiu Island shoreline, trying to hold on to it as long as possible. With each glance the reefs and trees looked more ghostly. Suddenly, they were gone.

So far I had been navigating by familiarity or aeronautical chart. Now the compass became my primarily focus. The chart showed a magnetic course to Cape Ommaney of about 270 degrees, and I made a mental note that a 180-degree turn to 90 degrees would take us back to Kuiu Island, if necessary. Scribbling in my notebook, I computed that we would need about ten minutes to cover the remaining distance at our airspeed, which meant we should be able to see the Baranof Island shoreline a minute or two before that, depending on the visibility on the other side.

In between glances at the compass and clock, I watched the strait out my side window. Despite a light wind, the deep, undulating swells surrounding us foamed at the crests like frothing monsters snapping at the floats. Even the gigantic *China Clipper* of the 1930s would have broken apart trying to land here. Suddenly, the engine roughened.

Adrenaline prickled my skin, and I started a tentative turn back toward Kuiu. At the same time, a quick sweep of the instrument panel showed the manifold pressure, fuel pressure, oil pressure, oil temperature, cylinder-head temperature, and tachometer gauges to be giving normal readings. I stopped the bank, no longer sure I had actually heard roughness. The engine now sounded okay. Or did it? Somehow, its steady droning seemed—different. The fishermen were looking out the windows at the swells, showing no indication of having noticed a change. I decided I had probably simply experienced "automatic roughness," a strange aviation phenomenon that occurs only over places where a safe emergency landing is impossible and goes mysteriously away as soon as a landing again becomes an option.

On and on we cruised across the strait. In the misty rain, with no land reference, the visibility might have been two miles or just a quarter of that. Nothing but the open North Pacific Ocean on the other side of Baranof; maybe it was unwise to head directly for Cape Ommaney. I turned to about 280 degrees. Better to hit the island too far north and have to fly south a bit to round Cape Ommaney than miss the whole thing.

Before actually expecting to see land, I began squinting into the murk ahead, cheating, hoping, longing. A turn back to Kuiu Island was gradually gaining in appeal over proving my value to the company, but I kept going. Baranof couldn't be much farther ahead. I studied the chart again and again to estimate our position and reassure myself that I hadn't somehow misinterpreted the proper direction.

The fishermen had struck me as seasoned and savvy, and when the full allotted ten minutes expired and land still had not appeared, I looked at the man beside me, half expecting him to point and say, "Right over there, son."

" 'Bout time for ol' Cape Ommaney to show up, huh?" he said instead. He joined me in peering out the windshield, and from the corner of my eye I noticed his companion lean over to look between the backs of our seats out the front.

Well, maybe a strong headwind, masked by the swells, was impeding our groundspeed. Could we have unknowingly entered Port Herbert or some other inlet on Baranof, with the shorelines on either side invisible in the rainfog and the head of the inlet about to appear? The continuing rolling, foaming swells below provided the answer: the water would have subsided inside an inlet.

I could feel dampness on my brow and under my arms. And damn, the engine was sounding rough again. I pushed the wheel forward and descended to a hundred feet. Sometimes a slightly lower altitude yields better visibility. Not this time; the rainfog remained just as dense and gray and empty.

We could not possibly have already flown by Cape Ommaney in the fog too far to the south. After all, I had added a margin of 10 degrees. The lubber line in the compass still bisected the 28 that stood for 280 degrees. For extra insurance, I pressed the right rudder pedal and skidded the nose to 285 degrees, then 290. Could my arithmetic have been faulty? I scribbled on the chart again, and again came up with a ten-minute crossing.

"We lost, partner?" The rear-seat fisherman said, his words sounding more like an accusation than a question.

"No!" I barked in defiance of my thumping heart. Where *were* we? I could not have been *this* off on the time. The swells so close below looked larger than ever. The chart showed that if we had indeed missed Cape Ommaney, a 90-degree turn to the right would take us to the west coast of Baranof; if we were still over Chatham Strait, that turn would eventually intercept Kuiu Island. Either way, that tactic would lead to land.

I banked until the compass read north-northeast. "We'd better turn back," I told the fishermen while leveling the wings. They sat in silence.

At this point I would have traded a year's pay for an automatic direction finder on the instrument panel, which could have picked up the old Coast Guard beacon back at Cape Decision or one of several stations in the Sitka area. But like most bush planes, this one had no navigational radios at all. Because electronic navigational aids were so uncommon in the bush, navigational radios were dead weight in the eyes of air-taxi companies; add another pound of payload instead.

After a west-northwest course the last few minutes, the switch to north-northeast, with the associated change in the appearance of the swell pattern, created some spatial disorientation. Suddenly, I was unsure of what direction we were following. The compass read about 15 degrees, but according to my senses we might have been flying in circles.

The needles on the two fuel gauges wavered just above the one-quarter marks, enough for another at least 150 miles before the engine sputtered and died. The chart clearly showed that regardless of our current position, 150 miles at 15 degrees would put us well into the archipelago, maybe even into the mainland. Where we ended up there was less important now than seeing land, any land. Nobody has moved southeastern Alaska, I reminded myself. It's still there. Hold 15 degrees and you'll find it.

Unless the compass was way off. When had the compass last been checked? When, in the busy, belt-tightening world of bush flying, had anyone bothered to check the compasses of any of our aircraft? Since we normally depended on our eyes for navigation, an inaccurate compass might go unnoticed or unreported for weeks.

"Where the hell are we?" said the man in back. "We want to go to Sitka, not Japan."

"We should see land soon," I answered. Although I ached to believe that comment myself, the unknown reliability of the compass planted a question mark on my 15-degree strategy. We could simply be paralleling the outside coast of Baranof. Or the inside coast.

I tuned the radio to 121.5 megahertz, the international mayday frequency. Maybe the Sitka Flight Service Station could hear us wherever we were, and despite our extremely low altitude use the transmission to give us a direction-finder steer.

"Fellows, I'm a little unsure of our position. I'm going to call for help."

I picked up the microphone. "Sitka, this is Cessna three-four-seven-seven Quebec. Over." I repeated the transmission.

A broken voice crackled unintelligibly in my headphones, but I caught the word "Quebec." Someone was trying to answer me. I called a third time just as I noticed a darkish line on the horizon. Ground fog? My pulse quickened.

"Land!" cried one of my passengers. I stopped breathing for a moment.

The darkish line appeared to be far away, but seconds later the windshield filled with coves, crags, trees, reefs, and breaking swells. I turned to follow the shoreline and tried to correlate the features with the chart. The visibility and low altitude thwarted me, but not the fishermen.

"There's Branch Bay!" one of them said. "I've holed up in there more than once."

Branch Bay put us on the outside coast of Baranof some twelve miles north-west of Cape Ommaney. Being back in contact with land, knowing where we were—no prisoner ever breathed a deeper sigh of relief at a commuted sentence.

The rain diminished and the visibility improved as we flew up the coast, and so did the aural health of the engine. By the time we passed Crawfish Inlet we had climbed to almost a thousand feet. The radio suddenly boomed in my ears: "Cessna three-four-seven-seven Quebec, Sitka Radio, how do you read?"

"Sitka, seven-seven Quebec, loud and clear, go ahead."

"I've been trying to call you for twenty minutes," said the voice in a rapid New England twang. "Do you require assistance?"

"Negative. We had a problem for a while, but it's been resolved." After landing in Sitka Channel, I deposited the fishermen at a downtown dock.

"Interesting ride, captain," one of them said as they shouldered their duffle bags.

I found a soda machine in a nearby building and chug-a-lugged a cola. Then I rented a room in a downtown lodge for the night.

Before landing back in Ketchikan under a high overcast the next day, I checked the compass against the runway heading at the Ketchikan Airport and found it to be off by about 18 degrees north. No wonder I had missed Cape Ommaney to the south. I complained so bitterly to the company management that in a week all our compasses had been checked and adjusted.

Spring slid into summer and week after week of long hours, stuffed cargo carts, stumbling drunks, heavy takeoffs, back-to-back flights, weather delays, and too little sleep. "I'm hearing only good things about you," Terry Wills said at one point. My improved standing might have merited reconsideration of my agreement to leave by winter, but the stress and fatigue of rebuilding my reputation extinguished any desire to stay on. Enough of this. Why wait for snow squalls to come blustering back, like rowdy drunks stumbling into the streets after the bars closed? In the fall I quit.

Teaching was an honorable, stimulating profession, especially at the college level, with regular hours and no marginal-weather situations. Summers off. I promptly signed up for a teacher-certification program through the University of Alaska's Juneau branch and passed all courses. The following spring, the final requirement was six weeks of in-class student-teaching. Had I done my stint in upper high school, I might have had a third career in the classroom. But an eighth-grade English teacher thought my background in journalism would be helpful to her pupils in putting together a yearbook, so I chose that grade instead.

It had been a long time since I was in junior high, and I had forgotten that an eighth-grade classroom was a more appropriate training ground for a police cadet than a student teacher. It was also a good milieu for scream therapy. Occasionally I'd lose patience and yell, "SHUT UP!" so loudly as to silence voices not only in our classroom but in adjoining ones, as well. The regular teacher smiled sympathetically from her desk as the little devils and I skirmished daily in the blackboard jungle. The playing field seemed to be structured fairly—one side outnumbered, the other outranked. Indeed, in the end the teacher apparently judged the contest to be a draw; her written evaluations helped send the kids to the next level and cleared me over this final hurdle to certification.

But my young adversaries won a symbolic victory: when I received my teaching certificate from the state, I put it in a file with other documents, never to be used.

Chapter 9

RELIEF VALVE

For the first few minutes after takeoff from Ketchikan, the man and two women sitting in the three middle seats of the Beaver chattered noisily. Occasionally an odor of whiskey wafted into the cockpit. Pilot Kirk Thomas paid little attention, however, and instead gazed at scenery. Thomas was used to merriment in the cabin, and these three had a special reason to be merry: they were en route to picturesque Petersburg to attend the Little Norway Festival. Petersburg sponsored the festival each spring to celebrate its Norwegian heritage. Besides a show of parades, banners, and brightly clad lasses, the festival was a five-day orgy of parties and making whoopee—a sort of far-north Mardi Gras. Like many participants, the three Beaver passengers had begun celebrating early.

Now there was a rustling in the middle seats, and the chatter changed to whispering and muffled giggling. Suddenly, an uproarious shriek shattered Thomas's daydreaming, prompting him to look over his shoulder.

The male passenger was stark naked, wearing not even his seat belt.

He grinned and saluted the pilot with a flask while the two women squealed their delight.

This proved too much for Thomas's Mormon upbringing. "Put your clothes back on or I'll dump you on the nearest beach!" he snapped.

The man sheepishly complied. But the giggling and swigging promptly resumed, and when the trio stumbled onto the dock at Petersburg, the man stripped again, howled, and dove into the harbor. Since the water in Alaska is frigid year-round, he presumably found the experience somewhat sobering.

The incident made us laugh when Thomas related it back in Ketchikan, but rather than becoming the talk of the town, it simply joined a long list of such anecdotes. We were used to the bawdy, the bizarre, the farcical. We could hardly have avoided them in a wilderness where we flew by the seat of our pants in direct contact with a motley assortment of people and cargo. At the time, some incidents in this category were embarrassing, irritating, or stressful to the pilot directly involved, but in retrospect all were welcome for the chuckles they brought, for their therapeutic mitigation of the pressure, the close calls, and the insecurities of our livelihood.

Sometimes even pilots stripped. It was late afternoon in September, and after climbing out from Ketchikan with two deer hunters bound for Josephine Lake on Prince of Wales Island, I noticed a vast expanse of thick ground fog boiling in from the ocean, blanketing everything in its path like lava. If the fog rolled into Ketchikan before I returned from Josephine, I would have to spend the night in the boondocks.

Cruising the Beaver at climb power saved a few minutes, and at the lake I decided to buy several more by landing immediately instead of circling first to check for debris. Once on the water, I taxied quickly into the cove where the lake's Forest Service cabin was situated.

Suddenly, the airplane stopped. I leaned out the door to investigate. Just below the surface, the floats had snagged a network of windfall, which I would have detected had I taken the time to circle. Since the beach lay just fifty feet ahead, I dared not risk trying to rock the Beaver free with power and elevator lest it suddenly surge forward. Instead, I shut down the engine, yanked the paddle out of its sheath on the float, and tried to push us off the snags. We moved not an inch. The tick-tock, tick-tock of passing time screamed louder and louder in my mind as I envisioned the fog rolling closer to town.

I knew the lake water was icy cold: on the approach I had noticed patches of old, turquoise-tinted ice from the previous winter still clinging to the shore in places where the steep slopes of Copper Mountain blocked the sun. But I had no choice. I tore off my outer clothing and, wearing just my underwear, slipped gingerly into the waist-deep water. Moaning and gasping for breath from the chill, I was able to pull the Beaver free, now 160 pounds lighter, and tow it to shore.

The hunters and I quickly unloaded the camping gear and supplies, then, wincing again, I towed the airplane back out beyond the logjam and climbed in. With no towel and no time to dress anyway, I left my clothes in a pile on the floor and immediately took off, shivering and dripping. The Beaver's 450-horsepower engine blasted hot air out of the cabin heater vents, and soon I was smiling like a sunbather.

The fog was rolling over the hills of Gravina Island, enveloping the fringes of the Ketchikan Airport, when I landed in Tongass Narrows. At the dock, a couple of linemen stared at me for a moment, then catcalled and rushed off. I had already dressed when they hurried back with cameras and a half dozen pilots, passengers, and office people.

More often, a pilot's dip was unintentional. When veteran seaplane pilot Herman Ludwigsen was chief pilot for Ketchikan's old Webber Air, he landed at the settlement of Hollis in a Grumman Goose one day and discovered the dock there was slightly submerged from the weight of ice and snow. One of his passengers was wearing only street shoes, so Ludwigsen gallantly cradled her in his arms to carry her ashore—then slipped and sprawled into the water with her.

Also taking an unexpected dunking was pilot Bob Ulrich, who was so intent on photographing a magnificent sunset in Ketchikan that he absentmindedly walked off a seaplane elevator, the camera to his face, and plunged thirty feet to the water below. Ulrich swam to the dock unhurt, but his expensive Minolta is still at the bottom of Tongass Narrows.

Bush flying offered a variety of other ways to get wet. Beach the airplane too lightly before helping carry supplies to a cabin or camp, and you might return to find an offshore wind or incoming tide had drifted it away. If a skiff was unavailable, off with your clothes and into the water. And the law of averages guaranteed an occasional slip into the water while maneuvering the airplane at a dock or beach. One day I picked up two salmon fishermen at a beach at Karta Bay, loaded their gear, and had them climb into the cabin. I then stepped from the beach onto the left pontoon, intending to walk forward to the cockpit door, fire up, and taxi away. But I lost my balance on the mooring line that lay stretched on the pontoon like a long snake. Instinctively moving faster, trying to regain balance, I teetered along the length of the pontoon and off into the waist-deep water in front. After I climbed back on, shook myself off as best I could, and plopped down in my seat, dripping, I could only smile at the startled fishermen.

In addition to their use for securing a seaplane on shore, the lines on the pontoons and wings are used for maneuvering at a dock or beach. For example, if you nose onto a beach, you have to turn the plane to point out for the departure; the hanging wingtip line provides something to grab as you spin the plane. The big Otter has an additional long line on the tail. One Otter pilot had just pushed off from the dock and started the engine when the airplane's forward movement suddenly stopped, as if an invisible giant had grabbed the tail. The grip held despite a burst of throttle. Bewildered, the pilot leaned out his door and looked back toward the dock, but the aircraft structure obscured his view. Leery of adding more power without knowing what was going on, he shut down and stepped onto the pontoon.

There, he saw that the free-floating, fifteen-foot-long tail line—which had a knot in the end for grasping—had snagged the dock in the narrow slot between two boards and was holding the Otter in place. After the airplane drifted back in close enough for him to jump onto the dock, the pilot pulled the line free. This time, he tossed the loose end into the water before pushing off.

The likelihood of an embarrassing event seemed to increase in direct proportion to the desire to make a positive impression. I had been a commercial bush pilot for less than three months when I returned from a flight one morning to find three attractive young women in the waiting room. College students from Washington State on vacation in Alaska, they had signed up for transportation to the Forest Service cabin at the lower end of Patching Lake. A busy schedule had delayed accommodating them, and the dispatcher had assured them they could go out with the next available pilot.

"Well, we won't keep you waiting a second longer," I announced in an unnecessarily loud voice. "Let's go." Five minutes later we taxied away from the dock, the rear of the 185 filled with camping gear. Patching Lake sat on Revillagigedo Island about eighteen miles north of Ketchikan, adjacent to Heckman Lake. Patching and Heckman were similar in shape, and each had a cabin on its lower end. Although I had never landed at either, I had flown by several times and felt confident I knew which was which. No need to unfold a chart and let three pretty girls think I was a new pilot. So I spent the flight instead describing the excitement and challenges of bush flying.

An axiom called Murphy's Law, applicable to all of life but especially familiar in aviation, holds that if someone can make a certain mistake, he eventually will. Since it was possible for a relatively inexperienced bush pilot to drop Patching-bound passengers off at Heckman. . . .

The pilot who landed at Patching four days later to pick up the women found an empty cabin, thought about the situation, took off for Heckman, and located them there. They told the pilot they had discovered the error immediately from Forest Service literature inside the cabin. They had run outside and yelled and waved and jumped up and down, but I was already roaring down the lake on takeoff. Nonetheless, the women said they had enjoyed themselves, and they admitted the mistake had contributed some adventure and humor to the outing.

Ever afterward, whenever I had a lake trip, the dispatcher cheerfully reminded me not to land at Heckman, even if the destination were a hundred miles in the opposite direction. If Heckman itself was the destination, I was admonished not to land at Patching.

Passengers were not always as forgiving as the three young women. One blustery morning on a flight from Thorne Bay to Ketchikan, a passenger thought Webber Air pilot Dale Hahn was responsible for the turbulence. After a particularly sharp jolt, something suddenly slapped him on the head. Hahn turned around. "Stop doing that!" a middle-aged woman snapped, glaring at him, her weapon—either a pocketbook or a glove—poised for another blow.

In a more serious attack, former Ketchikan seaplane pilot Stan Oaksmith Jr., who quit flying to run a marina, once had to fight off a drunken, crazed logger who—for reasons unknown—suddenly tried to strangle him on a flight from a camp at Bradfield Canal. Oaksmith managed to plop the 185 onto Behm Canal, taxi to a rocky beach, and get the man out of the airplane. Back in the air, he radioed for Alaska State Troopers, who flew out and arrested the guy.

Alcohol could inspire amorous intentions, too, as all but the ugliest floatplane pilots in Alaska eventually discovered. En route to the village of Hydaburg, Bob Bullock's task of negotiating rainfog was compounded by the continual advances of his only passenger, an intoxicated woman. In desperation, Bullock, who later became an FAA air traffic controller and airport manager, finally landed and strapped her into the rear seat of the Cessna 185. She spent the balance of the flight screaming obscenities at him.

Ex-Coast Guard air station commander Paul Breed was unaware of an alcohol connection when he noticed two men waving frantically in front of the Forest Service cabin on Honker Lake. Breed was hurrying back to his base at Klawock, but he decided to land in case the men needed medical transportation. Instead, the two begged him to fly to Ketchikan and come back with a case of beer so they could celebrate the Fourth of July. "That was on the fifth of July," Breed told me. "Needless to say, I didn't bring them any more booze. They were drunk then, and I figured they'd had enough."

In Ketchikan, as in many Alaskan towns, you could buy a drink or a bottle almost twenty-four hours a day (state law required bars to shut down for several hours for cleaning). Walking to work in the morning around the eight o'clock hour, I'd pass bars already (or still) packed with loggers, fishermen, and others whooping it up. Whether just starting or resuming from the night before following the cleaning shutdown period, I couldn't tell. Many seaplane passengers stayed in a bar till just before takeoff time, gulping a last drink before flying out to the bush, where they might have to endure a long dry spell. In the air, the destination still miles off, a fidgeting, cross-legged bar patron would tap me on the shoulder. "Listen, partner, I just can't hold out no more." With a sigh and a grumble, I would land on a lake or waterway so he could scramble onto the float and relieve himself. At least once on my flights a passenger waited too long to ask.

Eventually, I discovered that the airsickness bags in the seatback pockets could double as a urinal and save me a landing. What about mixed company on board? For the desperate passenger, alcohol numbed embarrassment and the need for relief trumped decorum. For the other passengers, well, this was the Alaskan bush, not Buckingham Palace. Passengers who used an airsickness bag for this alternate purpose seemed to manage the delicate process without much mishap, despite the confined quarters and the occasional turbulence.

But some passengers found the bags to be less than user-friendly for the intended purpose. After a woman threw up over several fellow passengers on a bumpy flight, I asked her at the dock if she had noticed the blue envelope with "Motion Sickness Bag" and instructions printed on it protruding conspicuously from the seat-back pocket directly in front of her. She admitted that she had examined the envelope but hadn't realized that the white plastic sack inside was meant to be removed and opened.

On another flight, this one in a de Havilland Otter floatplane, pilot Tim Brooks detected some movement from the corner of his eye and looked around. On the Otter's aisle floor a passenger was arranging four unfolded but unopened airsickness bags to form a large square. He explained above the engine noise that he was feeling queasy and was placing bags on the floor to catch whatever might issue from his stomach. Luckily, Brooks instructed him just in time to open one of the bags.

In the bush, a man could literally be late to his own funeral. After highly respected Hydaburg leader Clarence Peele died during a March visit to Ketchikan, dozens of friends and relatives from around the Pacific Northwest gathered in Ketchikan for transportation to Hydaburg on the west side of Prince of Wales Island for the services. On the day of the funeral, we shuttled planeload after planeload of mourners to the village. With the job finally completed late in the afternoon, it was time to deliver the casket. By then, however, rainfog had developed on Prince of Wales, and pilot Bob Mayne could not find a hole through the passes to the village. He returned to town for the night, and Ketchikan Mortuary reclaimed the casket.

In the morning, fog still blocked the passes, so Mayne landed at Hollis on the east side of Prince of Wales with the casket to wait for the clouds to dissipate. Unable to reach Craig on Prince of Wales to pick up six high school girls bound for a basketball tournament in Ketchikan, I also landed at Hollis. For an hour Mayne and I idled at the seaplane dock in the quiet air, chatting through streams of vaporized breath, eyeing the persistent fog. Soon the company dispatcher told us via radio that the girls' coach had decided to drive them to Hollis in a van to catch the airplane there rather than wait indefinitely for better weather. The entire village of Hydaburg, the dispatcher added, was still standing by for Mayne to arrive with the casket.

An hour passed. Then another. No van from Craig. I radioed the company again, and the dispatcher called Craig. That community, she reported, was mystified about the whereabouts of the van and would send a car to investigate. Meanwhile, she said, Hydaburg had sent a seiner toward Craig. The crew would borrow a truck there, drive to Hollis, pick up the casket from Mayne, return to Craig, and transport it to the village by boat.

By early afternoon Mayne and I had exhausted all topics of conversation, thumbed through each dog-eared magazine stuffed in the aircrafts' seat pockets, and explored every yard of Hollis within a three-hundred-yard radius of the dock. Still no vehicles. No van, no car, no truck. What was going on, we wondered? Surely we were the victims of some complex prank. Again I radioed Ketchikan; the dispatcher said the state trooper stationed at Craig would leave immediately to look for the three vehicles.

By now the sun was finally burning off the fog. Mayne and I untied our Beavers, taxied out, and took off. Mayne headed up Twelvemile Arm toward Hydaburg, and I flew into the Harris River Valley toward Craig, paralleling the snow-covered road to look for the missing vehicles. I quickly solved part of the mystery. The van was in a ditch about three miles from Hollis. I circled, and an adult and six girls waved. Some five miles farther on I found the car mired off the road. The lone occupant also waved when I circled.

I notified Ketchikan of the discoveries, and the dispatcher told me to continue on to Craig to pick up a different load of passengers. As I throttled back to descend I noticed a state trooper van racing along the road.

Later I learned the trooper had managed to stay on the slippery road and had picked up all eight occupants of the two vehicles, none of whom had been hurt. The girls eventually got to Ketchikan on another company airplane, although not in time for the tournament. Mayne finally delivered the casket to Hydaburg, allowing the belated funeral to take place. By radio, the village recalled the seiner, which because of thick fog had not yet reached Craig.

Fog delays could be especially notable when the passengers included dignitaries. The phone rang at Todd's Air Service late one fall afternoon. Four men in Wrangell urgently wanted to get to Ketchikan before dark, but other air services had refused to fly them because of the hour; could Todd's do it? Dixie Jewett, tall, independent, and capable, hurried down the ramp to her 185. The hills had already lost their features in dusk and rainfog when she landed in Wrangell Harbor. Minutes after takeoff, squinting to see through the gathering gloom, she realized she could no longer continue safely with passengers on board. Spotting the lights of a tugboat by Zarembo Island, Jewett felt her way onto the water, taxied up, and asked the skipper to take her passengers on into town.

The startled skipper humbly agreed when he learned they were then-Governor Bill Egan, who was on a campaign swing in Southeast; Alaska's sole congressman, Nick Begich (who would later disappear in a Cessna 310 with Louisiana congressman Hale Boggs); and two aides.

While Jewett took off for a nearby logging camp to spend the night, the tug headed for Ketchikan, delivering its distinguished guests to anxious officials hours after a scheduled dinner engagement. The incident made headlines around the state.

Like politicians, four-legged animals—both inside and outside the cockpit—could make life interesting for bush pilots. Former company chief pilot Dwight Gregerson had a dog in the rear of his 185 one morning and at first attributed its incessant whining to discomfort at being airborne. The dog, however, apparently had a hungry eye on an ice cream cone the front-seat passenger was licking; suddenly, the dog leaped forward, snatched the cone out of the passenger's hand with its mouth, and gobbled it down.

And Dale Clark of Revilla Flying Service in Ketchikan told about the time he landed in Klawock Lake to photograph a swimming black bear he'd spotted. The bear, unaware that Clark's intentions were harmless, bit one of the pontoons, puncturing the aluminum. After a hasty takeoff, Clark returned to town. "I put a Band-Aid on it and kept on flying," he said.

The stories could go on and on. Pilots sitting around the office chatting had no reason to manufacture or exaggerate them, for bush flying provided a fairly regular stream of strange experiences that were ready-made for round-table laughter. Each of us had had enough of our own to believe what the other guy was saying. Some humorous anecdotes, in fact, were too salacious or otherwise X-rated for publication. Others never made the general rounds in the aviation community because they involved an illegal activity that might result in a fine or license suspension if the authorities learned of them. Instead, these happenings were whispered in confidence to a few close friends.

Often the pilot to whom a certain incident occurred would move away or die, and then, gradually, the details of the story would become fuzzy; various versions would evolve, and the story would take on the status of legend or myth—feasible but unverifiable. This one fell into that category: an unnamed pilot was flying three out-of-state businessmen to Checats Lake on the mainland for a week's fishing outing when one of them leaned forward. "What are those orange balls down there?" he asked.

In a cove below floated a half dozen orange buoys marking the locations of underwater crab pots. After the pilot so informed the men, they conferred among themselves for a moment.

"Hey, could we stop and see if the pots have anything? Fresh crab for lunch at the lake would sure hit the spot." The pilot explained that raiding the pots would constitute piracy. "Well," the men suggested, "we've got some liquor with us. Suppose we exchange a bottle of Scotch for some crab?"

That sounded like a fair arrangement to the pilot, so he throttled back to land. Minutes later the plane took off again with three crabs. Thereafter, the fisherman who operated the pots presumably kept his fingers crossed every time he pulled them up, just as bush pilots continued to report for work with curiosity piqued, wondering what would happen that day in the unpredictable, sometimes wacky world of bush flying.

Chapter 10

BAREFOOT HERO

That guy must be crazy!" the passenger said. We were sitting in a cafe in Craig, sipping coffee, waiting for a September squall to pass. The archaeologist had chartered us to fly to the fishing village to assess several Tlingit artifacts a resident had found, and she had asked me to wait for her. When she returned to the cafe where we had arranged to meet, gusts were exceeding forty knots. We had ordered coffee and positioned ourselves at a window table to watch the weather.

"Who's crazy?" I asked.

The archaeologist, a thin, thirtyish woman with wire-frame glasses, pointed out the window. "Him. That pilot. He looks like he's going to land here."

In the driving rain by the north end of Fish Egg Island, a floatplane was on final approach for the Craig waterfront. As we watched, the aircraft twisted and lurched in the wind as if doing aerobatics. The wings flipped sharply to a near-vertical position in one gust. Below the plane, the inlet churned from shoreline to shoreline in angry, foaming, two-foot waves.

"Can he land safely out there?" the archaeologist asked.

I shook my head. "Even the seagulls are on the ground right now." The plane descended to about ten feet above the water. Closer and closer it came, turning this way and that. Land, I silently urged, before you fly into the dock. At the last second it plopped down in a tiny bight by the seaplane dock, the only spot where the water was sheltered. I recognized the orange-and-white colors of Todd's Air Service's 185.

"Oh, that's Ed Todd," I said. "Wouldn't you know."

The plane maneuvered to the dock, and out jumped a man in short pants and bare feet.

"Now I *know* he's crazy!" the archaeologist said. After tying up the 185, the pilot helped two passengers step from the cabin. They shook his hand and hurried up the ramp, hunching against the wind and rain.

I laughed. "That's Todd, all right, but he's not crazy."

Eccentric and colorful, Edwin Victor Todd knew exactly what he was doing. When bad weather kept other pilots huddled inside, he took off with calculated assurance. When a hunter or prospector wanted transportation to a lake the rest of us deemed too small to work safely, we referred him to Todd. A legend throughout Alaska, he had the experience and skills to do flying jobs the rest of us couldn't, and the sangfroid for those we wouldn't.

"We fly when YOU want to fly," read the Yellow Pages ad for Todd's Air Service. No matter that the wind was gusting to forty knots, or that dense rainfog forced motorists in town to use headlights at noon, or that the sun had already set behind the western mountains. In marginal situations, when we stood by the window in the office, weighing the risks against the potential rewards, the sight of anyone else's floatplane taxiing out into Tongass Narrows often goaded us into launching one of our own planes for a look; weather that was good enough for a neighboring air service was good enough for us. Todd exerted no such influence when *he* flew by, however. He had different standards and belonged to a different class, an image psychologically supported by the location of his operation south of town, some three miles from where the other Ketchikan air taxis were clustered along the waterfront.

Sometimes a group of weather-grounded pilots would gather in a waterfront restaurant and watch Todd's 185 disappear up the channel in the fog. Then we'd speculate on how he was able to get through in conditions that blocked the rest of us like a concrete wall.

"He's got super eyesight, that's all," someone would proclaim. "Nah," another pilot said, "I think he's got a photographic memory; he doesn't need to see where he's going, except for a rock here and a tree there."

A third pilot suggested he flew much of the time on instruments, and someone else claimed the man "just plain has more balls than we do."

Not always did Todd get away with it. While he never scratched a passenger in his twenty-five-year career, he sometimes returned with a damaged airplane. Taking off one day from a small lake with an overload of deer carcasses, he underestimated the room he needed. The floats struck rocks on the shore just as the airplane left the water. Quick reflexes and a superb flying ability enabled him to stay aloft and struggle back to town. Although the floats were torn, he ramped the plane before it could sink.

Another time, en route to Hyder at the head of Portland Canal, he tried to maneuver around clouds to clear a snow-covered ridge and in a whiteout got too close; the floats hit the ridge hard enough to cause serious damage. Again he managed to limp back home.

Undoubtedly there were incidents we never heard about, but none seemed to temper Todd's ways.

As if to flaunt his defiance of the elements, Todd typically flew in short pants and bare feet, although in especially nasty, cold weather he donned overalls and a pair of sandals. Throughout the year he took daily skinny dips in the frigid waters of Tongass Narrows, and he jumped rope regularly. He eschewed tobacco, coffee, and junk food. Wiry and tough, beady-eyed and crafty-looking, sporting an Errol Flynn mustache, Todd was ruggedly handsome despite a short, slightly round-shouldered frame. He spoke with a western accent and called male friends and acquaintances "partner."

Like most owners of small air services, he worked tirelessly fourteen to sixteen hours a day, week after week during the Season. He attracted lots of business, invested wisely, and left a valuable estate. But it was joie de vivre rather than wealth that drove him.

"Because it's interesting," he told me one day during a tape-recorded interview when, as a reporter, I asked him why he had put up with the long hours, stormy weather, and insecurity for so many years. "You get a charter into some place where you seldom go and sometimes where you never have been before . . . I think about selling out, and then I think, my god, what would I do that was more interesting . . . If I get a good offer I might do it and go into the real estate business, but shoot, I don't think I'd enjoy myself in it like I am here. People have asked me, 'Todd, why don't you retire?' and I say, 'For god's sake, what's retirement but sitting here in an airplane and watching the scenery rolling by?'

"I had a guy come up here one time and he stayed with me about a week, a guy I hadn't seen in years. When he left he cranked hands with me and he said, 'I don't know anybody that lives a better life than you do,' and that just about put it in the words that I felt about it."

Todd liked to fly low to see more details, and even in sunny weather he often hugged a shoreline for miles to look at the driftwood and rocky niches. He was not averse to buzzing a bear or a friend's house; old-timers chuckled about the time a young Todd buzzed a girlfriend's home in the Herring Cove section of Ketchikan and ran into telephone wires he had failed to notice. He recovered quickly enough to avoid crashing.

While other pilots took a break from airplanes on their days off, Todd would jump into a 185 on his (when he allowed himself a day off) and explore someplace he had never been. Ken Loken, owner of the old Channel Flying in Juneau, once landed in Twin Glacier Lake near the Taku River with a load of passengers and found Todd and a female companion skinny dipping off a 185.

Todd's spirit soared no less outside the cockpit. He drove two Datsun "Z" sports cars: one purple, one white ("My roller skates, one for one foot and one for the other"). He took winter vacations in Tahiti, Spain, and other exotic places, often pausing to visit a nudist colony on the way. And he seized every opportunity for practical jokes. Snorkeling one day near his flying service, he spotted someone beachcombing. It was dowager Katherine Ziegler, widow of a pioneer Ketchikan attorney. Todd swam over to her underwater, jumped up by the shore, and growled like a monster.

Although he rarely socialized at other air taxis, Todd liked people. Several pilots in Ketchikan and on the airlines might have had to enter other professions if he had not helped them learn to fly.

Todd's Air Service maintained an open-door policy, and on a typical night a handful of friends, fellow pilots, and customers gathered in the kitchen of the house above the hangar to sip tea or munch a salmon fillet or mountain goat steak. Todd would describe a tough flight he had made that day, his face affecting a grimace for emphasis but his eyes twinkling. Then there would be a rap on the door. Todd would get up, and a moment later we would hear, "Hey, partner, come on in!" One night he put on a huge sombrero he had brought back from Mexico and pranced around the room while we howled with laughter.

A poetry lover, he often recited verse during such theatrics. He was especially fond of Robert Service's "The Men That Don't Fit In." Ask Todd if he was ever going to retire from bush flying to live a "normal" life, and he'd open his mouth in mock astonishment, point a questioning finger at his chest, and rant histrionically:

There's a race of men that don't fit in,
A race that can't stay still;
So they break the heart of kith and kin,
And they roam the world at will.
They range the field and they roam the flood,
And they climb the mountain's crest;
Theirs is the curse of the gypsy's blood,
And they don't know how to rest.

Born in Seattle on May 2, 1919, Todd moved to Ketchikan with his family as a boy. After working at various construction jobs, he learned to fly and established his air service. He also attracted a mate who shared his love of adventure. Helen Todd, however, lacked her husband's skill. Or maybe his luck. One afternoon she left in a Piper Super Cub for nearby Annette Island to check her trapline. When she hadn't returned by evening, Todd took off to search for her, but dusk and fog had already blackened the island. In the morning he found her lifeless body on a lake beach, her Super Cub upside down in the water. Apparently she had lost her depth perception on approach to the lake (which afterward gained the name "Helen Todd Lake") and flown into the glassy water, flipping the airplane. Without matches or dry clothing, she died of exposure during the night.

It was then, some friends claimed, that Todd began his regimen of exposing his flesh to the elements to toughen it lest it someday be called upon to suffer the same trial. Other friends said Todd flew in short pants and bare feet simply because he was sensually oriented.

Two years after the tragedy, another woman entered his life. Dixie Jewett, a native of Virginia City, Montana, had left her job as an artist in the ad section of a large department store in the Southwest and headed for Anchorage to escape the heat and boredom. Her money took her only as far as Ketchikan, so she worked there as a cab driver and sign painter.

One day Todd needed a business sign painted, and he called her. Enchanted by the tall, pixie-eyed, bushy-haired woman, he invited her along on a flight. Then he offered her a job as dispatcher. She, in turn, fell in love with the daring, lusty pilot, who at forty-eight was twice her age. Eager to impress him, she decided to learn to fly and took informal lessons from his assistant pilot, Tony Kielczewski.

Soon she was spending more time practicing takeoffs and landings than dispatching. Realizing she was hooked, Todd bought a $1,800 Piper Super Cruiser in Pennsylvania through a classified ad in a national aviation marketing newspaper. "Go pick it up and don't come back without your license," he told her. By nature as plucky as Todd himself, Jewett accepted the challenge.

Despite her inexperience, she returned to Ketchikan from the four-thousand-mile flight with a commercial license and the airplane and her body intact. But one January day Tony Kielczewski did not come back. About 10:30 A.M., he loaded a 185 with groceries and took off in gusty, bitterly cold weather for Hyder and the abandoned salmon cannery at Hidden Inlet on Portland Canal, where a family still lived. A message he left on the telephone recorder in the office stated he planned to return around 3:00 P.M. He never reached either destination.

Vacationing in California when they heard the news, Todd and Jewett hurried back to join the search. For days, search aircraft battled turbulent north winds, snow squalls, and early darkness. But no one spotted a trace of the plane in the vast wilderness of icy mountains and thickly forested valleys between Ketchikan and Portland Canal. Vessels scouring Portland Canal and Revillagigedo Channel found no wreckage in the water. After several weeks the search was cancelled.

With Kielczewski gone, Todd's Air Service needed another assistant pilot, and Jewett took over. Bush flying was a man's domain. Jewett was the first female commercial pilot in Ketchikan since aviation had begun in the community almost a half century earlier, and initially many customers declined to ride with her. But she flew to the same destinations in the same weather as the men and showed both spunk and ability.

"It was no time at all before these people were asking for her," Todd reminisced later. "They'd say, 'I don't want you, you S-O-B, send that good-looking pilot over here,' and that's the way it's been ever since. Nobody ever refused to ride with her again. In fact, a lot more people request her than ever requested me."

Jewett added that once she gained acceptance, "about two hundred people claimed to have been the first to fly with me."

Over the years, Todd's Air Service gained fame and a certain notoriety as Ketchikan's most colorful flying duo: the hearty, barefoot Todd, who flew when even the seagulls tucked their wings; and the spunky Jewett, who proved to tough, skeptical loggers and fishermen that she could fly as well as a man. Like the rest of us hired hands, Jewett sometimes became disgruntled with bush flying. Several times she quit in a huff, vowing to forsake "this thankless job," as she called it. But always, after a few weeks in another livelihood in another town, she was back, lured not only by the Sirens but by her love for Todd.

To her, and to everyone else, Todd was an indestructible hero, as indelibly a part of Ketchikan as Deer Mountain and Tongass Narrows. Thus, when he failed to return from a routine flight on Sunday, October 5, 1978, hours passed before she became concerned. Todd had taken off alone about 7:30 A.M. to hunt mountain goats and planned to pick up two sport fishermen at Fish Creek in Thorne Arm at noon on the way back.

For a while Jewett assumed Todd had simply spent too much time stalking a big billy and had fallen behind schedule. When there was still no trace of his 185 by late afternoon, however, she concluded he was grounded somewhere by a broken fuel injector, ignition trouble, or other mechanical problem. It had happened to Todd before; it had happened to her.

She took off in the air service's other 185 and landed at Fish Creek. No, the fishermen said, they had not seen Todd's orange-and-white airplane. After dropping the fishermen back in town, Jewett called two fellow pilots, and that evening the three airplanes searched Todd's favorite mountain-goat lakes in the Coast Mountains. Todd had not specified a lake from which he would hunt because, like most hunters, he flew from lake to lake until he found the quarry within stalking distance. After dark, Jewett reluctantly notified the Ketchikan Volunteer Rescue Squad that Todd was overdue.

Had any other pilot been missing, the news would have dismayed the shell-shocked residents of Ketchikan and stung their wounds. Already that year, the town had suffered four fatal air crashes, three of which occurred during a single terrible week in August. In the worst accident, a Grumman Goose slammed into fog-bound Sumner Strait, killing all twelve occupants. The other crashes claimed thirteen additional lives.

But nobody was worried about the fifty-nine-year-old Ed Todd, who looked forty-five and acted thirty; he was the best bush pilot of them all, a veteran of thirty years and about thirty thousand hours of tough, stormy flying. He was okay. Besides, people reminded themselves, Sunday's weather had been excellent. The first fourteen days of the month dumped more than eleven inches of rain on the area, but not a drop fell on the fifteenth, although scattered fog clung in some of the valleys. If Todd could work mountain lakes with heavy loads in nasty conditions, he certainly could handle mountain lakes alone in good weather.

The skies remained calm and dry when the official search finally got under way shortly after noon on Monday, more than twenty-four hours after Todd missed his Fish Creek pickup. Normally, the Ketchikan Volunteer Rescue Squad would have launched a search at dawn, but members shared the initial assumption that Todd had encountered some mechanical problem. So, they waited while Jewett searched again that morning. When she once more reported no sign of her boss or his 185, N70269, the KVRS went into action.

Organized in 1947 following the crash of a Pan American World Airways DC-4 on Annette Island, the privately funded KVRS included air-taxi pilots, state troopers, city firemen, and other citizens willing to help out in rescue operations. Over the years the KVRS had located scores of hunters, fishermen, boaters, hikers, and pilots missing in southern Southeast, a region too vast for the Coast Guard alone to cover.

The area the KVRS now had to scour extended from Ketchikan north to Bradfield Canal, east to Portland Canal, and south to Fillmore Inlet: some seven thousand square miles of mountains, forest, and waterways. Much of the area lay within the Misty Fiords National Monument, and the geography gave the older searchers a sense of déjà vu: it was here they had looked unsuccessfully for Tony Kielczewski almost ten years earlier.

Throughout Monday afternoon, twenty-five airplanes and helicopters scouted dozens of lakes, both named and unnamed. Each aircraft carried a spotter so that in the passes and valleys and bowls, with cliffs and peaks all around, the pilot could concentrate on flying. Searchers also investigated a sighting of flashing lights on Annette Island and a report by campers at Humpback Lake of two rifle shots to the east.

No one found Ed Todd.

At the time, I had embarked on a long break from flying and was back at the *Ketchikan Daily News* for a few weeks. Although I wasn't participating in the search as a pilot, I covered it as a reporter and of course was involved emotionally.

At seven-thirty that evening, the pilots and spotters crowded into search headquarters in the dispatching office of Temsco Helicopters on Peninsula Point north of town. White-haired, droopy-eyed, hawk-nosed Dick Borch leaned on the office side of the counter while the others stood or sat on the lounge side. A longtime ferry and tugboat skipper, Borch helped organize the KVRS in 1947 and had served as its leader ever since.

"Let's see what we have," he said in his characteristic slow rasp. "Todd took off shortly after dawn. The people that live near his hangar heard him depart. What we don't know is where he went. The note he left only said he was going goat hunting and would be back at noon to pick up a couple of guys at Fish Creek. As far as Dixie can tell, he didn't have any passengers. Nobody heard any radio transmissions from him, and we haven't received any reports of an E-L-T [emergency locator transmitter, a required piece of equipment on most US civil aircraft. On impact it automatically emits a continuous signal on the international mayday frequency]. We asked the airlines to listen for signals when they're over this area, but they monitor the emergency frequency anyway."

Borch studied the large chart spread out on the counter. The portion that depicted the search area contained a grid pattern in blue pencil, each quadrant representing the responsibility of one search aircraft.

"If he had to be back at noon he probably didn't go too far—somewhere within fifty miles. The weather was pretty good, so that wasn't a factor. But Dixie checked all the lakes he likes to hunt from yesterday and this morning, and we checked them again this afternoon. We also checked more distant lakes. So far we have no clues. Anybody got any ideas?"

One pilot suggested Todd had landed on a river rather than a lake, but Borch dismissed that possibility because snowfall had not yet forced goats to an elevation low enough to justify stalking from a river. Another searcher wondered if Todd had been unable to locate goats within stalking range and decided to visit friends at a camp or settlement instead.

"We've already contacted the few people who live within reasonable flying distance of the mainland," Borch said. "None of them saw Todd or heard an airplane Sunday."

Had Todd encountered engine trouble somewhere between Ketchikan and the mainland and been forced down on salt water or muskeg? Maybe. From now on searchers would start looking for N70269 as soon as they took off, not just upon reaching mountain goat country.

Then one pilot reported that late-afternoon fog had prevented him from inspecting a small lake in his section. Borch asked him to point out the lake, and as the other searchers crowded around the chart, the pilot tapped a location in the Boca de Quadra area about seven miles east of Humpback Lake.

"Well, that could mean something," Borch said. "The shots those guys at Humpback heard may have come from there, though that's pretty far for rifle noise to carry. Okay, let's have a real good look at that one first thing in the morning, if we can; the weather forecast doesn't sound too promising."

Most searchers might as well have stayed in bed Tuesday morning. The hills and mountains had disappeared behind ragged stratus that raced above the treetops at four hundred to seven hundred feet, and heavy rain, driven almost horizontally by southeasterly gusts of thirty knots, cut visibility to a mile or less. The KVRS dispatched just seven aircraft, and the pilots, the organization's most experienced, had to stick to the shorelines.

Meanwhile, about 11:30 A.M. Tuesday, a salmon troller sighted what appeared to be an oil slick off the mouth of Ella Creek on Revillagigedo Island and radioed the news to Ketchikan. Two hours later, a ground party dropped off by helicopter investigated the discoloration; it originated from a recent mudslide three hundred yards upstream.

As the seven aircraft crews returned one by one to refuel, other KVRS members handed them sandwiches the Hilltop Motel and the Seventh-Day Adventist Church had donated.

In midafternoon KVRS vice president Ken Eichner, president of Temsco Helicopters and a three-decade veteran of flying in the Ketchikan area, finally managed to work his Hughes 500C chopper up the valleys and sneak through a pass to the previously unsearched lake east of Humpback. There, he slowly turned 360 degrees, watching the shoreline as it swung across the windshield. He spotted an old slide, a beaver dam, and two geese, which swam nervously away from the strange, noisy bird.

But he saw no airplane. Less than fifteen miles to the north, the wreckage of a twin-engine Lockheed Electra lay on a mountainside above Badger Bay, a crumpled, rusting reminder of an earlier search for another famous pilot. On a stormy January 5, 1943, Harold Gillam, one of Alaska's premier pioneer bush pilots, crashed there during a flight from Seattle to Anchorage. It took searchers more than a month to find him.

By now news of the search for Todd had spread throughout Southeast and reached dozens of people in the rest of Alaska and the Pacific Northwest. At the *Daily News*, my phone rang again and again as friends, former passengers, admirers, and relatives called to ask if Todd had been found and, learning that he had not, lingered on the line to pay tribute:

"Hell, nothing can hurt ol' Ed Todd. I used to fly with him when I was setting chokers out at Cape Pole. He come out and got me and Jake Rauwolf one day when it was blowing and snowing like mad. No one else would turn a prop, but we called Todd and he come right out and got us in his 185. Yeah, Todd's okay, wherever he is."

Eventually, I asked the front office to screen my calls and refer only those that related to search developments. The phones also rang repeatedly at KVRS headquarters at Temsco Helicopters; residents offered their services as spotters, sandwich-makers, or in whatever other capacity help might be needed.

Tuesday night the searchers again gathered in Temsco's dispatching office, tracking in mud and dripping rainwater on the floor. In a few minutes the windows fogged over. Borch paced about on the office side of the counter as he spoke.

"I'm afraid the weather doesn't look any better for tomorrow, just more of the same garbage. It looks like we'll have to run the beaches again, but we're getting to the point now where that might turn up something. If Todd's up there in one of those little mountain lakes, he knows it might be a week or more before the weather lets us get to him, so he just might try to walk out. But the way he dresses, he's going to have a rough time. There's fresh snow up there. Dixie, he doesn't carry much survival gear, does he?"

"Flippers for swimming, that's it. He doesn't like any extra weight when he comes out of the potholes he goes into. But he's a toughie. He could last a lot longer than most pilots in their twenties all bundled up."

illam had five passengers. All survived the crash, but the only woman among them, twenty-five-year-old Susan Batzer, died from loss of blood hours afterward. She had been bound for a new job in Anchorage. It was her first airplane flight. After Gillam trudged off through the deep snow to seek help, the remaining four passengers hunkered down in a makeshift shelter. They heard search aircraft nearby over the next several days, but none spotted the wreckage and the survivors were unable to attract their attention. A month later—long after the search had been called off—the two men still able to walk struggled down the mountainside through the snow and the forest all the way to Boca de Quadra Inlet. There they were able to hail a Coast Guard boat on routine wartime patrol.

Rescuers evacuated the other two survivors, weak and frostbitten, while the search resumed for pilot Gillam. His body was finally located near a shoreline, where he had frozen to death.

In the summer of 1981, a friend and I landed a floatplane in a small lake near the base of the mountain where the crash had occurred and hiked up to the wreckage. He had previously visited the remote site. Apparently the only others who had been there over the years were a few helicopter pilots who landed in a nearby muskeg meadow. Still undisturbed in the wreckage was a soggy, crumpling leather suitcase containing cosmetics jars and a small perfume bottle.

When Jewett returned to Todd's Air Service after the meeting, about thirty friends and relatives were chatting quietly and sipping coffee in small groups, as various people had been doing all day there. Todd's half-brother, Leon Snodderly, a first officer for Alaska Airlines, had arrived from Seattle on Monday, but the other relatives had gotten in only that morning. Several women were making fresh coffee in the kitchen or offering cold cuts and cheeses on trays in the living room. Around midnight the last visitor left. The doorbell began ringing again about 9 A.M.

Elsewhere Tuesday night, the Los Angeles Dodgers were playing the New York Yankees in the sixth and, as it turned out, final game of the World Series. Television sets in Ketchikan bars were on to catch the satellite broadcast, but the game was anticlimactic; patrons and bartenders talked instead about a bush pilot missing somewhere in the mountains.

Dawn overslept Wednesday morning. When the lingering night finally withdrew, allowing searchers to see out the windows of Temsco's dispatching office, Tongass Narrows resembled the open North Pacific. Deep, rolling swells rushed by, foam spraying from the crests in a steady thirty-knot wind, and Gravina Island, a half mile away on the opposite shore, was invisible behind the murky rainfog.

The weather did not keep the Coast Guard base in Ketchikan from sending out a cutter to search the maze of shorelines along the mainland, but it delayed until 11:30 A.M. the arrival of two huge HH-3F helicopters from the Coast Guard air station at Sitka. Only the KVRS's four most experienced pilots took off, and for the second day in a row their searching was limited to the shorelines.

The four KVRS planes worked in two pairs, with one aircraft in each team following the other. The theory was this: If Todd had hiked down from the mountains and was huddled in the forest, he might not be able to scamper through the windfall to the beach before the first plane passed. But he probably would get there in time to wave his arms at the second one, following a mile behind. For safety in the poor visibility, the lead aircraft and the trailing one tried to stay at different altitudes—not an easy task when you could climb no higher than treetop level anyway.

The pilots in each team stayed in contact with one another by radio.

In some areas, mountaintop radio repeater facilities relayed the transmissions to Ketchikan. Leaning back in his chair with his hands clasped behind his head, Borch listened by the radio at Temsco:

"Six-Six Xray, Eight-Two Fox, I've lost sight of you, Mike, what's your position?"

"We're coming up on Smeaton Bay."

"Say again?"

"Smeaton Bay, Smeaton Bay."

"Roger, understand Smeaton. We're just about there, too. Be advised we're down to two hundred feet now. We'll try to slow down and let you get a little more ahead of us."

Borch, who had not lost a search aircraft in the entire history of the KVRS, recalled the four planes about 3:30 P.M. The Coast Guard helicopters, also forced to stick to the shorelines, came back in not long afterward.

No strategy meeting took place that night because the forecast called for continued rain, fog, and wind on Thursday, which again would limit searching to the beaches. Although Todd had now been missing for four days, most people in Ketchikan remained confident he would be located alive and well. He would be on a beach or at the edge of a mountain lake or in a muskeg meadow, lightly dressed, a cocky grin on his face. "Well, partner, it took you guys long enough to find me," he'd say with a twinkle in his eye to the pilot who picked him up.

Borch told representatives of the news media the KVRS felt discouraged with the weather but not with the prospect of finding Todd alive.

"Todd's one of the most experienced, capable pilots in Alaska," he said. "All we need is good weather."

Borch got it Thursday. Contradicting the gloomy forecast, the morning brought mere broken clouds and isolated showers, with excellent ceilings and visibility. The KVRS quickly dispatched seventeen aircraft, the Coast Guard choppers took off from the Ketchikan airport, and the cutter sped out of the harbor at Base Ketchikan.

Don Ross, part owner of Ketchikan Air Service and, like Todd, one of the most seasoned pilots in the Ketchikan area, preferred to fly alone, without a spotter. On Monday, the last time the weather gods had smiled on Ketchikan, he had searched the lakes in his quadrant looking for a beached 185. Now he checked those lakes again in his own 185, paying more attention to the rocky slopes around the lakes. About 10:15 A.M. he circled a small, unnamed lake at the three-thousand-foot level several miles north of Big Goat Lake. Sighting nothing there, he flew out the V-shaped mouth of the lake and began studying the valley slopes below.

"A couple of miles down the valley I saw a different color on the rocks, something that didn't belong," Ross said. "I came back for a closer look and saw an orange wingtip. After another pass I saw pieces of metal scattered all over the mountain."

"Roger," Borch said quietly at Temsco when Ross radioed the discovery.

After a moment of silence, the KVRS chief cancelled the search, directing Ross, Ken Eichner, and two additional pilots to proceed to Big Goat Lake for the recovery effort.

Jewett, searching in the same quadrant because it contained Todd's favorite goat lakes, was flying with Cape Pole logging camp resident Larry Simpson as a spotter. They failed to hear the transmission because of terrain interference. A few minutes after Ross sighted the wreckage, she circled the same unnamed lake and then flew down the valley. Jewett admired Simpson's cool nerve as a spotter. He kept his eyes constantly glued to the windows, unperturbed by bumps, steep banks, or sudden applications of power. Spotters who turned away for a couple of seconds to see what the airplane was doing might miss something important. Now Simpson spoke as he spotted the bits of metal.

"I see wreckage."

Shocked, dismayed, Jewett circled several times and reported the sighting to Temsco. It was then she learned Ross had already found N70269.

Most of the KVRS fleet had heard Ross's transmission; when Eichner lowered his Hughes 500C helicopter onto a rocky peninsula at Big Goat Lake, five or six floatplanes were beached in a line on the nearby southern shore, two others were taxiing in, and two more were circling to land. A dozen pilots and spotters stood in a group by the airplanes. Three searchers climbed into the 500C, and Eichner took off for the crash site.

The wreckage lay vertically strewn on the steep slope from an elevation of about thirty-seven hundred feet—almost within throwing distance of the ridge's crest—down to about twenty-five hundred feet. Eichner could land no closer than a half mile from the scene; the party needed four hours to struggle up to what used to be a Cessna 185 floatplane.

After cutting the seat belt and extracting Todd's overalls-clad body from the cockpit, the crew, in one member's words, "kicked the airplane down the mountain" so that the dislodging effects of the prying and wrenching they had done would not cause the wreck to tumble suddenly onto them as they descended. As one searcher slung the body over his shoulder, a large jackknife fell out of the overalls and clattered onto the rocks. Goat's hair and dried blood covered the blade.

No one could explain the crash. Jewett, noting that N70269 was the lesser performer of Todd's Air Service's two 185s, suggested the floats struck the rocks at the edge of the tiny unnamed lake on takeoff and Todd tried to keep the plane in the air.

"He just never throttled back," she said. "Once, coming out of a lake, he even ran up on the muskeg, but he kept barreling along till he got her in the air. He always just kept boring ahead."

Other pilots speculated fog had formed in the valley and that Todd, trying to climb through on instruments, as he had on hundreds of other occasions in various situations, had finally met the law of averages. An autopsy determined no medical problems that might have contributed to the accident.

Officials from the National Transportation Safety Board and FAA arrived in Ketchikan on Friday to investigate, but the resulting NTSB report listed the cause of the accident as undetermined.

To people throughout Alaska, the puzzle was not why it had happened, but that it had happened at all. Pilots felt especially humbled. Some of us had regarded Todd as a larger-than-life figure, a heroic knight invincible before all dragons and ogres. If *he* could fall on a seemingly innocuous mission, no amount of savvy could ever protect the rest of us from the menaces of the bush.

Ketchikan's Chapel of the Mortuary overflowed during services the following week. Dozens of mourners unable to squeeze in stood outside in a light rain on the steps and sidewalks. The pastor read a eulogy I had written. Afterward, Todd's ashes were deposited in his wife's grave in Bayview Cemetery south of town.

Ketchikan writer Margaret E. Bell, author of twelve books, wrote a poem for the deceased poetry lover:

> *Ed Todd is dead.*
> *The whole town's crying. Icarus, soaring*
> *Toward the sun, falling, dying.*
>
> *Ed Todd is gone.*
> *The whole town's crying.*
> *Angels go along to guard his way, flying, flying.*

Jewett, who inherited a portion of Todd's estate, left Ketchikan and commercial flying for good to pursue an art career. She lived for several years in Bozeman, Montana, and later moved to Oregon.

Meanwhile, former Ketchikan pilot Joe Soloy had started a company in Washington State to provide turbine-engine conversions for piston-powered helicopters. When Soloy Conversions expanded into airplane turbine conversions, the company's first demonstrator was a Cessna 185. Soloy named it the *Ed Todd* for his old friend.

"If Ed had had this airplane with all its extra power, who knows, he might be alive today," Soloy said.

Yet at fifty-nine, Todd would have had only a few years' flying left. Soon he would have been eligible for social security, a thought incongruous with his exuberant lifestyle. At least he had died quickly, in an airplane, while still healthy in body and mind, doing what he loved in a place he loved. Death was not always so kind.

In 1978 the Ketchikan area had three percent of Alaska's population but twenty percent of the state's aviation fatalities. Not all were seaplane accidents. On February 5, five members of an Anchorage family died in the crash of a Cessna 320 on Etolin Island northwest of Ketchikan. The only survivor was rescued ten days later after attracting the attention of a passing fish tender.

Then on August 25, all twelve persons on board a Ketchikan-based Webber Air Grumman Goose were killed in a water crash near Point Baker on the north end of Prince of Wales Island. Only four bodies were recovered.

Four days later, a California couple perished when their Cessna 182 struck Deer Mountain, and two days after that six persons were killed in a Beechcraft Bonanza that also crashed on Deer Mountain. Searchers were still looking for the 182 when they stumbled onto the Bonanza wreckage.

Ed Todd was killed on October 5, and on November 25 all five occupants of a Tyee Airlines Beaver from Ketchikan died in a fiery crash at Twelvemile Arm on Prince of Wales.

Aviation accidents elsewhere in Alaska in 1978 included the death of Senator Ted Stevens's wife and four others in the December 4 crash of a Lear Jet in Anchorage. Senator Stevens, also on board, was seriously injured. On August 9, 2010, Stevens himself would die, along with the pilot and three fellow passengers, in the crash of an amphibious Otter seventeen miles from Dillingham.

Chapter 11

OVERNIGHTING

Few pilots welcomed an unplanned night in the bush due to weather or mechanical problems. The aircraft were equipped with some emergency supplies, and most of us carried our own R-O-N (remain overnight) bags just in case, so survival was usually not a problem in the relatively mild environment of Southeast Alaska. Nonetheless, the experience left us grumbling. Because it was unexpected, we typically had to forgo activities we had planned in town— a movie date, a city league basketball practice, a woodworking project. Rarely did an overnighting occur at a place we would have chosen to visit on a day off. And the rotten weather that usually was responsible made spontaneous fun hard to find.

The mainland strip of Southeast, with less habitation than the archipelago, could be an especially lonely place to the pilot trying to sneak home through fog or snow with dusk around the corner. Run out of daylight in that wilderness and you usually had to spend the night by yourself. If you could, you reached a seasonal Forest Service or trapper's cabin. There you'd find enough provisions to make the experience a little less unpleasant: a small supply of wood for the stove, a candle or two, a few leftover cans of beans or soup, some magazines, maybe a deck of cards for a session of solitaire.

With no cabin at hand, home for the night was the least rock-ridden beach you could taxi to before darkness engulfed everything. Tie the airplane to a tree, log, or rock, zip up your jacket, and curl up on the seats inside. Eat the spartan, hard, cardboard-tasting emergency rations, if you wanted; you'd still listen to your stomach rumble. If the moon came out, maybe you could also listen to the wolves howl.

In a fjord where a beach might not be available, the pilot could only drift about in the foggy dark, serenaded by unseen waterfalls thundering down cliffs.

The archipelago could also be lonely to the pilot who waited too long to concede defeat. He spent the night where he finally was forced to plop down, which could well be a boulder-ridden beach. He might have to stand shivering in the water throughout the night, holding the plane off the rocks as the tide came and went, cursing the rain and the wind and his job.

With human habitation rarely farther away than twenty or thirty miles, however, the islands offered plenty of options to the more prudent pilot who devoted the last few minutes of daylight or visibility to hightailing it to sanctuary. Virtually everyone maintained an open-door policy in the bush, where survival often depended on mutual help. At a camp or village, a pilot would have shelter for the airplane, a warm bunk, and a hearty meal. In fact, bachelor pilots who had not evolved into competent cooks would likely eat more sumptuously while stuck overnight than they would have back in their apartments; bush tradition frowned at allowing a grounded pilot to leave the table until he had stuffed a third helping of everything down his throat.

The after-dinner agenda included conversation, competition at card games or Monopoly, perhaps a photo album of life back in Oregon to thumb through. For pilots so inclined, there might be a six-pack to share.

While the pilot snored away the evening, his hosts strolled down to the harbor to add another tie-down line to the airplane, sweep the snow off the wings and tail, and chase away kids who had sneaked into the cockpit to jiggle the controls.

Of course, some bush communities were more popular among pilots than others for overnight stays. Regardless of a pilot's religious conviction, Christian camps—those operated by believers who imposed strict rules of conduct—rated four stars for quality fellowship and accommodations. The few camps with alcoholic operators, on the other hand, could make you think of Dodge City with the marshal out of town. Sometimes in a burst of gusto a logger would whoop and fire a gun at the bunkhouse ceiling. You wondered how anyone there managed to make it to the woods in the morning.

The Haida Indian village of Hydaburg on Prince of Wales was one of the last civilized places at which my fellow pilots and I wanted to get stuck for the night. The village, twenty-two miles south of Craig, then had no hotel, restaurant, or entertainment, and the two general stores maintained irregular hours. Even more inhibiting than the absence of public amenities was the animosity some residents displayed toward Caucasians.

A few years earlier the village had launched a cultural-revival program to preserve its tribal traditions from the "Americanization" white teachers and missionaries had imposed with heavy-handedness in the early part of the twentieth century. According to residents, the whites had suppressed Haida dances, songs, legends, and other aspects of the culture. Elderly resident Helen Sanderson said the teachers "used to beat us for speaking Haida" when she was a schoolgirl in the village. A fuzzy document from the Haida archives, composed by whites and dated 1911 or 1915, read in part:

"We . . . hereby declare that we have given up our old tribal relationships;

that we recognize no chief or clan or tribal family, that we have given up all claim or interest in tribal and communal houses; that we live in one-family houses in accordance with the customs of civilization; that we observe the marriage laws of the United States; that our children take the name of the father and belong equally to the father and mother . . . that we have discarded the totem and recognize the Stars and Stripes as our only emblem . . ." The document contained the signatures of twenty-eight of the village's leading citizens.

Over the decades most Haida ancestral customs had thus faded into desuetude. Just a handful of the oldest villagers could still speak the Haida language, which, along with much community folklore, was written only in their waning memories or in the silent images of surviving Haida artifacts. One spring day Helen Sanderson and a friend approached Hydaburg school superintendent Dr. Leonard B. Waitman and asked if the school could teach Haida lore to children before it was lost forever. (The Languages Department of the University of Alaska had estimated the Haida language would be extinct in ten years unless it was recorded.) Waitman, who was white, thought the idea was not only feasible but overdue.

"It burned my ass," he said of the cultural-renunciation document. With grants from the state, the school inaugurated "Haida cultural study," in which pupils studied Haida cultural subjects one hour a day in class. Adults could participate through adult-education classes at night. The program's three instructors became the only certified Haida teachers in Alaska.

The village continued to live with modern conveniences and to pursue economic development with its share of the $1 billion and forty-four million acres of land the 1969 Alaska Native Claims Settlement Act had granted Alaska natives in exchange for land along the route of the trans-Alaska oil pipeline.

But the cultural revival generated a fierce community pride that resulted in a certain clannishness. A few of the four hundred residents, perhaps those who were especially aware that Haidas once had a reputation among Indians as mighty warriors, developed resentment toward whites. The *Ketchikan Daily News* had published an article about tension between several residents and white teachers in the village.

In such an atmosphere, pilots preferred not to spend a night in Hydaburg and sought refuge elsewhere when bad weather caught them in the boondocks with dusk approaching. But Mother Nature honored no preferences.

One cool, overcast morning a Seattle-based inspector for the federal Occupational Safety and Health Administration chartered an airplane with the company to make routine safety checks at several communities on Prince of Wales. The Ketchikan Flight Service Station expected a gale to begin thrashing the region that evening, but the forecast for the day sounded okay. As the pilot I estimated we could complete the rounds and scoot back to town before the wind became unsafe.

I decided to start with the most distant destination on the itinerary and work our way toward Ketchikan so we would be drawing closer to home as the gale approached. That strategy left Hydaburg for last.

By the time we landed on Sukkwan Strait in front of the village around 5:45 P.M., raindrops were streaking off the windshield and whitecaps were foaming from the wave crests. Because the two facilities he wanted to inspect were a long walk from the regular seaplane dock, I chose a closer, raft-like dock near a boat harbor.

"Better hustle," I said to the inspector after I tied up the Cessna 185. "The gale's knocking on the door."

The inspector, a tall, middle-aged man whose suit seemed incongruous in the bush, hurried up the ramp while I paced about on the dock or sat in the cockpit. I was still waiting a half hour later when the strait had become angry with waves and black gust streaks, and the hills toward Ketchikan had faded behind a curtain of gray stratus. Although an adjacent cold-storage building blocked the wind in the nearby boat harbor, the trollers and seiners there were rolling in their berths from the swells. Our old dock, too, was in constant motion, heaving as if King Neptune were trying to push it away; during the period when I stood beneath the 185's dock-side wing for shelter from the rain, the wing twice brushed my cap in a roll. I glanced back at the village. A dog trotted across the driftwood-strewn beach, and in one of the ramshackle wooden houses bordering it, a woman stood by a window staring at me. But there was no sign of the inspector.

"Come on!" I muttered to myself.

When he finally stepped carefully down the wet ramp some thirty-five minutes later, holding up his briefcase as an umbrella, time had run out.

"Sorry I took so long," he said. "I had trouble finding the places I needed to inspect." He grimaced when I told him we would have to spend the night because of the weather and that Hydaburg had no public accommodations. "Do you know anyone we can stay with?"

The company's agent in the village was in the Lower 48, and the substitute agent was a sullen fellow who had become the brunt of jokes among our pilots. White teachers were on summer vacation. I knew about a dozen other residents who were frequent customers, but not the location of their homes. The prospect of knocking on doors at random to find out did not appeal to me.

"No, unfortunately. The people here are sort of unfriendly—they'll hardly give you the time of day. But I think I know a place where we can at least stay warm and dry."

The inspector said he had stopped at both general stores hoping to buy a snack and found them closed, so I reached into the baggage compartment, opened the emergency-survival kit, and took out the freeze-dried food. Next, I added a couple of lines to the three with which I had already tied the airplane, frowning at the dock's ceaseless undulating in the swells. It was too late now to taxi over to the regular seaplane dock, which, stout and solid, would have offered better protection.

We walked up the ramp, and I led the way down a path to a small building that housed long-distance telephone equipment for the village. From a previous charter with a telephone repairman, I knew where the door key lay cached, and we entered, dripping. Inside, a generator that supplied power to the equipment radiated welcome heat. I called the company on a phone there and explained our situation. Then we fashioned makeshift beds from overalls, a throw rug, and other pliable items, and heated water for the freeze-dried food in an electric coffee pot. Since the generator rendered conversation awkward, we idled away the hours reading some magazines that were stacked on a table.

Later that night I trudged back to the dock to check the 185. Although it seemed secure enough in the rainy dark, I frowned again at that constant pitching and rolling. A few hundred feet away a loose strip of aluminum siding on the cold-storage building banged like rifle shots. What lousy luck to get weathered in here, I thought to myself. Anywhere else we would have had real beds, a hot meal, fellowship—and probably a decent berth for the airplane.

Back in the "Hydaburg Hilton," as we had dubbed the building, the humming from the generator eventually lulled me to sleep. When I awoke my watch read 6:15 A.M. A peek out the door revealed broken clouds and no wind, so I roused the inspector, and minutes later we headed back toward the dock.

At the tip of the ramp we stopped abruptly. The 185 was gone! "What the hell!" I cried. I noticed immediately that half the dock was also missing. In dismay I quickly glanced about and spotted the airplane, apparently intact, about two hundred yards away by the beach in front of the village, the heels of the floats pulled up on the gravel. Two men sat nearby on driftwood.

I jogged down the unpaved road that paralleled the beach, splashing through puddles, then cut across the pebbly sand until I reached the plane. The men stood up.

"You the pilot?" one asked. Both wore rain gear and had shoulder-length black hair.

"Yeah," I answered, panting. "What happened?"

Around midnight, they told me, the wind had reached sixty knots (the inspector and I hadn't heard it inside our noisy shelter) and a villager had gone down to the waterfront to check the boats. He had seen that our makeshift seaplane dock was beginning to break up under the stress of the swells and, realizing the airplane was in jeopardy, had raced back to the village to get help. At least eight men had hurried into the stormy night, untied the plane, and using a skiff on either float, guided it to the most sheltered part of the beach. There, they had held it just offshore to prevent the waves from pounding the floats on the gravel. Several men had had to stand in the chilly water to grip the wing struts.

About 2 A.M. they had heard a loud crack, which they later discovered was a large section of the dock tearing away.

Finally, near dawn, the gale subsided, the water calmed, and the men had been able to beach the 185. The others had gone back to bed, but these two had remained behind to keep an eye on the plane and re-beach it every few minutes as the tide came in.

"Where were you?" one of the men asked. "We tried to find you last night but no one knew where you were staying."

"My passenger and I slept in that telephone shack south of the cold storage."

Both men looked puzzled. "Why did you sleep there?"

I shrugged my shoulders sheepishly. "Well, we didn't want to bother anyone."

The men were silent for a moment. "Anybody in the community would have put you up. We know you can't fly when it gets too windy." I thought I detected a hint of indignation in their faces.

"Did you think we'd scalp you?" the other man said with a slight smile. I chuckled and thanked them with handshakes for their help, asking them to extend my thanks to the others. As they walked back toward the village, I signaled to the inspector, who still stood at the top of the ramp.

"I thought you said these people would hardly spare the time of day," he commented when I related the events of the night as we taxied out for takeoff.

On another inclement night long afterward, Hydaburg again showed compassion to someone who thought it absent. I had returned to Ketchikan the year before after a four-year absence. An unrelenting period of discontent with bush flying had induced me to seek another career change, and a few weeks later the East Coast had become my new home. For the first two years I worked as an editorial staffer on a magazine in White Plains, New York, then moved to another magazine in the same publishing group in midtown Manhattan. My title there— associate editor—sounded more impressive than it actually was. One of several staff writers and copy editors, I toiled at a salary that compelled me to live in a boxy studio apartment far uptown.

But the big-city lifestyle seemed appropriate for one who had renounced every aspect of bush flying. No gales or rainfog to harass me here. Regular nine-to-five, weekends off. Jacket and tie. Even a briefcase, though I rarely took work home and toted it mainly for show. As if to make up for years in the boondocks, I threw myself into the urban amenities. Museums, squash, theater. As in Ketchikan, the bars here seemed never to close. These, however, were packed with sophisticated yuppies rather than rip-snorting, blue-jean-clad men of the forest and sea. With no lives depending on my skill and judgment, no expensive machine to operate in the morning, I frequently bar-hopped my way back uptown after work.

Perhaps most significantly, I had at last joined the ranks of former college classmates who had followed the conventional path after graduation. I had a good job with a future now. Despite the late start, plenty of time remained to find a wife, settle down, buy a house on Main Street.

Eventually, I began noticing an inner emptiness, like the faint pangs of hunger that emerge many hours after a gluttonous meal has finally digested. Entombed shoulder to shoulder in a lurching subway train, glum expressions on every face, I started sensing a vague rebellion. Striding back to the office following a squash match and a stop at a deli for a take-out lunch, I began to feel besieged by concrete and carbon monoxide and blaring horns. Standing at the lone window in my apartment on Eighty-seventh Street looking at the view, a tiny courtyard and the wall of another building, I would languish in spiritual claustrophobia.

Strolling in Central Park became a precious diversion for its open space and greenery, and a periodic visit to relatives in Connecticut via the train from Grand Central Station allowed even more emotional stretching. Opportunity limited these breaks. But anytime, anywhere, I could escape in daydreams to my beloved Alaska, so far away in distance and now in time: the fresh, invigorating smell of the archipelago air, the chortle of a grizzled, whiskey-guzzling woodsman as he described some misadventure, the majesty of jagged, snowcapped peaks deep in the wilderness. . . . Even the bad-weather flights and the no-margin takeoffs found welcome, for challenge was the spice on the feast named Alaska.

One day, thinking about bush flying, I caught my reflection in a window on Third Avenue and was startled to notice the jacket and tie. The image resurrected a childhood memory. For several weeks after joining the Boy Scouts, I had to wear ordinary school clothes to meetings because new uniforms were on backorder. Eying my fellow scouts in their uniforms, I felt like a crow amid peacocks. Finally, the Thursday before a weekend camping trip, my uniform arrived. Now I could be a real scout. But first the uniform needed the appropriate patches and insignias. I became a harpy. Hurry, Mom, I pleaded, drop whatever you're doing and sew them on so I can wear the uniform on the camping trip. I'd rather not go at all than be a peacock without feathers. I squatted beside her on the couch and watched every stitch, making sure she placed the patches exactly as illustrated in my Boy Scout handbook.

On the drive to the departure point at an elementary school Saturday morning, I sat erect in my uniform beside my mother, an officer being chaperoned in his staff vehicle. Window glare occasionally reflected my image. Half-expecting pedestrians to salute as we passed, I glanced every few moments at the shiny felt patches as if they were medals.

When my mother pulled into the school parking lot, though, I noticed something terribly amiss. The scouts who had arrived earlier and were now pulling gear out of their cars or milling about in small groups were all dressed like— like scruffy civilians: sweat shirts, blue jeans, sneakers. One friend so attired noticed me and strolled over as I stepped out of our car with my backpack. "Heyyy, you're not supposed to wear a uniform on a camping trip!"

Years later, as a pilot working in scruffy civilian clothes, I again ached to put on a uniform. This time it was a jacket and tie, and the peers I wished to emulate were the former classmates. Now, here I was in a jacket and tie, once again feeling out of uniform. Heyyy, a voice seemed to whisper, you're not supposed to wear a jacket and tie on a quest for fulfillment. Your butt may in be an office, but your heart is back in the cockpit.

Reminiscing would sometimes wrench from me a forlorn sigh. Nostalgia had also come during the brief stint with the *Anchorage Times*, of course. But then I was young enough to step back outside for another interlude in the sky. Now I was well-established in a new life thousands of miles away, and closer to forty than thirty. Already in middle age by some standards, not far from crossing the line according to others. No, my bush flying days were gone, gone forever. I'd have to be content with my logbooks and journals, my photo albums, and my memories.

Yet other voices whispered that a career and lifestyle could be considered "good" only if they were enjoyed. Wasn't pursuing an image while crying in the heart a foolish tragedy, the voices asked? In the eponymous poem by Edwin Arlington Robinson, Richard Cory achieved an image and the envy of townsfolk, and then put a bullet in his head.

For months the philosophizing served only to torment me, and the notion of actually returning to bush flying remained as preposterous as reliving my college years. Grow up and accept reality! I told myself. But wistful repetition gradually imbued the thought with possibility, and the inner emptiness began to fill with a growing dream. Intellectual objections fell away. I chucked the empty briefcase, took off the jacket and tie, and reached out across the miles and years.

Like Paul Breed's Flair Air, Revilla Flying Service in Ketchikan had just two airplanes, though these were 185s rather than Beavers. One of them was berthed on a ramp inside an aging waterfront hangar that also contained a loosely organized hodgepodge of airplane and engine parts, tools, fishing gear, construction supplies, welding equipment, paint cans, and outright junk, hanging on walls, standing in corners, piled on the bench, or stuffed into lockers. An office with desk, couch, filing cabinets, and coffee table was attached to the hangar. The second airplane sat on a ramp out back, between the hangar and Tongass Highway. A foot ramp led from the street down to the hangar and docks. Our facilities were sandwiched between those of my former company and another large air service.

Also like Flair Air, Revilla Flying Service had a limited crew to perform a variety of duties. I was the only pilot besides owner Dale Clark, a thirty-three-year-old, bespectacled, curly-haired industrial arts major from a Montana ranch family of twelve children. He was a nephew of former owner Carl Jackson, who had died in a floatplane crash on nearby Annette Island. Clark had not yet fully recovered from a crash of his own a few months earlier. Climbing out from a mountain lake with two goat hunters on board, he had had the misfortune to fly into a sudden severe downdraft that slammed the airplane onto the ground. One of the hunters had not survived.

During the summer we employed a young Metlakatla woman to dispatch, answer the phone, and keep records. The rest of the year we did those things ourselves. When we were both out on flights then, we turned on the telephone recorder and locked the office door.

A competent though unlicensed mechanic, Clark handled maintenance tasks during nonflying periods while I swept floors, shoveled snow, emptied garbage, and answered correspondence. I suffered no cultural shock from such menial chores after New York. Alaska had wiped the gloom from my spirit; now that I was back, wearing blue jeans literally and figuratively, I cherished even the rain.

It was the early 1980s now, and Ketchikan had grown during my absence. Several new housing developments, their streets still unpaved, had eaten into the forested slopes, and a new shopping mall and a racquetball complex were in the offing. A fairly steady stream of cars poked along Tongass Avenue; people now complained about the lack of parking spaces more than the weather. Much of the activity was in anticipation of an economic boom from US Borax's planned mining of the world's largest known molybdenum deposit on the mainland forty miles to the east in Misty Fiords National Monument.

Business people regarded the mine as salvation, since the timber industry, one of Ketchikan's economic mainstays, had slumped. Only a few logging camps were still active on Prince of Wales Island, and dozens of unemployed loggers loitered in the unemployment office and the bars. I noticed that practically all of the remaining camps now had one or more TV satellite dishes.

Unchanged, as always, were the mountains, valleys, and forest, the islands, lakes, and waterways. I felt instantly at home among these familiar old friends. How strange to think I had ever left. Now it was New York that seemed a forbidding world away.

Since Revilla had no scheduled flights, we relied on charters. They came in infinite variety, from short, local sightseeing tours to day-long trips into the upper end of the Inside Passage. From spring to midfall, charters kept us in the air heading in all directions. On days when weather problems slowed us down, two, three, sometimes four backlogged groups of campers or fishermen waited in the hangar next to their piles of duffel bags, coolers, backpacks, cartons, beer cases, rifles, and fishing gear. Clark or I would taxi up to the dock, scramble out, and look at the crowd.

"Okay, fellows, who's next?"

One charter involved a flight with Geraldo Rivera, then a correspondent for ABC TV's *20/20*. The program wanted to shoot a segment on the logging camp at

Coffman Cove on the northeastern end of Prince of Wales Island. The camera crew had flown out the day before and planned to film Rivera's arrival by floatplane. "You're on primetime TV, so make a good landing," a grinning Rivera said to me as we approached the camp. In addition to the technicians, I could see a couple of dozen camp residents on the seaplane dock below, waiting and watching.

"Thanks for the pressure!" I quipped to Rivera, a vivacious, charismatic man with a thick mustache and an easy smile. A brisk east wind stirred the air and the water, but I managed to set the airplane down with reasonable smoothness.

"We'll give you an A minus," he said.

He asked me to dock on the right side of the 185 so he could step out first for the cameras. A rain shower had moved through the area minutes before. With the crew capturing the scene and the sound, Rivera clambered out, grinned at camp spokesperson Leta Valentine, slipped on the wet dock, and fell hard on his buttocks.

"Shit!" he exclaimed.

He climbed back into the cockpit, and I restarted the engine and taxied around for take two. This time he stayed on his feet and received a second greeting from Ms. Valentine.

Rivera had told the Southeast media that the *20/20* producers intended the segment to be a simple study of life in a logging camp, but skeptical Southeasterners chewed their fingernails for weeks. The program often featured scathing investigative reports, and Coffman Cove had two reasons to be a target: the camp had been built practically on top of a four-thousand-year-old archaeological site, and clear-cut logging was a controversial practice many conservationists wanted to ban. However, when the segment finally aired, a record Southeast audience sighed in relief to see that it was indeed an innocent lifestyle study.

Winter now. The lakes were frozen, the days dreary, the charters irregular. One Friday morning in February Clark made the only flight on the schedule, a 9:00 A.M. pickup at Metlakatla, then hurried off to the Ketchikan airport to a catch flight to Seattle for the weekend. In early afternoon I was finishing correspondence to prospective Lower 48 customers when the door burst open. Out of breath, bundled up in a blue parka, lugging a suitcase and two shopping bags stuffed with brightly colored presents, a young Native Alaskan woman looked excited.

"Can you fly me to Hydaburg?" she asked, her dark eyes fixed on my face. She told me her name was Anna, that she hadn't been back to Hydaburg since high school five years before, that she had been homesick in Seattle ever since the Christmas holidays. Suddenly deciding to fly home for a visit, she had phoned the village yesterday and caught a 727 to Ketchikan this morning. Now she needed transportation the rest of the way.

I looked at the clock. If we left right now I could make the ninety-mile round trip with about a half hour to spare before darkness. "Okay, let's do it."

A minute later Anna stood on the dock chatting excitedly while I loaded her suitcase and presents into the 185 and pumped twenty gallons of fuel into the left wing tank. She grinned like a child before a birthday party as we taxied into the Narrows for takeoff.

Once we were airborne, however, she grew strangely sullen. When I asked how it felt to be back in Alaska after five years, she simply shrugged. And unlike most passengers, she showed little interest in the rocky beaches and snow-filled valleys around us. I assumed the noise of the engine discouraged her from talking and that she was preoccupied with thoughts of homecoming.

My own thoughts turned to the weather as we crossed Clarence Strait and approached Prince of Wales Island. The flurries that had been fluttering from the gray overcast all day were intensifying now, drawing a curtain across the island's hills and mountains. By the time we reached Hetta Inlet, visibility had dropped to a couple of miles. Unable to cut across the hills between Hetta and Sukkwan Strait directly to the village, I decided to follow the shoreline of the inlet all the way around.

But the snow continued to thicken, forcing us lower and lower until the floats practically touched the water. Trees, rocks, and driftwood along the shore slipped by like ghosts. The accumulation had already covered all exposed parts of the beach, right up to the water. I could see nothing out the windshield except thousands of thick flakes that seemed to be driving at us horizontally. Time to turn around.

I throttled back and lowered the flaps, but as I was about to make a 180-degree turn the ghosts vanished altogether, leaving us enveloped in a whitish-gray vacuum. I yanked back the throttle and held up the nose. We plopped down firmly.

Anna sat quietly, her hands in her lap, her eyes staring blankly at the instrument panel.

"It's getting pretty spooky out there, so we'll have to wait for the snow to let up a little," I said, turning the 185 toward the barely discernible shoreline. "The village is just around the corner, another fifteen miles or so, though I'm afraid we'll have to go back to town if things don't improve."

Anna raised her head to look out the windshield. When she spoke I had to cock my head to hear. "I want to go back to Ketchikan. I don't want to go to the village anymore. I've changed my mind. Please, take me back."

Shoulder-length black hair blocked her profile except for her nose. "Go back?" I said, bewildered. "Why? What happened? An hour ago you were begging me to fly you out."

"My family doesn't really want me. They said they do on the phone, just to be polite, but they don't. I'm the big-city girl now. I've become an outsider. I'd put a damper on things if I was there. I was a fool to think I could just waltz up here after so long and fit right back in."

"Aw, you're just nervous about greeting everyone," I said. "Once that's over, you'll think you never left."

Anna shook her head. "No. I don't belong anymore." Her voice was beginning to quiver. "I can see it all now. I guess I just had to get this close to realize it. Take me back, please." She turned to me and I noticed a glistening in her eyes.

But flying anywhere then was impossible. I paralleled the shore until I spotted a narrow, rock-free stretch where the airplane could be beached.

Five times over the next two hours I crawled out on the wings to brush off a blanket of snow with my gloves so we would be ready to blast off as soon as the visibility improved. But the relentless snow collaborated with the fading light to turn our world into ever-deepening shades of gray. Soon dusk was upon us. Kicking driftwood at the edge of the forest, where I had been pacing, I cursed the weather. Now my passenger and I were stuck on a dark, cold beach in the boondocks. I thought of my friends and the comforts back in town.

Anna merely nodded when, plastered with snow, I climbed into the cockpit and announced we would have to spend the night. My tide book indicated that if I let the airplane go dry, the incoming tide would refloat it about dawn. The surrounding mountains and hills prevented direct communications with the Ketchikan Flight Service Station. But on the air traffic control center frequency for the area, I managed to contact an unseen airliner far above us. Crackling with static that seemed to punctuate our isolation, a voice with a southern accent agreed to let the Ketchikan FSS know of our predicament. Then we were alone again.

Neither of us had much of an appetite, but I pulled out some packets of snacks from the emergency supplies anyway, and Anna opened a present that contained a box of assorted chocolates. The hours dragged on and on. After the snow finally slackened, Anna and I spent part of the time stomping about in the night outside to stay warm.

During one of our cockpit spells, each of us huddled and shivering in the dark with our thoughts, Anna suddenly began reminiscing about growing up in the village. She spoke of salmon fishing and berry picking and potlatch celebrations, of old people who could still converse in Haida, and Christmas mornings in the family cabin overlooking Sukkwan Strait. I felt she was talking to herself as much as to me in her low, melancholy monotone.

I was dozing fitfully when Anna shook me. "I hear a motor—listen."

In the otherwise quiet night a distant rumbling slowly grew louder.

A boat was approaching. Wondering who could be out in this weather, I shined a penlight at my watch. It read 10:50. Moments later, lights appeared through some remaining flurries. I recognized the outline of a salmon seiner. A spotlight sweeping the shoreline glared into the cockpit, and we shielded our eyes.

"There it is!" someone on the seiner called. "Hey, there!"

Anna and I clambered out and stood in the snow as a skiff putt-putted through the spotlight beam on the water up to the airplane. The bow crunched to a stop on the pebbles, and a middle-aged man wearing a rain suit and ski cap stepped onto the beach.

"Hi," he said to me. Then he looked at my passenger. "Anna!"

She hesitated. "It's my brother Frank!" They embraced in a long hug, and then began talking softly. "How did you know where we were?" I heard her ask.

Though I couldn't catch every word of his answer, Frank explained that the family became concerned when she hadn't arrived by late afternoon and learned through phone calls that a floatplane was weathered in out here. "We thought it was probably you trying to come home," he said. "You didn't think we'd let our little girl spend the night out here in the snow, did you? Come on. Everybody at home is waiting for you."

I hauled Anna's suitcase and presents out of the rear seats and handed them to her brother, who took them to the skiff. Then I poked Anna in the ribs and whispered, "I thought you wanted to go back to town." She smiled and kissed me on the cheek.

"Do you need any help?" Frank asked me as he guided his sister into the skiff.

"Nope. I'll be okay. So long, Anna."

When I awoke in the cockpit at dawn, shivering and famished, the sky was clear and a magnificent fluffy white coat adorned the beach, the trees, the hills. I smiled at the scene on the flight back to Ketchikan as I savored the richness of an interesting occupation. I knew that Anna, surrounded by love in her home, also felt rich.

Chapter 12

MECHANICALS

In the early days of aviation, some pilots carried a mechanic on every flight. With just cause, they worried more about the health of their rickety, wood-and-fabric airframes and unreliable engines than they did about the weather. Modern, all-metal, scientifically engineered airplanes, however, usually flew on and on and on with little protest. They tolerated the pounding of waves and swells, and the engines withstood the intense heat of long, low-speed, high-power climbs and the shock-cooling of long, high-speed, low-power descents.

On modern airplanes used in air-taxi work, engines were limited to a finite number of hours before they had to be overhauled or rebuilt, regardless of condition: typically seventeen hundred for the Cessna 185's and 206's IO-520 Continental, and fifteen hundred for the de Havilland Beaver's Pratt & Whitney R-985. Airframes and engines had to be inspected every hundred hours of flight time. Some modern bush planes still on the line had accumulated more than fifteen thousand hours, and some pilots with that many hours had never experienced a major in-flight mechanical problem.

When something did go wrong, it was often in the starting system. Floatplanes might make two dozen starts and stops in a day in the saltwater environment, and periodically we would push off from the dock to discover that the starter, battery, or related component had succumbed to wear or corrosion. The pilot would yell to anyone on the dock: "Quick, pull us back in!" Or he'd scramble out of the cockpit, take the paddle from its sheath on the pontoon, and paddle. Sometimes a strong wind or current overpowered his efforts and the plane would drift rapidly away. The high-compression engines were hard to start by hand-spinning the prop, especially when standing awkwardly on the pontoon with the airplane bobbing in the waves. In such a case, the pilot could only yell for help and hope a boat arrived before the plane drifted into a reef, piling, or other obstacle.

An airborne failure posed a more serious threat. A few years earlier, Ketchikan pilot Kirk Thomas had had a sudden loss of power in a Beaver over the Harris River Valley on Prince of Wales Island. While circling the only stretch on the river where a landing could be made, he was able to keep the engine going for a while by repeatedly engaging the fuel primer. Not enough power was available to climb for the safety of altitude, and he was reluctant to make a dash for the nearest open water, at Hollis at the mouth of the river, because no landing site would be at hand if the engine quit on the way. Thomas had been updating the company on the radio throughout the ordeal; finally, the operations manager told him to play it safe and land on the stretch he was circling. The Beaver sustained some damage but Thomas was uninjured.

We all wondered if some fatal accidents attributed to weather actually resulted from engine failure, with bad weather at the time an innocent, coincidental scapegoat. Often investigators were unable to examine mechanical parts because the wreckage was burned, too badly mangled, or submerged in prohibitively deep water. At larger air services, each airplane served many masters; a moral code obliged pilots to report abuse such as a takeoff over-boost or very hard landing so mechanics could immediately inspect for damage that might affect a subsequent flight with a different, unsuspecting pilot. Unfortunately, some pilots kept mum rather than admit to abuse. Mechanics occasionally discovered evidence of serious abuse during a routine, scheduled inspection, but by then many hands had been at the controls and the culprit could not be identified.

During flight training, student pilots are given simulated emergency-landing practice and taught to continually scan the countryside below on routine flights for possible landing sites, just in case. Most pilots continue the "what-if" habit after certification. A Southeast floatplane pilot would take at least casual note of muskeg meadows, sheltered salt water, ponds, and uncluttered beaches. We could not help mentally squirming a bit over an angry ocean, a thick forest, or a rugged mountain. When possible in such an environment, we detoured a bit to better position ourselves for an emergency. It was easy to get complacent, though, because most often, week after week, month after month, the engine kept rumbling faithfully on. Most often.

Labouchere Bay was a large, open body of water at the north end of Prince of Wales Island, interrupted only by a few islets. Protected from the swells of Sumner Strait, to which it opened, and from the prevailing southeast wind except in a gale, the bay offered a floatplane pilot plenty of room in which to take off, with ample space left over for a safety margin. At the head of the bay sat a logging camp.

It was here that I had taken two Coast Guard officers on the second stop of a charter to inspect fuel-storage facilities. We had landed first in Bay of Pillars at Kuiu Island at an abandoned salmon cannery, where some storage tanks still contained fuel. While the officers poked around the tanks in their blue uniforms and orange jackets, checking for leaks and undermining of the structures, I had browsed through dew-laden bushes plucking blueberries and salmonberries. The partly cloudy skies were dry, my thoughts far from mechanical problems. At

Labouchere Bay an hour later, I had passed the standby time by jogging on the camp's logging roads.

Now, the second inspection completed, my hair still wet from a shower in a bunkhouse, we taxied from the dock. Next was the tiny hamlet of Point Baker, just three miles to the north. The 185's engine responded normally with full power as I pushed the throttle to the firewall, and moments later the floats slipped off the water. At that point I automatically took my right hand off the throttle to retract the flaps.

Suddenly, the snarl of the engine dropped to a sputter. Thinking a loose friction lock on the throttle assembly had allowed the plunger to slip back to the idle position, I jerked my hand from the flap lever back to the throttle. It found the throttle, as well as the prop and mixture controls, still firewalled. We had climbed only a few feet above the water, and before I could take other action the airplane dropped back down on it. The idling engine sputtered again as if choking, then stopped.

The incident had lasted a few seconds, barely enough time for an instant of terror had we been over rocks or trees or ocean swells. But noting the large body of gentle water all around I had felt no tension on takeoff, and no adrenaline flowed when the power loss occurred. Instead, there was only surprise, which kept us silent for several moments while the gyros whined down inside the instrument panel.

"What happened?" one of the officers finally asked. Each of the fuel gauges indicated a half-full tank, and the handle on the fuel-selector mechanism still pointed at "both," meaning the engine had drawn fuel from both wing tanks simultaneously. The emergency fuel-shutoff valve remained in the "off" position.

"I'm not sure, but we'll find out," I answered. Aware that the Coast Guard was a frequent and valuable customer for Revilla Flying Service, I added with a chuckle, "This has never happened to me before." The engine, an overhauled Continental IO-520-D installed a few days earlier to replace its run-out predecessor, had accumulated about ten hours, all trouble-free. I was leery of trying to restart it in the middle of the bay lest a broken fuel line cause a fire, so the officers volunteered to step down on the floats and paddle us to shore while I sat in the cockpit and steered against a slight crosswind with the water rudders.

As the paddles rhythmically swashed through the water on either side of the fuselage, I glanced about the large bay and humbly reflected on our fate had the problem arisen at a destination farther along on our itinerary: Point Baker, where an engine failure would have dropped us into the swells of Sumner Strait, or the fishing village at Meyers Chuck, where rocks lay at the end of the two principal takeoff paths.

The toes of the floats slid onto a gravelly beach, and the officers replaced the paddles in their sheaths. I removed the top half of the cowling with a screwdriver from a small tool kit in the map compartment and studied the engine.

There was no broken fuel line or injector or other obvious trouble. Next, with the clear plastic cup designed for the purpose I drained several ounces from all five fuel sumps—one in each wing tank, one in the engine, and two under the fuselage. None of the samples contained water or sediment.

Then, with the toes of the floats still on the beach to hold the 185 in place, I started the engine. It ran normally with the auxiliary fuel pump off, indicating the engine-driven pump was functioning. "Well," I said, shaking my head, "everything seems to be okay. Let's give it another try." I assured the officers I would keep the airplane on the step for a few minutes before leaving the water to make sure the engine would continue running.

With the cowling refastened, we spun the 185 around and climbed in. So far I had not checked the engine instruments at full power; like many floatplane pilots, I took off by the seat of my pants and concentrated instead on watching for debris in the water that might damage a float during the takeoff run. This time, however, I watched the gauges as I advanced the throttle.

All needles behaved until the final half inch of throttle travel, whereupon the fuel-flow needle swept right by the red line (maximum allowed) and into the manifold-pressure side of the dual instrument. The engine sputtered. I quickly yanked back the throttle, and we slowed to an idling taxi.

"Uh oh!" one of the officers exclaimed. But I felt relieved, for I now knew what ailed the engine: excess fuel at full power. Leaning the engine's fuel/air ratio with the mixture control seemed to be a reasonable remedy. After a successful step-taxi test, we took off and, carefully monitoring the fuel flow, returned to town with no further trouble.

In the office, Revilla owner Dale Clark grimaced as I related the events at Labouchere Bay. "I've heard of engines quitting because they didn't get enough fuel," he commented, "but I've never heard of one quitting at sea level because it got too much."

He and a mechanic explored the engine for several hours but found nothing amiss. The fuel filter showed no sign of contamination. Before putting everything back together, they adjusted the fuel flow down slightly for good measure.

The engine performed perfectly on a test flight, the fuel-flow needle dutifully pegging—and remaining—at the red line at full power. But no one felt satisfied. If the problem had been an excessive fuel-flow setting, why hadn't it manifested itself during the previous ten hours of flight? Why hadn't the engine quit on takeoff from Ketchikan or Bay of Pillars? We checked with other 185 pilots and mechanics in town and phoned several overhaul shops in the Seattle area; none had ever heard of an IO-520-D, or any engine, for that matter, flooding out on takeoff at sea level. A Continental factory representative also had no explanation.

The auxiliary fuel pump on a 185 was used for priming before starting the engine and to provide a flow of fuel in case the engine-driven pump failed. In the "high" position the auxiliary fuel-pump switch was spring-loaded; the pilot had to hold his finger on it to maintain maximum pump operation. Had a temporary electrical short at Labouchere Bay turned on the pump at that position, we wondered? If the engine-driven pump was working, activation of the auxiliary pump would have caused an excessively rich fuel mixture—sort of like giving a full glass of Scotch to a party guest who had asked for two fingers' worth. We purposely kept the pump on high in a full-power test to see what would happen, but while the resulting overly rich mixture sent the fuel-flow needle slightly past the red line, it produced no power loss.

The possibility of pilot error undoubtedly arose in a few minds and undoubtedly faded immediately. Other than deliberately holding the auxiliary fuel-pump switch in the high position during the takeoff run—an awkward act, which we had demonstrated probably would not have stopped the engine anyway—there simply was nothing a pilot could do at sea level to produce too much fuel on takeoff. At altitude, where the air was thinner and engines needed less fuel, failing to lean the mixture before applying full power could flood the engine. But Labouchere Bay's elevation was zero.

Nonetheless, I felt uncomfortable that Clark and the mechanic could not re-create the power loss and vindicate me. The incident remained a mystery, and the problem never recurred.

Besides feeling fortunate that my engine failure had happened over calm water rather than a hostile environment, I felt relieved that the incident had happened at all. While I rejected the superstition that some supernatural master plan allotted a certain number of mechanical woes to each pilot, I did trust the law of averages to insure me against further serious engine trouble. Few experienced pilots had had even one total engine failure, let alone two. Now that I had had mine, the likelihood of another in the next few years was statistically almost nil.

However, I was also aware that a flipped coin that landed heads up five consecutive times still had a fifty-fifty chance of landing heads up the sixth time.

When my next engine ordeal occurred, I had flown just two thousand additional hours, a relatively brief interlude. This time the culprit was human carelessness instead of an obscure mechanical gremlin.

I was in Juneau now. After three years with Revilla Flying Service, I had moved to Seattle for a white-collar job with regular hours in a comfortable office, but this time disenchantment with bush flying was only part of the motivation. A romance had ended, and my heart languished. The young woman and I kept running into each other in the supermarket, in the cafes, on the sidewalks. Ketchikan was too small for the both of us.

The Seattle area had seemed to be an ideal getaway: distant enough for healing, still within the Pacific Northwest zone of mountains, forests, waterways, and islands I loved. Seattle even had four water-based air services, but I was ready for a break from the cockpit.

I was now the editor of a bimonthly newspaper. For months I had immersed myself in writing, editing, and other duties, often taking work home and coming in on weekends. Heartache had little time to fester and gradually faded away. Just as gradually, monotony and boredom had set in, and once again I began to stare out the window and daydream about bush flying. Why could I not be content with the ordinary, relatively secure lifestyle that satisfied so many millions of other people? Did I have some constitutional need for adventure and insecurity? Hoping to regain spirit, I made my first parachute jump at a bucolic airport near Lake Sammamish in Issaquah. I also took a few glider lessons at the same facility, white-water rafted down the Suiattle River, and hiked on Mount Rainier—at 14,410 feet, Washington state's highest mountain.

But Washington felt too developed, too civilized. It lacked the excitement and stimulation of the forty-ninth state, much as East Coast surf is bland compared with West Coast surf.

When I realized I was beginning to think seriously about returning to Alaska, I gulped. Hold on, here, I told myself. Are you sure you want to do this? You've forsaken bush flying three times before for the sort of job you now hold. If you go back to the cockpit, do you really think you could avoid another bout of burnout? You remember the romance but forget the sweat and the rain. How much longer will the cycle continue? Your employment record in journalism is already unstable enough to make any interviewer frown. You can't keep leaving good jobs every several years and expect the door to remain open. You may already be in your last opportunity for a meaningful career. After this, you might have no option but to fly floatplanes for the rest of your working life, changing companies as they furlough you or fold. Flying floatplanes in the Alaskan wilderness is not a skill that can be easily marketed elsewhere in the aviation industry, much less outside it. Even if you were young enough to be considered, the airlines would insist on a more appropriate aviation background.

Ten years earlier, tomorrow hadn't mattered. Life was for the present, to be experienced and enjoyed in pursuits of passion. The future would take care of itself. Now tomorrow did matter. Tomorrow was closer. I could see it in the mirror in the crow's feet at the corners of my eyes and in my receding hairline. I could see it in the simplicity of my tax returns. I could see it in the lonely, blank stares of the Seattle street people, who perhaps were lamenting lost opportunities as they held out their cups.

Despite these thoughts, I continued to listen to the patient Sirens of Alaska. Forewarned, Odysseus took the precaution of having his sailors lash him to the mast so he would be unable to heed the Sirens' seductive, insidious calls. I had no sailors, no mast. But when the lure became irresistible, I was wise enough to opt for Juneau and a change in routine rather than Ketchikan, where memories might be rekindled.

Founded in 1880 on the site of a gold strike 210 miles up the archipelago from Ketchikan, Juneau was an exaggerated image of its perennial rival. It too was strung along a narrow channel, but with more buildings to accommodate its population of 25,600. The main road paralleled the waterfront with four lanes instead of two, and the mountains behind the city rose higher and more steeply. The Juneau area even had glaciers, including the famous Mendenhall, accessible by road north of town. As the state capital, Juneau had a higher cost of living and exuded an underlying snobbism compared with Ketchikan's redneck ingenuousness.

But the two areas shared a need for air transportation; the bush around Juneau was equally roadless. With thirty employees and thirteen aircraft, Channel Flying, my new company, was the largest and oldest of Juneau's nine air services, the descendant of a one-airplane, one-man operation that part-owner Kenneth H. Loken founded in 1954. One of the pilots had previously flown seaplanes for famed oceanographer Jacques Cousteau. In addition to its waterfront facilities along Gastineau Channel, the company had an office at Juneau Municipal Airport, since some of the aircraft were amphibious. Channel berthed most of its floatplanes in a rectangular, man-made lake called "the pond" adjacent to the runway.

The airplanes were familiar to me, but not so most of the places the company served regularly: the Tlingit villages of Hoonah and Angoon, Tenakee Springs, the fishing hamlets of Elfin Cove and Pelican, the National Marine Fisheries Service's station at Little Port Walter, and others. Glacier Bay National Park and Preserve, a 3.3-million-acre world of ice, mountains, and inlets, was a favorite sightseeing destination near Juneau. It contained Southeast's mightiest mountain, 15,300-foot Mount Fairweather.

For several days I flew in the right seat as an observer to these places, then in the left as a pilot with a check pilot next to me, learning the routes. My experience in the Ketchikan area transferred readily to the process. While the beaches here were less rocky and glaciers gripped the steep mainland valleys like massive rivers of ice, the waterways, islands, and mountains imparted a sense of déjà vu; I quickly felt at home.

For tips on specific places, Loken, nicknamed "Pinky" for his perpetually ruddy complexion, could answer all questions. He often entered the waterfront operations room to check on the day's flights and, I suspected, to escape the paperwork drudgery in his office upstairs. No matter where inside a hundred-mile radius of Juneau a pilot was bound, the tall, blond Loken had been there himself before retiring from the cockpit several years earlier. He would expound on special considerations, then—his blue eyes still sharp and free of glasses after sixty-two years—tell an anecdote about one of his flights to the place. An avid hiker who had trekked in Nepal the year before, Loken talked about the bush with the wistful reverence of an aging adventurer.

Soon I would be the one relating an adventure.

The first hint of trouble came from that mysterious inner voice some people call intuition. The dispatcher had scheduled me to fly N5603R on Tuesday, after the Cessna 206 came out of the hangar for a routine hundred-hour inspection. When the mechanics did a compression check at the end of the inspection that morning, however, they found four of the six cylinders below limits. That meant another couple of days in the shop for the airplane. I spent the time getting settled in my new home. It was midspring, and most of the company's aircraft had yet to come out of winter storage; with just ten days of employment, I had to yield other available airplanes to pilots with more seniority.

The mechanics worked late into the night on Wednesday, and Thursday morning I was pleased to find N5603R cowled outside the hangar. But when we carted it over to the seaplane elevator, we discovered the tide was too low to get it into the water. Noon would be the soonest the incoming tide would reach the lower end of the elevator's runners.

"This airplane just doesn't want to go to work," I muttered as the mechanics and I stared down at the algae-coated bottom of the elevator frame. Made in jest, the comment seemed to hang ominously in the air for minutes afterward.

The foreboding haunted me again later that morning at the airport terminal, where I whiled away the hours with the land-based air-taxi people. As we sipped coffee, someone with a radio scanner suddenly turned up the volume. A Canadian Super Cub on wheels that had left Juneau for Atlin, British Columbia, had encountered freezing rain up the Taku Inlet and was limping back to the airport. Again and again we heard the pilot radio the tower that he was going to crash-land because of a loss of power, only to announce in a shaky voice a few seconds later that "the engine has come up now."

In a morbid way, there was something humorous in the repetition of this cycle. Most of the dozen pilots, dispatchers, and passengers who had gathered around the scanner chuckled in unison at each status change. I started to smile with the crowd but felt instantly guilty. Somehow, I shared the pilot's lonely desperation, a sensation that clouded my anticipation of flying even after he landed safely at the airport.

With 03R finally in the water, the dispatcher assigned me to make a 1 P.M. flight to the villages of Tenakee Springs and Angoon and a cabin at Gambier Bay. After leveling off at fifteen feet at the north end of Douglas Island by the airport and throttling back to cruise power, I noticed that the fuel-flow gauge read fourteen gallons per hour instead of the usual sixteen. Since the other engine instruments were giving normal indications, I concluded the gauge simply needed adjustment. I would so inform the mechanics when I returned to Juneau.

At Tenakee, a hot-springs resort community of eighty residents by Tenakee Inlet on Chichagof Island, I dropped off a passenger and a load of mail and freight. While taxiing out, I twice had to give the engine a spurt of power to keep it from dying. Idle set too low. I'd mention that, too.

The fuel flow read just twelve gallons per hour during the climbout from Tenakee, and the needle slowly sank until it pegged at zero over Chatham Strait. The rest of the engine instruments continued to report healthy vital signs. Obviously, the fuel-flow gauge was broken. Occasionally the smell of fuel wafted into my nostrils now, but I assumed the odor lingered from a chain saw I had unloaded at Tenakee.

As I worked my way across the strait and down the west coast of Admiralty Island toward Angoon, sleet and a gusty east wind began thrashing 03R: the edge of a front forecast to arrive in the Juneau area later that day. The wind, whipping the water into three-foot waves off Admiralty, forced me to crab thirty degrees toward the shore to maintain a straight track. Fighting the gusts with constant input to the ailerons and rudder, I splashed down to a landing in the harbor at the Tlingit Indian village.

The engine quit when I throttled back to taxi. "Damn this idle!" I mumbled, restarting the engine. At the dock I unloaded my remaining two passengers—who had been sitting behind me in the two middle seats—and the rest of the mail and freight. The company's Angoon agent later told the dispatcher in Juneau he thought the engine sounded rough when I took off.

My last stop was on the east side of Admiralty Island at Gambier Bay, where a man and his wife had radioed for transportation to Juneau from their cabin. The sleet and scud blocked the passes across the island, so I continued down the shoreline, intending to follow the water all the way around.

But I paid little attention to the weather now. The airspeed indicator was oscillating between just 85 and 90 knots in the turbulence, although the 206 was empty of payload weight and I had set the power for normal cruise. The needle should have been wavering between 110 and 115 knots. Was the airspeed indicator also breaking down? And was the engine rasping slightly, like someone who ought to clear his throat? And that fuel smell! I advanced the prop control and throttle to climb power, but the airspeed needle rose to only 100 knots.

For a minute I tried to convince myself that the below-normal airspeed resulted from offshore downdrafts that were forcing me to fly with a nose-up attitude, and that the engine roughness was actually the slipstream whistling through tiny window or door spaces. As a new pilot in Juneau, I was eager to prove my worth by completing assignments. I wanted to avoid an early reputation for turning back because of minor or imaginary mechanical trouble.

But pretending could not mask the evidence of a growing problem.

It could not change the proper professional response. With a sigh, I banked away from the shoreline to begin a turn back toward Juneau. As I glanced out the right window to watch the murky horizon during the turn, the corner of my eye noticed liquid sloshing on the floor in the foot well of the right-hand seat. Dripping passenger boots flashed into my mind and vanished immediately—

boots could not have deposited that much fluid. Knowing what I would learn, I reached over, stuck my finger in, and smelled.

Fuel!

The specter of a sudden inferno sent adrenaline tingling through my veins and nearly strangled me with claustrophobia. I was now abeam Chaik Bay, just ten miles south of Angoon. But I had no faith in the engine to get me back to the village, or even to a sheltered cove in Chaik Bay. If I headed for one of those sanctuaries against the fierce wind and the engine suddenly quit or blew up, I would come down on the windward side of Chatham Strait to drift helplessly away from land into increasingly rough water that would almost certainly capsize the airplane and sap the life from me. With the wind on my tail, however, I could quickly cross the eight-mile-wide strait to the downwind side, the east shore of Baranof Island. There I would at least drift toward land.

Frowning through the windshield, I turned 03R toward the outline of Baranof, barely visible through the sleet. I shut off all electrical equipment and pushed the control wheel forward until the airplane was about twenty feet above the waves. Now I could plant the floats onto the water and dive out in case the cockpit erupted in flames. Then I fiddled with my fingers beneath the seat until I unlatched the fire extinguisher and placed the cylinder in my lap. Although the airplane had six life jackets, I never thought to slip into one.

My pounding heart seemed to spur the airplane on. I reached Baranof in less than four minutes and turned north, staying close to both the water and shoreline. My chart showed the nearest habitation on this side to be back at Tenakee, some thirty miles away. Should I land in the first protected cove while the engine was still running, beach the airplane as best I could and wait? Search aircraft would scour Admiralty Island first; it would be at least tomorrow afternoon before someone would check this stretch of Baranof. And the wind was forecast to increase to forty knots or higher in the evening.

As I watched the swells smash against the rocks and reefs, spraying the trunks of the spruce and hemlock trees cluttering the banks, I felt an overwhelming urge to let someone know what was happening. I hesitated, then pressed the dual battery/alternator master switch and cringed against an explosion. The engine rasped on. Next, I gingerly flicked on the avionics master switch and cringed again.

In recent years the FAA had installed remote communication outlet (RCO) repeater stations on strategically located mountaintops to enhance radio communications in mountainous Southeast. Thus, despite my extremely low altitude, I pulled the microphone off its hook and tried to call the Juneau Flight Service Station. Silence. I twirled the knobs on the radio to 121.5 megahertz, the universal mayday frequency, and transmitted in the blind. Again there was no response. Since I was unaware of the locations of the RCO repeater station sites in this part of the region, I began trying RCO frequencies at random. The fourth frequency I tuned in was 121.4 megahertz.

"Cessna Five Six Zero Three Romeo, this is Sitka Radio, go ahead." The voice was a puff of air in an airless box, although of course the speaker could do nothing to mend the ailing engine or defuse the leaking fuel. I explained the situation, said I was going to try to make Tenakee, and asked the specialist to notify the company. Every few minutes thereafter his voice entered my headset to ask my position and estimated time of arrival at Tenakee. I fretted over the answers because the country was new to me and I was flying so close to the surface that the shoreline blocked from my view many of the features depicted on my chart. But by dead reckoning and following my progress with my finger on the chart like a poor reader working through a paragraph, I managed to keep track of my position.

At the mouths of bays, where I had to leave the security of the shoreline for a minute or more, I coaxed the engine with the plea, "Come on, come on, keep going!" until I was again within gliding distance of the shoreline.

Although I was reluctant to have the information, I also kept track of the growing pool of fuel on the right-hand floor. I leaned over periodically to watch spurts shoot out from the upper firewall area like milk from a cow, splashing on the floor. I tried mopping up the pool with paper towels, but I quickly exhausted the roll. The effort was academic, anyway; the danger from leaking fuel lay not on the floor, where there was no source of ignition, but in the engine and accessories area, which was fraught with intense heat, electrical wiring, and possibly sparks.

If the engine suddenly exploded, would the cockpit be instantly engulfed in fire, or would the firewall contain the flames long enough for me to ditch? I had already opened all the air vents within reach to dispel the fuel odor. Now I shut them to prevent the rush of air from fanning the flames I might have to face.

The falling needles on the fuel gauges showed about twice the normal consumption for the eighty minutes I had been in the air. The bad weather forecast and my unfamiliarity with this part of Southeast had inspired me to pump an extra twenty gallons into the right tank as a reserve. Those twenty gallons now seemed like liquid gold; without them I would be unable to reach Tenakee.

I frowned each time I glanced at the climb power settings on the manifold pressure and tachometer gauges. Throttling back to cruise power would reduce the fuel consumption and perhaps also lower the rate of fuel leakage. But I might unwittingly have selected the one power combination that, for reasons beyond my understanding of mechanics, chemistry, and physics, had thus far inhibited an explosion. Throttling back might change things and prompt a sudden boom— or a sudden silence up front. I opted for the status quo.

Just beyond Basket Bay I finally flew back out of the sleet. The gusty wind persisted, but my spirits rose with the visibility and ceiling. As my chances of making Tenakee increased, so did my eagerness to get there. I began fidgeting, grinding my teeth, and glancing at the panel clock, which seemed to show only a few seconds' advance for each minute I believed had passed.

At last I rounded the southern corner of Tenakee Inlet and gained a tailwind. Several minutes later I turned upwind to land in front of the quaint community.

"Sitka, Zero Three Romeo, landing Tenakee. Thanks for your help," I said into the mike. There was no answer; the mountains along Tenakee Inlet blocked the communications facilities that had relayed our previous transmissions.

Roiled by the wind, the water glared with dark, angry waves. But the 206 had electric flaps, and I debated only a second before deciding not to risk a spark by deploying them. I held the floats off the waves as long as possible to dissipate the excess speed of a no-flaps approach and made a full-stall landing. The airplane shuddered from the jolt and bounced several times before falling off the step.

The engine quit. I restarted it twice before reaching the dock. There, the company's waiting Tenakee agent, whom the dispatcher had notified of my problem, grabbed the wing strut and pulled the plane to the bumpers along the dock.

"Got a little engine trouble, huh?" he said. The air smelled fresh and delicious as we walked up the ramp to the Snyder Mercantile Company, the local general store, and I breathed deeply of it. After a long drink of water, I called the company, asked the dispatcher to inform the FAA that I had landed safely, and gave details of the flight to a mechanic. Then I went back outside and strolled along Tenakee's narrow, graveled street, savoring the wind in my face and the crunch of pebbles beneath my boots. An elderly hunchbacked woman shuffled by, acknowledging me with only a faint smile. Residents were used to visiting tourists, fishermen, and hunters. To her I was just another stranger, undeserving of special attention. Fuel leaks and faltering aircraft engines were beyond her knowledge or concern. Life went on.

By the time another company 206 landed with a mechanic an hour later, sleet had begun to pelt the little community. Zero Three Romeo promptly dispelled whatever superstition I had harbored that its woes would mysteriously disappear the moment the mechanic arrived. As I taxied the airplane around to the other side of the dock to run it up on the seaplane ramp so the mechanic could work on it, the engine quit four times, and the backfiring sounded like a gun battle. Mechanic Clyde Dammel and pilot Jacques Norvell stood solemnly on the dock, watching and listening.

After Dammel removed the top half of 03R's cowling, Norvell and I placed it into the other 206 to keep the wind from blowing it off the dock. Dammel needed just a few moments to locate the trouble. Two fuel lines, he candidly told us, had been left untightened when he and the other mechanics had worked late the night before to complete the hundred-hour inspection. Both lines had gradually vibrated loose during my flight. One served the fuel-flow instrument and was the source of the fuel leaking into the cockpit. The fuel had gathered behind the firewall and spilled through openings onto the floor in spurts as it sloshed around. Meanwhile, the untightened fuel injector line to the number five cylinder had caused the power loss when it worked itself off.

It had sprayed raw fuel continuously over the hot engine. I contemplated the news and its considerations:

If one of my Angoon passengers had sat in the right front seat, he would have noticed the leaking fuel and alerted me, allowing me to terminate the flight much sooner. Whenever I had passengers, the right front seat was almost always occupied. But these two had asked to sit in the middle seats, leaving the one next to me empty.

If I had had a load of passengers or freight instead of an empty airplane after leaving Angoon, a normal power setting might have been insufficient and I would have increased power. A higher setting would have meant more fuel flow and more heat. Would it also have meant an explosion or fuel exhaustion before reaching Tenakee?

If I had been more familiar with the Juneau area, I would have taken on much less of a fuel reserve at Juneau, which would have put Tenakee beyond 03R's range, under the circumstances.

I had thought the fire danger came solely from the source that was leaking fuel onto the floor, which actually posed relatively little threat. Had I been aware of the far more serious leak from the loose injector line, I probably would have ditched the airplane as soon as I reached the Baranof shoreline—and thus lost the airplane and possibly my life.

Dammel reattached and secured the two fuel lines and replaced the cowling, and I mopped up the pool of fuel on the floor with paper towels from the other 206. There was still enough fuel in 03R for the twenty-five-minute flight to Juneau. Norvell took off in his airplane and Dammel accompanied me to be on hand in case further trouble developed. We made the flight in silence, the airspeed now at 115 knots and the engine droning heartily. As we taxied toward the dock in town, I turned to Dammel.

"What could I have done to reduce the fire risk?"

He grimaced and shook his head. "Not a thing. You were damn lucky. It should have ignited."

In the coming years I would be lucky again in three sudden emergencies, one with smoke streaming from the engine, one with ten people on board, and one with a lone passenger—the mother of one of the world's richest men.

Chapter 13

ICE CAP BLUES

How high is sea level up here?" the woman in the right front seat asked above the engine roar of the Beaver as we climbed out from Gastineau Channel. She appeared to be in her fifties, a heavy person with bushy gray hair, glasses, and a southern accent. At first I thought she was joking, and I started to smile in appreciation. But her deadpan, expectant expression told me the question was serious.

The woman and five other passengers from a cruise ship were aboard the Beaver for a tour of the nearby Juneau ice cap, a spectacular mass of ice and snow covering fifteen hundred square miles and spawning some three dozen glaciers. It was mid-May, and although I had begun flying commercially in Juneau a month earlier, this was my first ice cap flight; the cruise ships were just starting their seasonal voyages up the Inside Passage. For the next four months the ships, sometimes three or four in the harbor at once, would deliver up to four thousand tourists to the capital city virtually every day. Depending on the weather, dozens or hundreds would sign up for a tour of the ice cap. Besides flying to the usual bush places, we served as tour guides.

"How high is sea level up here?" the woman said again, apparently interpreting my hesitation to mean I hadn't heard her initially.

"Well, ma'am," I said, trying not to sound derisive, "sea level is pretty much the same all over the world, whether it's the Arctic Ocean or the South Pacific."

"Oh."

I wanted to pick up the microphone and share the exchange with my fellow pilots, whose aircraft were strung out in a loose line at various altitudes behind and in front en route to the ice cap. But I knew that several of them—and thus their passengers—were listening over the speaker instead of through headphones. So, I diplomatically waited until we returned to the Juneau Seadrome downtown, unloaded our passengers, and gathered in the office at the top of the ramp for the next group. Then I discovered the joke was on me.

"Hell, we all hear that question about ten times a summer," chuckled one pilot who had flown in Juneau for several years. "You won't believe some of the questions these cruise ship people ask you."

I became a believer a few days later when an elderly man sitting behind me tapped my shoulder as we entered Taku Inlet.

"What kind of fish are those down there?" he shouted at my headphones. I glanced below, curious. It was too early in the Season for salmon jumpers; had he spotted a pod of whales or porpoises? "Where?" I twisted my neck to look at the man.

The man shook his head slightly and scowled at my lack of observation. "There! All over! Don't you see them?" Then, watching me scan the water without success, he added, "Those white fish, jumping everywhere!"

Suddenly I understood. "Ah, those are whitecaps, sir."

"Whitecaps—are they good to eat?"

Another cruise ship tourist asked if I would circle the North Pole for him. The ice cap may have resembled his image of the top of the world, but I would have had to fly several thousand miles to comply. One couple asked me to fly by an Eskimo village so they could take pictures of igloos to show the folks back home. I explained that Southeast had no Eskimo villages, that most Eskimos in the state resided in western and Arctic Alaska, many hundreds of miles from Juneau, and that they lived in buildings, like non-Native Alaskans. And many tourists wanted to take a look at the trans-Alaska oil pipeline, the closest portion of which lay at Valdez, almost five hundred miles to the northwest.

One of our pilots swore a tourist once asked him where she could exchange dollars for Alaskan currency. Another pilot claimed he got a request to point out penguins.

It was unfair to ridicule the less-informed tourists, of course. Many were unsophisticated senior citizens who had seldom traveled far from their hometowns and who knew few specifics about Alaska beyond its image as a faraway land in the north. Before coming to Alaska, I had not known that the southeastern archipelago existed until I studied the state on a map. But the tourists were convenient outlets through which to vent the monotony of multiple sightseeing flights.

And anyway, most questions on ice cap tours over the next several months were routine and reasonable. And repetitious. A dollar for each, "Why is the ice blue?" would have paid my grocery bills. (Glacial ice becomes prismatic from compression and reflects blue but absorbs other colors of the light spectrum.) Many tourists were also eager to find out how many trips a day I made to the ice cap; they seemed surprised to learn the company flew to camps, villages, lakes, and other destinations as well and that many days I didn't get to the ice cap at all.

And dozens wanted to know if I ever got tired of giving aerial tours of such magnificent scenery. The easiest answer was a simple smile and shake of the head.

In my mind, however, I silently gave a different answer: Well, ma'am, I too marveled at the sights on my first ten or fifteen tours, but now, after fifty or sixty I find the ice cap a little less stimulating, especially on days when I have to make back-to-back tours.

Most tourists had never been in a floatplane, or in any aircraft smaller than an airliner, so many questions concerned safety: "Do you have enough gas, young man?" "Are you sure this thing is safe?" "You *do* have a license, don't you?" At first, I answered candidly, but the repetition of such questions soon inspired me to have a little fun: "No, sir, we have only enough fuel to get us halfway there." "I don't know; I've never been in a floatplane before." "Yes, indeed, I've had a license since Thursday."

Interestingly, sarcasm seemed to relax the tourists more than straight answers. Still, I frequently saw apprehension in their eyes when, taxiing out for takeoff, I turned around to brief them on the flight. Smiling reassured some, but others, like overimaginative children lying in bed listening to every creak in the house, saw discrepancies in routine aspects of floatplanes. Many tourists noticed the permanent mooring lines on the floats and wings while we taxied and urgently informed me that I had forgotten to "take off those ropes" before leaving the dock. And because the doors on airliners are closed before taxiing begins, countless tourists interrupted my briefing to tell me I had neglected to close the cockpit door of the floatplane. Tourists continued to so enlighten me even after I started holding the door two feet open with my elbow to show obvious intention. Eventually, I typed up the following card, laminated it, and carried it in my shirt pocket to take out and present with a smile to whoever broached the question:

Welcome to Juneau. You may have noticed that the door is open. I'm keeping it that way on purpose and will close it before takeoff. There are several reasons for the open door:

1. After casting off, a floatplane pilot's first priority is to start the engine and taxi quickly away from the dock before the wind or current drifts the plane into nearby obstacles. Once clear, he has time to close the door.
2. The pilot can put on his seat belt more easily if the door is ajar.
3. In rain, an open door provides circulation to defog the windows; the air vents don't work at taxiing speeds.
4. In warm temperatures, an open door provides circulation for cooling.
5. An open door during the taxi poses no danger to you or the airplane.

Again, I'll close the door before takeoff. Please relax and enjoy the flight. Thank you.

To avoid the tedium of answering other frequent comments or questions over and over, I began adding to my briefing the half-truth that the engine was too loud for a talking tour. I passed out ice cap informational brochures the company had prepared and asked the passengers to hold their questions until we landed back in Juneau—realizing that by then some questions would be forgotten.

While it was possible to shout out facts about the scenery en route, particularly in the Cessnas, the pilot had to repeat them several times before everyone heard, a tiring, voice-straining effort. Audible comments also required the pilot to talk over his shoulder, a potentially dangerous distraction with up to a dozen other sightseeing aircraft in the area. (As tourism became increasingly important to Southeast's economy, many air service operators began upgrading their aircraft with headsets for every seat and prerecorded narration.)

Some tourists were disappointed in the lack of visible wildlife on their flight. "I didn't see *one* animal!" snapped a man after we landed from a tour. Travel brochures and books that trumpeted Alaska's wildlife but neglected to mention that much of it was concealed by terrain or foliage gave some visitors to the state the impression they would see great herds of beasts covering the slopes and meadows á la Serengeti Plain.

Of course, often we did spot a moose, bear, or mountain goat along the Taku River Valley bordering the ice cap. Several times after I descended and circled an animal, the cabin erupted in delighted applause. Other pilots reported the same reaction, and we half-seriously discussed placing stuffed animals along the route.

Some tourists also complained because clouds or rain obscured part of the scenery—although usually they had signed up for the tour in similar conditions back in town an hour before. With each ice cap seat bringing seventy dollars, the company was understandably loathe to ground the sightseeing squadron just because the weather prevented us from climbing four thousand feet to get up on the ice cap itself. Most tourists, the company realized, were not repeat customers. As long as we could fly safely in the Taku River Valley below the ice cap, the green light was on. The Norris, Hole-in-the-Wall, Taku, West Twin, and East Twin glaciers descended to the valley floor, so even if we couldn't climb above five hundred feet, we could still give our passengers a detailed look at the termini of those glaciers. The calved icebergs, crevasses, moraine deposits, and icefalls were especially fascinating up close. And flying low gave passengers a better chance to spot wildlife and examine the lush valley scenery.

Pilots heard the comment, "This has been the highlight of our trip to Alaska!" almost as often after low-altitude, bad-weather tours as on clear days when we could climb high. Besides, we rationalized, tourists on low-altitude tours didn't know what they were missing above, hidden in the clouds.

Still, we admitted to one another that the tourists were being misled, if not cheated, when an ice cap tour lacked a look at the actual ice cap. We flew the tours in bad weather without protest because that was our job. To ease our consciences, some of us advised the passengers before takeoff that while the weather did not permit an ice cap tour per se, much spectacular scenery awaited their eyes anyway.

The practice of sending out sightseeing flights in non-sightseeing weather was fairly universal among Southeast operators. In Ketchikan, where the local attraction was Misty Fiords National Monument, my fellow pilots and I gave many "tours" beneath stratus that restricted us to weaving along the shorelines of the fjords at very low altitude; the passengers saw nothing of the monument's magnificent valleys, lakes, and peaks. But the company made lots of money.

With rain and tendrils of fog cutting visibility and restricting aircraft to the Taku River Valley, we worried more about a midair collision than satisfying the customers. We monitored a common frequency on our radios during ice cap tours and, in bad weather, turned on our landing lights and transmitted periodic position/altitude reports: "Eight-Seven-Three passing Jaw Point at seven hundred." In fair weather, with lots of elbow room to space out the fleet, the radios crackled mostly with chitchat: "Anybody see any moose down there?" "Only six more hours and we can go home." "Hey Roger, you going back to Louisiana for the winter?"

Now and then a pilot would announce, "Hey, guess who I've got on board!" Celebrities and VIPs included Frank Borman, the astronaut and Eastern Air Lines president; Mayor Tom Bradley of Los Angeles; several professional football players; a fabulously wealthy Saudi Arabian prince who chartered a separate airplane to transport his servants; actor George Kennedy; actress Gloria Swanson, and others.

Some tours featured a stop at a renovated log cabin called the Taku Lodge on the Taku River, where the passengers ate a salmon dinner, gazed at the glacial scenery, and walked on short nature trails. If we had no intervening flights, we waited for them. Most of us migrated to the kitchen. There we drank coffee, chatted, played cards, and swatted the mosquitoes that somehow managed to find a way into the room despite the screens protecting the windows and back door. With luck, there would be leftover king salmon fillets, baked beans, Jell-o sourdough rolls, and cookies for us after the tourists had their dinner ("pilot food," according to the kitchen helpers). While we ate, we occasionally saw a bear prowling across the grass by the outbuildings, scrounging for its own left-over meal.

On particularly busy days when the schedule permitted no such breaks, we left our passengers at the lodge for another flight back in town and returned for them later. One afternoon, after delivering some fishermen to a lake, I scooted back to the lodge to retrieve a load of tourists. As I taxied in, I saw that the other aircraft had taken up most of the dock; only a small section between a Goose and a Beaver was left. On salt water or a lake the spot would have been too tight to glide into. But with the river racing downstream and the nose of the Cessna 206 pointed upstream, I could apply just enough power to offset the current, then use the water rudders to slip sideways into the slot at zero forward speed. The maneuver would require finesse, especially since the direction of the current and the position of the dock meant a right-hand docking; sitting in the left seat, I would have limited visibility out the right side. But I had done it before in similar circumstances.

A couple of pilots stood on the dock ready to secure the airplane to a cleat when the float reached the bumpers. About forty waiting tourists watched in a cluster on the bank of the river. Closer and closer I inched the 206 toward its berth. Ah, observe the great master execute this neat procedure, everybody! Another ten yards now.

Suddenly, the two pilots pointed toward the rear and motioned frantically with their hands. Too late I realized the airplane had been slipping imperceptibly backward in the current, toward the Goose; the right stabilizer hooked the Goose's left wing-float strut, and in the strong current the 206 instantly pivoted. I quickly turned off the engine, and the prop stopped a second before the 206 slammed against the bow of the larger plane.

I scrambled out the door and climbed onto the wings of the 206, and several other pilots climbed on top of the Goose. An inspection indicated just minor damage in the form of dents and scrapes to both aircraft. But how to separate the planes? The current held the 206 against the Goose as if they were welded together. The teenager the lodge employed as a lineman rushed to the boat shed and returned two minutes later with a skiff. He attached a line to the 206 and gunned the outboard, but the planes stubbornly held their embrace.

Meanwhile, the solemn, silent audience on the bank continued to watch the show while they slapped at mosquitoes.

The Goose was farthest downstream of the airplanes at the dock. It finally occurred to us that if we simply untied the Goose and released it into the river with the 206, the force of the current would be negated and the aircraft would easily separate. I climbed back into the 206 and the Goose pilot got into his plane. Someone untied the lines of the Goose, and the river swept us away. Moments later we drifted apart.

The Goose pilot and I had already agreed that once separated, both aircraft would return to town without passengers for a more thorough inspection by the mechanics. After my takeoff, I was tempted instead to head for the most remote wilderness lake I could find and hide from the world. The passing days gradually soothed my ego. When another pilot got tangled up with a Beaver in a similar docking mishap three weeks later, I slapped him on the back and welcomed him to the club.

Deteriorating weather rarely stranded tourists at the lodge overnight, but it sometimes made getting them back to Juneau difficult. On a foggy evening in June 1994, five floatplanes operated by a different air service struggled to find a route home from the lodge beneath low ceilings and around patches of scud. Four of them made it. The fifth, a de Havilland Otter, crashed in Taku Inlet near Scow Cove. Seven cruise ship passengers died.

In late September the last cruise ship of the Season sailed out of Gastineau Channel down the Inside Passage toward the Lower 48. We were glad to say good-bye to the tourists and concentrate on the more varied flights to bush destinations, but the departure of the ships also presaged the return of winter. Like other aspects of Juneau, winter here was more intense than in Ketchikan: colder and snowier, and the infamous Taku winds tore down the valleys from the east, sometimes exceeding hurricane force. Because dawn came late and we had to spend much of the morning cleaning the airplanes of ice and snow, we could typically squeeze in just one flight—when we could fly at all—before dusk returned in midafternoon. The staff dwindled. Despite my low seniority I lasted until March, when furlough notice finally arrived.

I went to Seattle to savor big-city amenities and milder weather, planning to return to Juneau in May for the next Season. Instead, a new phase of seaplane flying awaited me.

Chapter 14

URBAN SEAPLANE PILOT

When Alaskan air services needed to lease a floatplane, have repairs done on a radio or engine, or buy some aviation component, they frequently turned to Kenmore Air Harbor, the country's largest seaplane operation. Based on the north end of Lake Washington about eighteen miles north of downtown Seattle, Kenmore had huge maintenance and parts shops as well as a flight division. It was also the world's most esteemed renovator of the de Havilland Beaver. The company had completely rebuilt dozens of worn-out or ex-military Beavers for customers or its own use and had designed a number of modifications for the model, including larger cabin windows and an expanded baggage compartment. In Alaska, pilots spoke of Beavers and Kenmore Beavers, bestowing on the latter the reverence motorcycle enthusiasts reserved for Harley-Davidsons.

Customers for Kenmore's rebuilt Beavers have included actor Harrison Ford and musician Kenny G. Two Kenmore-rebuilt Beavers lumbered across the North Atlantic with extra fuel tanks to customers in Scandinavia. Most of Kenmore's Beavers were ex-military aircraft the company acquired mainly at government surplus or scrap sales, and some arrived disassembled on barges from places as distant as southeast Asia. Although the Beaver is ancient by today's standards, having been produced from 1947 to 1967, it remains the most popular floatplane for commercial use in North America because it's one of the few aircraft designed specifically for bush flying. In 1987, a panel of judges appointed by the Canadian Engineering Centennial Board included the Beaver among Canada's ten best engineering achievements over the past century. The panel had evaluated more than a hundred nominations for engineering excellence and positive social and economic impact.

One day while still in Seattle on furlough from Channel Flying in Juneau, I drove out to Kenmore to take a look. I met owner Bob Munro, a balding, distinguished-looking man who had founded the company with two friends in 1946. A superb pilot, Munro rarely said no to an aviation challenge. In the early 1950s, a mining company needed to transport tons of equipment to a new camp in the Coast Mountains sixty miles east of Ketchikan, but the remote site had no road or water access. The glacial terrain ruled out wheelplanes, civilian helicopters then were too unreliable, and no one in the area was set up to fly on skis. The only way seemed to be by seaplane, a daunting task Ketchikan pilots declined. So the mining company contacted Kenmore Air.

"We had never landed a seaplane on a glacier ourselves," Munro said, "but we felt we could figure it out as we went along." Munro and two of his pilots got the job done. Two decades later, for a project to study glacier movement, Kenmore Air seaplanes shuttled scientists from the University of Washington and the US National Geodetic Survey, along with research supplies, to and from glaciers on Mount Olympus in Olympic National Park and Glacier Peak in the Cascade Range.

At first, flying for Kenmore had not occurred to me. I was an *Alaskan* pilot; wouldn't flying seaplanes anywhere else would be a step down, like teaching in high school after a stint as a university professor? In fact, most floatplane pilots who had flown in both Alaska and the Lower 48 followed the opposite route— working at Kenmore or other local air service first to gain experience, and then heading north for the big leagues. Also, I was a bush pilot; you could hardly call the Seattle area bush country, with civilization spreading out in all directions.

But Kenmore, a family operation, impressed me with its professionalism. And I began to realize that in many ways my hauteur was misguided. First, late 1980s progress was changing both Alaska and bush flying. Once the least populated state, Alaska had yielded that distinction to Wyoming. While the Alaskan business community applauded the state's new ranking, many common folk like me had viewed the news with the same somber meditation that Vermonters probably engaged in when they learned the Green Mountain state no longer had more cows than people.

Ketchikan had had some planked streets and sidewalks when I first arrived. Now it had none. Growth had recently brought its first traffic light.

The Haida village of Hydaburg had sat isolated on the shores of Sukkwan Strait then. Now a 21.6-mile gravel road connected it to the Hollis–Craig road, which led to the Hollis ferry terminal. Hydaburg residents thus were no longer dependent on floatplanes for transportation to Ketchikan. The Hollis–Craig road itself had been gravel; now it was paved.

Swan Lake near Ketchikan had radiated wilderness peace and beauty. Now, logged and dammed, it emitted a different aura as part of the town's hydroelectric system.

Bush residents had spent idle hours engrossed in reading or creative arts. Now, many lounged in front of satellite-based color TV sets. Progress.

On the aviation side, floatplanes had lost a little of their omnipresence in Southeast with construction of airports at Hoonah, Kake, Klawock, and elsewhere. Especially in northern Southeast, many pilots, both commercial and private, had switched from floats to wheels to save operational costs.

As logging waned and tourism increased, pilots were making more and more sightseeing flights.

Traditional high-frequency radios had become obsolete with the expansion of superior very-high-frequency communications facilities.

New Loran C radios for airplanes promised to revolutionize bad-weather navigation. (GPS was not far behind.)

The FAA was cracking down on rule breakers, at both individual and company levels; my air service in Juneau, Channel Flying, had paid a stiff fine for maintenance violations.

Many outfits had computerized their reservations and bookkeeping systems, and the larger ones had added turbine-powered airplanes to their fleets. In the offing, under a national FAA flight service station consolidation program, was the reduction of Alaska's twenty-seven FSSs to three. Juneau would be the site of the Southeast regional station. When the planned network of upgraded communications facilities was completed, pilots throughout Southeast would be able to contact an FSS specialist at Juneau indirectly through relay to file a flight plan, check the weather, or call for help.

While such modernization promised to make life in Alaska easier, it was dimming the state's image of romance and trimming its distance in mind from the Lower 48.

To my surprise I learned that like Alaska, Seattle had a rich seaplane heritage. Bill Boeing, founder of the Boeing Company, tested an open-cockpit flying boat on Lake Union next to downtown in 1916, and the company's first production airplane was a two-seat floatplane. Commercial seaplane service in the area began not long after Lindbergh's flight. Colorful pioneer pilots included Clayton Scott who, with just a couple hours of seaplane instruction, started making shuttle flights in 1929 between the Seattle waterfront and nearby Bremerton in a Loening Air Yacht amphibian. Later, as a test pilot for Boeing, Scott checked out the company's four-engine B-314 flying boats, one of which carried President Franklin Roosevelt across the Atlantic for the Casablanca Conference during World War II. Along the way, Scott also served as Bill Boeing's personal pilot. He owned an aircraft maintenance shop near Seattle and remained active in it almost until his death at age 103.

Also in the Seattle seaplane hall of fame was crusty, stern-faced Lana Kurtzer, who in 1931 started a seaplane service on Lake Union. Kurtzer installed a full-length mirror in his office there to "remind myself to smile," he told me in 1987, but he was enough of a people-pleaser to attract thousands of students to his Lake Union flight school over the decades. At one point he employed nine pilots—four of whom, in the era before Gloria Steinem, were women. A regular customer was multimillionaire industrialist Edgar Kaiser, who commuted with Kurtzer between Seattle and his home on Orcas Island in the San Juan Islands. Kurtzer logged more than thirty-six thousand hours and retired in his late seventies only after disqualification for renewal of his flight medical certificate.

Since those early days of water flying, Seattle had become a major city with access to outlying areas thanks to freeways, bridges, and ferryboats. One might assume seaplanes here would be less in demand if not downright obsolescent. Yet the Seattle skies buzzed with seaplanes from both commercial operators and private pilots. Where was everybody going?

A visitor with limited time who wanted to see the San Juan Islands or Victoria, British Columbia, both about sixty miles from Seattle, could spend hours on a ferry. Or he could take a floatplane to either and arrive in thirty-five to forty minutes. The time savings was even greater for more distant destinations. And the floatplane offered incomparably better sightseeing, a big consideration for tourists. For countless places not accessible by road or ferry, such as private docks on islands, a floatplane remained the only reasonable option.

The versatility of floatplanes made for some unique charters. Needing a floatplane for several scenes in the television movie *Adventure in Satan's Canyon*, Walt Disney Productions once had a Kenmore Air Cessna 180 fly all the way from Seattle to southern California for the filming. Heavy fog around Long Beach forced the pilot to land on an upper-elevation reservoir. A few minutes later an angry sheriff pulled up, lights flashing; although powerboats frolicked freely on the reservoir, seaplanes were unwelcome. The Disney production crew sped to the scene, removed the wings, and trucked the 180 to the studio, where it was suspended from the ceiling and jiggled to simulate motion in front of a fake background. Over the years Kenmore aircraft had appeared in about a dozen other theater and TV movies and in many ads and commercials.

When the company offered me a job, I thought why not? It was a chance to taste a different flavor of seaplane flying, and I could return to Alaska for the following Season.

I stayed for a quarter century.

The variety astounded me. Kenmore already had regular flights to the San Juans and Victoria, and with a fleet of about twenty floatplanes, was expanding its schedule to marinas and fishing resorts up the Inside Passage. Ultimately, the scheduled destinations would number about forty-five—far more than at the five air services I had flown for in Alaska combined. (The precise number of aircraft and scheduled stops fluctuated from year to year.) Kenmore also had a contract with the US Navy to support submarine operations, which included two flights

Other seaplane air taxis in the Seattle area also had some interesting charters. When President Reagan's son Michael raced a speedboat from Ketchikan to Seattle to raise funds for the Cystic Fibrosis Foundation in 1984, the Secret Service chartered Lake Union Air Service's entire fleet of five Cessna 206 floatplanes to provide surveillance. Included in the mission was an Otter from Tyee Airlines in Ketchikan to accommodate an ABC TV *20/20* crew. With flaps lowered and power retarded to keep pace with the speedboat, one 206 led the vessel at an altitude of fifty feet. Another plane stayed overhead with a technician on board to monitor the boat's speed and fuel consumption. The rest of the 206 fleet carried spare parts, special communications equipment, and, of course, gun-toting agents. With several stops, the procession took about thirteen hours on the seven-hundred-mile trip.

For the 1990 Goodwill Games, organization general manager Rex Lardner (representing Turner Broadcasting) needed to deliver addresses just three hours apart at opening ceremonies in Spokane and Seattle. A logistics committee studied the transportation options. The airlines had impossible schedules. A chartered business jet would be restricted to airports miles from each ceremony site. A helicopter was too expensive. So a 206 floatplane from Sound Flight in Renton got the assignment, landing on the Spokane River at one end and on Seattle's Union Bay for the other. Lardner was on time for each talk.

daily from a base at nearby Keyport to a joint US–Canadian base in Canada. A photo showed a Kenmore Beaver with a torpedo strapped to a pontoon, although the usual cargo consisted of personnel and mail.

On the charter side, I had no missions as distant as southern California, but it seemed I went everywhere else: the cities of Vancouver, Portland, and the state capital at Olympia; twice to Southeast Alaska; the Mount Saint Helens volcano (sightseeing); the Boeing Company's official yacht, *Daedalus* (in many locations); scenes of breaking news with reporters and photographers; and innumerable private docks, including those of Microsoft founders Bill Gates and Paul Allen.

Many of the flights to Gates's and Allen's estates were to deliver or pick up associates or service people such as electricians or plumbers. One day I arrived early for a pickup at Allen's dock in the San Juans. Strolling about on the dock, waiting, I felt a need to relieve myself. I walked to a section where terrain blocked a view from the estate buildings, then, in my assumed privacy tinkled into the water. Later, I learned that a security camera had the entire dock in view.

Allen himself was on board my airplane once, and at least a dozen times I transported Gates. They were among a large clique of affluent denizens who had estates and vacation homes in the region. Some came from old money, but many were nouveau riche beneficiaries of thriving high-tech area companies or their own dot-com successes. (Seattle economist Richard S. Conway estimated that Microsoft alone had produced twelve thousand millionaires by the year 2000.) Most lived here for the beauty of the mountains and the sea, the easy access to skiing and sailing, and the educated, artsy atmosphere of the Seattle area. Their magnificent homes were hidden from the general public within secluded waterfront enclaves, of course, but as pilots we had a panoramic view of the mansions, guest houses, lawns, gardens, swimming pools, and tennis courts.

After Gates built an estimated $63 million estate (assessed in 2009 at more than $145 million) on Lake Washington to much national publicity, a pilot loading visitors for a sightseeing flight would often hear, "Can you show us Bill Gates's house?" Actually, it was visually much less impressive than other area mansions that were valued at, say, only twenty million; a lot of the cost of the Gates estate supposedly went into amenities not apparent to the eye, such as elaborate security systems. We complied with the request anyway, but our floatplanes circling overhead or landing on the water out front must have annoyed the Gates family like persistent, buzzing flies; a Gates spokesperson eventually asked Kenmore Air to back off.

Most of the mega-wealthy dressed casually and chatted amiably with us at the dock or en route as if we were one of them. Few flaunted their status. Gates was an exception. While other wealthy folks often asked for the right-front seat, he always sat in the back, even if he were the only one on the charter, and he rarely smiled or talked. His peers would apologize with civility if they had kept you waiting on a charter, realizing that the company likely had subsequent plans for the airplane. Gates would show up two hours late and say not a word as he strode onto the dock. You really felt like a chauffeur with him on board.

The Gates family owned several vacation homes in the resort community of Alderbrook on Hood Canal southwest of Seattle. The seaplane dock there was tide-sensitive, so the dispatcher scheduled flights to the place accordingly. Because Gates was late for an Alderbrook charter one afternoon, we arrived when the tide was too low to reach the dock; the pontoons contacted the muck and the airplane stopped about ten feet short. I took off my shoes and socks, rolled up my trousers, and stepped into the water. Minus my weight, the airplane gained just enough buoyancy so I could pull it the rest of the way in, grimacing from stepping on sticks and clamshells. At the dock, Gates stepped out. I expected him to thank me and perhaps quip something like, "That was above and beyond the call of duty." Instead, he walked off silently with his briefcase.

When I shared that story back at Kenmore, one pilot said he once taxied in with Gates under similar conditions at Alderbrook but was unable to pull the plane to the dock. So, wading through the water, he gave the Microsoft co-founder a piggy-back ride. Again, a wordless departure.

One of the few times Gates spoke to me was to urge me on in weather I thought unsafe. It was an April charter, and he and his future wife, Melinda French, were bound for a computer conference in Victoria. At the entrance to the Strait of Juan de Fuca we encountered thick fog, and I circled several times, assessing the situation. "I see an opening over there," Gates said, pointing. It was what pilots call a sucker hole, a narrow space with no exit. He continued to goad me on, but I refused and suggested we land at the nearby community of Port Townsend to wait for an improvement. After tying up the Cessna 180 in a marina there, we walked to a restaurant and sat at a table. Gates and French had breakfast, I a cup of coffee. When the waitress brought the bill, he paid for himself and French. But the seventy-five cents for my coffee came from my pocket. (He did leave the tip.)

Mary Gates, Bill's mother, was a congenial woman with a gracious smile. On one flight to Alderbrook with just her in the Cessna 180, the engine suddenly backfired and quit. We were passing the naval base at Bremerton at about twenty-eight hundred feet, and after assuring her we were in no danger, I glided to an easy landing. A navy boat hurried out and towed us to a dock. I had radioed the company during the glide, and minutes later another 180 arrived, picked up Mrs. Gates, and took her the rest of the way to Alderbrook. Two mechanics who accompanied the pilot of the second 180 found that a shaft at the rear of the engine had failed, allowing a gear to fall aside and simultaneously disable both magnetos. They made repairs and I flew the airplane back to Kenmore.

In a letter to Mrs. Gates, owner Bob Munro apologized for the disruption and offered her two complimentary flights to Alderbrook. She wrote back to thank us and to commend me for my—her words—"calmness and confidence" after the engine failure. As a former journalist I knew how rapaciously the local media would pounce on the story, but the Gates family and Kenmore Air kept the incident in-house, and reporters never got a whiff.

Besides the local rich, Kenmore carried many celebrities. Senior and management pilots got the biggest names, who included John Wayne, Brooke Shields, Dinah Shore, Goldie Hawn, Katharine Hepburn, Michelle Pfeiffer, Jodie Foster, Neil Armstrong, Drew Carey, Robert Goulet, TV journalist Diane Sawyer, Jimmy Buffett, musicians Steve Miller and Dave Matthews, Gene Hackman, and NFL Hall of Famer Steve Largent. Jodie Foster was scheduled on a flight to Quadra Island in British Columbia. Learning that she would soon be arriving, Kenmore employees and passengers alike milled about outside, waiting excitedly. We assumed she would come by limousine, but she and a companion showed up in a common taxi, a half hour late. Because this was a scheduled flight, the company normally would have left a tardy passenger behind. But Jodie Foster. . . . Before boarding her airplane, Foster shook the hand of each fellow passenger and apologized for delaying the flight.

My own list of the well-known was much shorter and more humble: comedian Jonathan Winters, alternative-medicine guru Dr. Andrew Weil, journalist

Michael Kinsley, US Senator Maria Cantwell, conservative radio host Michael Medved, and author Ivan Doig, among others.

Celebrities were most likely to appear on flights to the hugely popular Victoria, which was served by several ferries as well as by seaplanes from Seattle and Vancouver. With or without a well-known name, the Victoria passenger list was often multinational, with Great Britain, Japan, and Germany represented most frequently (other than Canada). Some Victoria flights had not a single US citizen, other than the pilot.

In Alaska, I had made an occasional flight to the nearest Canadian community, Prince Rupert, British Columbia, but because Kenmore flew to Victoria all year (six times a day in summer) and up the Inside Passage from May through September, crossing the border now was routine. Each crossing required customs/immigration clearance at the port of entry. No matter if the officers were out on other calls, or if the weather or darkness was closing in, or the airplane had a tight schedule: pilot and passengers had to wait for clearance. Nor did pilots get a free pass on either side of the border for regular, multiple crossings.

Such vexation was but one of the refutations to my naive assumption that after the challenges of Alaska, flying floatplanes out of Seattle would be simpler. Greater development along our routes indeed put pilots closer to ports and facilities such as fueling stations and rescue services. ("Greater development," of course, was relative; much of the lower Inside Passage was still isolated.) Civilization, however, also imposed more demands, just as a city had more stoplights than the country. In Southeast Alaska, after talking to the hometown airport tower or flight service station, a pilot generally could take off and make the rest of the flight without having to contact air traffic control. In the Seattle area, most routes passed through or near airspace belonging to several major airports with communication requirements. Along the way, local pockets of bustling aircraft activity—the San Juan Islands, for instance—had traffic-advisory frequencies for collision avoidance. On the 110-mile leg from Kenmore to Nanaimo on Vancouver Island, where we usually landed on Inside Passage flights for customs and refueling, a pilot might communicate on eight different frequencies.

Flying in and out of the Victoria waterfront itself was like dealing with a busy airport; restrictions abounded, and a floatplane might be fifth or sixth in line there waiting to land or take off.

Boat activity at many places confronted seaplane pilots with wakes that made a smooth landing or takeoff impossible. And airspace around Seattle was periodically closed or greatly restricted due to special events such as a presidential visit.

Seaplane noise. In Alaska, residents simply accepted it as part of daily life, but here it provoked angry phone calls and neighborhood meetings. Many municipalities, including Seattle, instituted special noise-abatement procedures for sea-

Seaplanes carry more than three hundred thousand passengers a year to and from Victoria Harbour, according to Transport Canada, the Canadian equivalent of the Federal Aviation Administration. The place is the third busiest of the twenty-two certified water airports in Canada, and the Official Airline Guide says the sixty-two-mile route between Victoria Harbour and Vancouver's Coal Harbour constitutes the busiest in all of Canada for weekly flights. So much traffic means lots of rules for seaplane pilots at Victoria. In order to operate there, commercial seaplane companies must have written permission and give pilots extensive training on the regulations. Private pilots are asked to stay away. Harbour Patrol officers cruise around in boats to check for compliance, and infractions can result in stiff fines for both pilots and their companies.

Why is Victoria so popular? As the provincial capital of British Columbia, the city of about eighty-three thousand attracts lots of government workers, lobbyists, and civic-group members. And tourists come to enjoy the British flavor, gardens, festivals, and views of the ocean and mountains.

planes, with curfews and restrictions on routes and altitudes. We did our best to follow them, but psychology sometimes caused sensitive ears to hear what wasn't there. Turbine engines were demonstrably quieter than pistons, and Kenmore Air hoped to appease area homeowners somewhat in the early 1990s by investing in turboprops. Instead, for a while the angry phone calls actually increased; the turboprops—Turbo Otters and Turbo Beavers—were larger than our piston planes, and people instinctively associated larger airplanes with more noise.

Like so much of urban life, seaplane noise was a compromise, with homeowners agreeing to tolerate a certain decibel level and seaplane companies agreeing to alter operations to minimize the impact. But vexing flare-ups continued. A new homeowner in the Green Lake neighborhood of Seattle called to complain about our floatplanes flying over her house "all day long, day after day." We explained that her house happened to lie beneath a landing approach to Lake Union that had been mandated in a formal, community-approved noise-abatement agreement. No, sorry, we couldn't adopt a different approach because that would violate the agreement and upset homeowners elsewhere. "Well, my realtor didn't tell me about these damn floatplanes."

In a 1990 flare-up at Nanaimo, British Columbia, a busy seaplane hub for both American and Canadian pilots, a group of fist-shaking homeowners on two islands by the city waterfront complained that pilots were violating the local noise-abatement policy. A stern notice went out to air services, reminding them about the three-hundred-foot altitude restriction over narrow Newcastle Channel, which separates the islands and the city waterfront. Air service operators urged their pilots to comply lest continued violations result in more restrictions.

On a stormy December morning that year, I landed at Nanaimo and noticed several helicopters circling over Newcastle Channel. Boats were zipping around in circles there, and dozens of people had gathered in a parking area over-looking the channel, staring solemnly, held back by a police barricade.

After docking at a marina inside the channel, I learned that a half hour earlier a Rainbow Air Beech 18 on floats bound for a logging camp on the main-land had stalled on takeoff and crashed right in front of the marina. The marina owner and his dockhand had been standing outside the office, watching as the twin-engine airplane climbed over the channel into a gusty east wind. "His wings rocked and he dropped and hit the water on the left wing!" the dockhand blurted out. "Then there was a big whoosh of fire and the plane sank!"

The logger in the right front seat had managed to crawl out the rear door, as had one of his buddies in the cabin. The marina owner scrambled into a skiff and plucked them from the frigid water. Helicopters and boats searched franti-cally for more survivors, but soon divers found the pilot and the other six passen-gers still inside.

Usually, seaplane pilots avoided the problem areas at Nanaimo by taking off out the mouth of adjacent Departure Bay. Because the wind that day rendered such a direction unsafe, the Beech 18 pilot had taxied into the bay, turned around, and taken off upwind, toward the channel—and the unhappy homeowners. Why would he, an experienced pilot accustomed to heavy loads and challenging situa-tions, have allowed his aircraft to stall? After all, he had no physical obstacles to clear. A long channel lay beneath him on which to plop down in case of trouble.

My theory: Rough water in Departure Bay may have prevented him from taxiing out as far as he would have preferred. Perhaps he was simply impatient to be under way and started the takeoff too soon. In any event, he found himself approaching the channel well below the prescribed three hundred feet. Desperate to avoid an infraction with his pair of roaring, thundering, 450-horsepower engines, he had increased the climb angle. A stall was now a tiny margin away. Then, gusty downdrafts whipping over the treetops by the channel snatched that margin away.

Pilots knew, and the law concurred in theory, that if you couldn't have both, safety always preempted compliance with rules. But pilots also knew that the nonflying public saw (or heard) only the infraction, not the extenuating cir-cumstance. Even if you thought you had ample justification, you might have to explain your actions and fill out reports. Federal inspectors might not be con-vinced that you actually had had no options. How tempting, how much easier, to just sacrifice some safety and stay within the rule.

Like gun owners, seaplane pilots in an urban setting were automatically the bad guys—reckless, dangerous, not fully compatible with civilized society.

We groused about the unfairness, but we needed public support to continue operating with enough elbow room to stay profitable. It was not enough here to be a good pilot; you also had to be a diplomat, a public relations expert, and an ambassador for your company. So we demoted common sense and bowed before the altar of public perception.

After September 11, 2001, seaplane flying in the lower Inside Passage got even more restrictive. Among the changes: Pilots had to obtain a discrete transponder code from an air traffic control facility before crossing the border in either direction; the US Navy no longer tolerated low-level circling or flybys of submarines riding on the surface; and customs procedures tightened. At times I missed the relative simplicity of the Alaskan bush, but in a way the demands of urban seaplane flying were stimulating, like the need to learn a new language after moving to a foreign land.

Just as I hadn't anticipated those demands, I underestimated the weather in the Seattle–lower British Columbia region. Winter gales howled in here with no less ferocity than in Alaska. Air flows around both sides of the Olympic Mountains met in an infamous "convergence zone" from Seattle to the San Juans, creating frequent fog and drizzle. The northern half of the 290-mile-long Vancouver Island, where we regularly flew in summer, was a particular magnet for the North Pacific's wet air masses. And the outside coast of Vancouver Island was so often blanketed in morning fog that Kenmore sent flights there only in late morning or early afternoon, when the sun had had a chance to burn off the clouds.

The rules down here were new, and the passenger makeup was more cosmopolitan. The weather made me feel right at home.

Chapter 15

DEBATES AND DECISIONS

After six years of bush flying in Alaska, I adapted fairly quickly to my new environment. Experience up north provided no shortcut to learning the local geography, but in a few weeks that too felt comfortable. Like Guard Island near Ketchikan, Smith Island was an important landmark to Seattle-area seaplane pilots. Smith lay in the Strait of Juan de Fuca between Admiralty Inlet and the San Juan Islands, right along the route to many of our destinations. In low weather, outbound or inbound, we welcomed the sight of it as both a position marker and an indication of conditions. Over water with no view of land, judging visibility was difficult; the fuzzy horizon, blending with the drizzle, fog, water, and stratus, might be a half mile or two miles away. Smith Island gave us enough definition, enough perspective in the surrounding murk to decide whether to push on or find another way.

In fact, long before the first seaplane cruised by, the small, flat island contained a lighthouse to help mariners in similar weather. Painted white and constructed in the late 1850s, the lighthouse building housed tenders and their families until twentieth-century installation of an automated light-beacon tower. Though originally situated comfortably inland, the building lost ground over the passing decades as wind and rain gnawed relentlessly at the nearest bluff. Eventually, the eroding bluff reached the building's foundation. When I began flying for Kenmore Air, about half of the structure, including the lighthouse, had already broken away and tumbled down the bluff into the water. The remaining shell perched precariously on the rim, much of it even overhanging the rocky beach below, as if hesitant to follow. Gulls and cormorants roosted inside the rotting frame, and wind blew through the openings.

In the 1990s, the National Park Service rescued the 198-foot-tall Cape Hatteras lighthouse from a similar fate by moving it twenty-nine hundred feet back from the encroaching North Carolina shoreline. The project required months of planning, huge hydraulic jacks and dollies, and a $12 million bequest from Congress. The isolated, abandoned buildings on Smith Island had merited

The Federal Emergency Management Agency predicts that over the next few decades erosion could claim a quarter of the buildings now within five hundred feet of the US shoreline. In the Seattle area, with an annual precipitation of about thirty-eight inches, the ongoing danger for homes by the water comes more from sudden slides, which sweep along soil, trees, and virtually anything else in their path. Although deaths in slides are rare, they do happen. Slides killed four Seattle train workers in 1897 and two children, asleep in their beds in a Kirkland home, in February 1947. And in January 1997 a family of four died when a slide crushed their home on Bainbridge Island.

The same series of storms that claimed the Bainbridge family saturated hillsides throughout the area, resulting in almost three hundred nonfatal slides in Seattle alone. At 6 A.M. on January 3, residents of one neighborhood in Seattle were given five minutes to evacuate after inspectors discovered that their buildings were slipping off their foundations.

Also that winter, some homes along a bluff over Elliott Bay in the Magnolia area of Seattle slid down an embankment. Seaplanes approaching or departing from Lake Union via Elliott Bay had a striking view of the broken, twisting houses, a vivid illustration of the potential risk in erecting buildings by a hillside in the Pacific Northwest. Commercial tour boats paused in front of the scene so passengers could gape and take photos. In a few years, however, additional slides and arson reduced the buildings to unrecognizable rubble.

no such effort, considering the higher priority of the many occupied houses situated on eroding bluffs in Pacific Northwest neighborhoods.

So now we eyed the strange-looking building whenever we flew by, wondering when the rest of it would succumb. In good weather, we would look down from several thousand feet and there it was, a lonely white sentinel clinging to the edge of the island. In fog or drizzle, we'd lumber by at low altitude, close enough to peer into the open building, sometimes close enough to send the seabirds scattering. The building became a conversation piece, a sort of mascot, and we'd frequently point it out to passengers for photos. One pilot suggested the company set up a pool with a cash prize for whoever could most accurately predict the date of collapse, as Alaskans do with the annual spring breakup of ice on the Tanana River in Fairbanks. Perhaps one of us would even be lucky enough to witness the building's final moment from the cockpit.

But month after month, year after year, the building clung stubbornly to the edge of the island, although the overhang became more pronounced. The occasional earthquake that rattled dishes and nerves throughout the region failed to dislodge it. Nor did the more frequent gales that upended trees with sixty-knot gusts blow it down. On the first flight after each quake or storm, we began squinting as soon as the island came into view—and there it stood, proudly and defiantly, like the star-spangled banner after a night of bombardment at Fort McHenry.

The building's tenacity brought mixed emotions. On the one hand, we anticipated the inevitable collapse with the sort of excitement many volcano-watchers felt before the Mount Saint Helens eruption in May 1980. (Come on, stop stalling, you cliff-hanger, give up and end the suspense.) On the other hand, we respected the building as we would a defiant property owner who refused to sell out to arm-twisting developers. (Stand your ground, old-timer.)

When at last it did let go, a third emotion gripped some of us. I was the first pilot in our company to discover the loss. On the morning of May 23, 1998, crossing the Strait of Juan de Fuca on a flight to the San Juan Islands, I routinely glanced toward the building as the airplane approached the island. It was gone! I circled for a closer look. Beneath the spot the building had occupied, streaks from a landslide discolored the soil on the bluff. A jumble of boards lay on the beach below, unrecognizable as remnants of a building. Since my last sighting late the previous afternoon, the ground had been still, the weather benign. A crucial section of soil beneath the foundation might have broken away overnight. Or perhaps, like an elderly patient in a nursing home, the building had simply gotten tired of hanging on.

Like a relative of that patient, I felt a sadness, grief even, although the collapse had been both expected and overdue.

I radioed the news to the two other company pilots aloft at the time, and within days practically everyone, regular San Juan Islands passengers as well as pilots, knew about the building's demise. Several passengers asked me before takeoff to give them a close-up flyby of Smith Island so they could see for themselves. "That little island doesn't look the same anymore," one of them commented. A longtime company pilot had vowed that someday he would arrange to be photographed while sitting on the exposed floor of the building, casually reading a newspaper. But he never took action on the plan. "Now I've lost my chance," he said.

For me, the collapse seemed to symbolize personal lost or fading opportunities, and once again I found myself pondering seaplane flying as a career choice. The old building had lingered for years but now was gone; my options for a return to journalism or other traditional career had lingered for years, but now . . . had I too lost my chance?

Even within aviation, I had specialized and could not expect broader cockpit opportunities outside that niche to come easily for a middle-aged pilot. Tasting apple pie early on, I had dallied at that particular table, never sampling the blueberry, the cherry, the pumpkin, while they were still warm from the oven.

I might have found other flavors to be even tastier. If not, I could have returned to the unfinished apple with a greater perspective. The airlines had long since relaxed their uncorrected-vision requirements for pilots—but not their maximum age limits for hiring. For me, that door now was closed, that flavor gone from the selection. One day a pilot friend I had flown with out of Juneau stopped by at Kenmore Air to visit. He had left floatplanes to fly for a commuter airline in Africa and was on his way back to his home in Alaska for a brief vacation. "I'm kind of surprised you're still flying these floatplanes," he said. "Don't you ever want to do something different?" It was a question I asked myself every time I passed Smith Island and the empty spot by the bluff where the old building had stood. If I insisted on staying in a cockpit, perhaps I should have been like Larry Blagrove, who had eaten a slice from every pie at the fair.

Most pilots had a single certificate to list their flying qualifications; Blagrove needed six certificates. He was licensed to fly and instruct in practically every type of civilian aircraft, including helicopters, gyrocopters, and gliders, and he added ratings—many never used—like a baseball fan collecting player cards. One of these, for the Boeing 707, cost him $30,000. He spent $11,000 for a Boeing 747 rating. Blagrove was also a licensed flight engineer, aircraft mechanic, aircraft dispatcher, and parachute rigger. Only a dozen or so pilots in the United States supposedly had as many aviation-related endorsements. Blagrove's cockpit stints included bush flying and pipeline patrol in Alaska, hauling the night mail in Chicago-based Beech 18s, medevac flights in business jets, Civil Air Patrol search-and-rescue missions, flying commuters for several carriers, and flights in a long list of private planes. With a brand-new, self-financed rating in the Boeing 727, he talked his way onto the flight roster of a South American freight airline and insisted—successfully—that he start out as captain.

When I met Blagrove, a bushy-haired, mustachioed native of Minnesota, he was a part-time pilot for Kenmore Air while holding down a full-time job as a DC-8 captain for Emery Worldwide. Over coffee during weather delays, he enthralled the rest of us with his fascinating, wide-ranging anecdotes, and he could have kept talking all day.

But I could reminisce only about flying seaplanes in a relatively small corner of the globe. *Carpe diem*, the vacant building site at Smith Island seemed to advise. Gather ye rosebuds, ye dreams, while ye may, lest they slide away in the night. (For some of us, the loss of the building was also an incentive to take more photos of people, places, and events while the opportunity existed.)

Yet common sense reminded me that no one can do it all. No one can peek over every hill for greener grass, or explore every fork in every road. Even Larry Blagrove, who ached to experience all aspects of aviation, still missed a lot: certification as an air traffic controller, military flying, air-show performances, a hot-air balloon rating. . . . Inevitably, trying to squeeze too much in exacts a price.

Blagrove's ex-wife told me that before their divorce, they moved eighteen times in twenty years as Larry switched from one flying adventure to the next. Ultimately, he would die at age forty-nine in the crash of his rented Robinson R-44 helicopter off the coast of New Zealand's North Island.

For all its disadvantages, commercial seaplane flying was an interesting, colorful, exciting way to make a living. It had called me back when desk jobs proved unsatisfying by comparison, and it continued to provide a constantly rotating kaleidoscope of delights and challenges. Many workers never found a job that inspired passion. True, I was foregoing other aviation genres, but I had been stable enough within the regional seaplane industry to make good friends and fully experience the geography and nuances of each station. No mere nibbling for me. I had a modest income and health insurance, and I was contributing a bit to the piggybank. For now, the status quo seemed more appealing than another quixotic move seeking greater fulfillment. Had I really done so badly?

Within a month, waves had washed away the boards on the beach at Smith Island and rain had scrubbed the slide streak on the bluff. Somebody poking about afoot doubtlessly could have pinpointed the building's former location from traces of the foundation in the wild grass, but from the air you could no longer tell the building had ever existed. The finality seemed to say, stop looking for what's gone. Stop fretting about roads not taken. Be grateful for a delicious pie, and if you're still hungry, keep eating.

Larry Blagrove was only one of several airline pilots who flew part-time for Kenmore Air in the summer during breaks in their schedule. Most had worked initially for Kenmore or other seaplane outfits years earlier, and then gone on to the airlines. They returned to float flying part-time at some point in their careers not for extra income but "to get my hands back on the controls," as one put it. Floatplanes allowed them to escape the computerization and regimentation of airliners, to reach a higher floor by taking the stairs instead of the elevator.

Besides active airline pilots, the summer-only or part-time group included some experienced floatplane pilots who were pursuing nonflying careers. One of these was a lawyer, another a software engineer. One summer pilot had flown the bush in Alaska, and then served for years as a magistrate. Another was a retired career military pilot who had flown for both the Navy and Air Force ("Colonel," we called him).

Also on the roster were a half dozen young pilots who had followed some variation of a common route to the cockpit of commercial seaplanes. First, they worked on the docks as linemen for two or three years, learning the mariner side, helping the regular pilots come and go. On days off or at college, they took basic flight training at an airport. Through Kenmore's own flight school, they got a seaplane rating. Then they joined the Kenmore flight school staff as instructors for several years, honing their seaplane skills by teaching others. Management and regular pilots observed them, and if they met standards of professionalism and attitude, they eventually earned a promotion to the flight line. Most regarded seaplane flying as a stepping stone, albeit an exciting one, to jobs in bigger, faster, more sophisticated aircraft.

The most junior of these new pilots were furloughed at summer's end. Some with more tenure declined full-time seaplane flying, preferring to spend the winter ski instructing, traveling, or just hanging out.

Another contingent consisted of middle-aged, seasoned, year-round pilots with families, homes, and roots in the Seattle area. They had no interest in other flying jobs because of the disruption in their lives a move would entail. Many had worked previously in nonflying professions or dabbled part-time in outside enterprises: two were ex-law enforcement officers, one owned an apartment building, another was a real-estate speculator. Like all commercial seaplane pilots they grumbled a bit about this and that, but they stuck around for the continuity, regular paycheck, and medical insurance, and because flying seaplanes was more interesting than an office or factory job. Also, though not a route to riches, Kenmore Air was a satisfying company to work for: a big, internationally respected, Christian family operation that gave its seventy-plus employees a frozen turkey for Thanksgiving and a bonus check for Christmas. The atmosphere inspired loyalty; many employees had been with the company for over three decades.

As in any group of diverse individuals, debates occasionally arose in the pilot corps. One involved the discrete company radio frequency. (Each aircraft had three radios, enabling pilots to simultaneously monitor different frequencies.) It was intended for aviation- or company-related communications, but with a dozen or more aircraft aloft at the same time, the company frequency typically flowed with general chitchat. Baseball statistics, stock prices, motorcycle engines, ski resorts, spices for cooking, TV shows, ribald jokes, anecdotes about passengers—listen long enough and you'd hear every subject. What a pilot in a sector with bad weather wanted to hear was a report on conditions elsewhere, but often he couldn't find an opening to ask, just as polite would-be participants in a free-for-all group discussion try again and again to get a comment in edgewise.

The taciturn among us would eventually tire of the yakety-yak and turn off the company frequency, rendering us unavailable to answer questions or receive important information. At periodic safety meetings someone usually reiterated the operational purpose of the company frequency, and for a couple of days afterward the chatter subsided. The more garrulous pilots could restrain themselves for only so long, however, and soon the company frequency was humming again.

On days with widespread low weather, everyone instinctively curtailed nonessential talk to allow the sharing of reports and route recommendations. Prior to launching the fleet we could check conditions at our destinations through official sources, but few reporting stations existed en route, where the weather might be considerably different. A scout plane could poke around and radio to the dispatcher yea or nay or maybe. On the maybe mornings, every aircraft might either complete flights or turn around. More often, like moths probing a lighted screen porch, some would find a way through and others wouldn't. A conservative company, Kenmore exerted no pressure on pilots, and no one who turned around while others got through was reprimanded. "You aren't going to impress me by being the first to take off [after a fog delay]," founder Bob Munro said at a safety meeting. In fact, on many mornings when the company put a hold on all our flights because of Seattle-area fog, I studied conditions outside and mused, "It doesn't look that bad; in Alaska we would have been in the air an hour ago."

Still, some pilots who aborted a flight often felt miffed if others reached their destinations in the same conditions. They began advocating for a new policy: if the lead plane turns around on a bad-weather day, those in trail should, too.

Like Democrats and Republicans supporting opposite sides of an issue, two camps formed. The conformists argued that confusion ensued under the current, unrestricted policy, with some aircraft pushing on, some heading home, some trying detours, some circling or landing to wait for an improvement. The dispatcher then struggled to keep track of everyone, and passengers demanded to know why their airplane returned to the terminal while the one their associates were on—going to the same place at the same time—got through. Federal weather minimums applied equally to all company pilots, and an image of consistency was good public relations. We're a team: let's fly that way.

On the other side, we "freelancers," as we were dubbed, countered that seaplane flying involved too many variables to tie the fleet together like mountain climbers on a rope. If a junior pilot with limited experience happened to be at the head of the pack and turned around, why should a veteran pilot a few miles behind be forced to turn around too if he felt he could safely continue? If a pilot in a heavily loaded Beaver turned around, why should a following pilot in a lightly loaded, more powerful Turbo Otter head to the stable as well? The Otter pilot might be able to climb above the fog, get to his passengers to their destination, and produce some revenue for the company. A poor night's sleep, a hangover, a developing cold, marital problems—long was the list of personal factors that might influence a lead pilot to subconsciously raise his standards and turn around in weather he might tackle on a day of greater alertness. And of course the fickle coastal weather could lift here and lower there within moments; a following pilot might reach the spot where the lead plane turned around and find that conditions there had improved. But he couldn't make that discovery if he automatically aborted on hearing that the lead pilot had just scrubbed the mission. No, better to keep the current policy: let each pilot decide for himself whether to continue or abort, based on his experience and the particular set of conditions governing his particular flight at his particular location.

"Well, when you older guys go on it makes those of us who don't look bad to our passengers."

"Choke on your sour grapes. What about *our* passengers? How do we explain to them that under the proposed policy we're going back to base because *you* ran into fog up front, when from *our* position we could see a patch of blue sky? Turn around if you don't feel comfortable, but let us go on if we want."

"Well, what you don't understand is that we junior pilots are still learning. We don't always know what's safe. We look to you older guys for guidance. So when we see you fly through a stretch of bad weather, we assume it's okay for us, too. But we can't handle what you can, and a lot of times, following you, we get in over our heads. To keep everybody safe, it's best to cater to the least experienced."

"We're not asking you to follow us. Know your own limits and stick to them."

The freelancers agreed with the conformists on one point: Getting through when other pilots turned around could create a logistics problem at a popular destination, especially when fog had delayed several flights there. The company might not have been able to contact all scheduled inbound passengers to let them know about weather problems in Seattle and the resulting new pickup times. Thus, a pilot might arrive to find more waiting, impatient passengers than he could accommodate. With manifest in hand, he steps onto the dock and reads out names. The group quickly becomes a mob.

"Hey, don't you have my wife and me on your list?" a man asks.

"I'm sorry, sir, but you must be scheduled on the next plane. It should be here shortly (lie)."

"But we got here before that couple, and you called their names."

"I'm really sorry, but I have to stick to names on my list."

"We weren't called, either, and we have a jet to catch!" someone else says.

Soon, the pilot begins to wish he had turned around with everyone else.

The conformists also called for a uniform takeoff direction at Lake Union, by the edge of downtown Seattle; there the company had a second terminal, much closer than the Lake Washington base to hotels and the Seattle-Tacoma International Airport. The terminal was at the south end of Lake Union, and in a strong south wind we had to taxi to the north end for takeoff into the wind. That taxi took about ten minutes. So, whenever possible we departed to the north to save time. On days with a modest south wind, some pilots took off downwind to the north while others elected to taxi to the other end for an upwind takeoff. The resulting opposite-direction takeoffs posed no safety problem, because we kept each other in sight and communicated on the common traffic-advisory frequency.

"Again, our passengers are upset. They want to know why we're spending time taxiing all the way to the north end for takeoff when you taxi out from the terminal and take off right away downwind."

"Simply explain to them that you're in a Beaver, which can't climb very well, and for safety you have to taxi for the upwind takeoff. We're in a big, powerful Otter, which can take off downwind safely with its superior climb rate."

"Well, a lot of passengers just don't understand these aviation concepts. They end up thinking we're doing the long taxi because we're not as capable. Besides, it looks dangerous to them to see planes taking off in opposite directions. They think the company's operation is disorganized. Everyone taxiing in the same direction and taking off in the same direction looks neat and tidy. Remember the importance of image."

"Nonsense. As it is, the flights are often already behind schedule because of various delays. How silly to make a flight even later with an unnecessary long taxi when the wind and payload permit a time-saving downwind takeoff. Leave the upwind/downwind decision to each individual pilot, as circumstances dictate."

Favoring image, teamwork, and setting a good example for junior pilots, management sided philosophically with the conformists on both matters. A number of meetings followed to discuss possible guidelines for uniformity, and the company handed out questionnaires asking pilots for comments and suggestions. Ultimately, management conceded that the variables would make uniformity inefficient and cumbersome; the existing policy of individual judgment prevailed.

Accustomed to much smaller, less group-oriented seaplane outfits in Alaska, I applauded this victory for the status quo, for individualism. By now, after thousands of hours in drizzle, fog, and wind, I had become fairly skilled at weather flying and was gaining a reputation for pushing the margins. I valued the continuation of choice in handling tough situations rather than having to yield to a herd mentality.

Nonetheless, the debate over more conformity influenced my flying thereafter. While I had always offered advice and knowledge to junior pilots, I hadn't previously realized how intently they watched us seasoned pilots in the field. Now, I understood the moral duty to consider how my airborne decisions might impact them, and to fly more conservatively in their presence than I would when unobserved. With a junior pilot right behind, land in the sheltered area farther out, where he'll be more comfortable. Otherwise, land in the stiff crosswind closer in to save taxi time.

When I told my fiancée about that epiphany, she emphasized a different point. "You have new responsibilities now that we're engaged," she said, "and I want you to fly conservatively all the time, not just when a new pilot is around. I want you to fly conservatively for me, for us." She paused to bestow a light kiss. "You're a very experienced pilot; you have nothing to prove by being macho. Surrender some of your ego out there. I just want you to come home to me."

And so I shall, I vowed.

Chapter 16

N90422

What's the most stressful flight for a professional seaplane pilot? It's not being slammed and jerked and wrenched so hard in a gale you think the wings might come off. It's not having miles and miles to go while a passenger's vomit dribbles down the back of your shirt. It's not flubbing a vital checkride, or getting trapped by fog in a mountain pass, or having a broken cockpit heater on a ten-degree January morning.

None of these. The most stressful flight is riding back to base as a passenger with another company pilot after you've seriously damaged your own airplane in a blunder.

You slump in the right-front seat, stunned, suffocating in disbelief and remorse. Your former passengers—now your fellow passengers—sit behind; you don't need to turn your head to know they're glaring at you, wondering from what mail-order catalog you got your license. How you ache to be zipped to the most isolated spot on earth. And by God when this is all over, you just might study a world atlas. For now, though, you're a buffoon locked in stocks in the village square. There will be fellow employees to face, and meetings with management, the FAA, and insurance representatives to endure. No doubt a lot of sleepless nights ahead, too. The pilot friend in the left seat might offer some philosophic words of encouragement, but they don't help. Not even a little.

That's the most stressful flight.

Late afternoon, August 28, 1993. The airplane entrusted to me was the newest in our fleet, N90422, an $850,000 de Havilland Otter that had gone on line just six weeks earlier after a complete overhaul and conversion from a piston to a turboprop engine. A fragrance of new upholstery and carpeting still lingered throughout the airplane. After delivering passengers to two destinations in the San Juan Islands, I had crossed the border alone to Victoria for a scheduled 6:30 P.M. pickup. I had docked behind a Canadian Twin Otter, then hurried up the ramp into the terminal building and cleared customs. Now I was leading my nine Seattle-bound passengers down the ramp to the airplane. The seaplane dock could accommodate only three aircraft at a time, and I knew that two company Beavers were inbound to collect additional passengers on this 6:30 flight. In fact, I saw the first one already taxiing in. With the Twin Otter and N90422 at the dock, the second Beaver would have to taxi in circles, waiting for space.

Unless I hurried.

I loaded the luggage into the cargo compartment, then asked the passengers to board. By the time they were settled and I delivered the safety briefing, the first Beaver had docked in front of the Twin Otter and the second Beaver was on the water, approaching. I scurried into the cockpit. I flipped on the master switch and the number one fuel pump, and then engaged the ignition and starter switches. The three-bladed propeller began to turn. When the gas-generator gauge indicated twelve percent I advanced the fuel-condition lever, and a second later came the familiar "whoosh" of combustion. The whine of the 750-horsepower Pratt & Whitney engine rose rapidly. I signaled the lineman to untie the mooring line. Because the Twin Otter's tail was just a few feet ahead, I planned to use reverse thrust to back up, giving the lineman room to turn us out.

But even though I was easing the thrust lever rearward for reverse thrust, the airplane was creeping *forward*, toward the Twin Otter's tail. What was this? I pulled harder on the thrust lever, but the airplane continued inching forward, as if drawn by a giant magnet. I could tell that the lineman was trying to halt our movement by pulling on the tail line, because N90422 was also moving slightly outward, away from the dock. The forward movement, however, was impeding his effort.

Now N90422's spinning propeller was just inches from the Twin Otter's tail. Panic welled. I yanked the thrust lever all the way back to its détente for full reverse thrust. Still the airplane moved forward. *We're going to hit!* I told myself in helpless horror.

Our left wing crunched into the Twin Otter's left stabilizer. A second later, the prop sliced into the outer right stabilizer in a terrible, grating cacophony. Shards of aluminum exploded in all directions as if a grenade had gone off, and I instinctively ducked, although the windshield protected the cockpit.

Then, reverse thrust finally kicked in and we shot rearward. The heel of the left pontoon slammed into the dock. I jerked back the condition lever to shut off the engine.

"I thought you were going to turn us out!" I yelled at the lineman as I scrambled down the cockpit steps. His face contorted in shock, he stood with N90422's tail line in hand. Intuition told me he was blameless, but at the moment I needed a scapegoat.

The twin Otter's tail bore ugly, jagged gouges like bites from a shark, and our prop blades were hideously twisted. Our left wing and the Twin Otter's left stabilizer had grapefruit-sized dents. The water-rudder assembly on the heel of the left pontoon was bent from its sharp contact with the dock. I turned away.

"We've had a mishap," I informed my stone-faced passengers after poking my head and shoulders through the cabin doorway. "Please go back inside the terminal and I'll arrange for a replacement airplane." I followed the silent procession up the ramp, trying to ignore the solemn stares from the other waiting passengers, the customs officer, the reservationists, and the Canadian pilots who had gathered on the terminal porch. Pedestrians on Wharf Street above had paused to look.

Inside the terminal, I phoned the company dispatcher to report the incident. The captain of the damaged Twin Otter walked up with pen and paper, and I jotted down my pilot certificate number and contact information. He squeezed my shoulder in sympathy, and then walked away.

I returned to the dock, where the pilot of the first Beaver was examining the damage. I muttered something about incompetent linemen. When he pulled out with six passengers, the second Beaver slipped in for six more. A third airplane—my replacement—was en route to collect the remaining passengers, and I climbed into my wounded Otter to wait, to hide. It took only a minute of brooding there to realize what had happened. When shutting down the engine after docking behind the Twin Otter earlier, I obviously failed to position the thrust lever correctly to make reverse thrust available upon start-up. You have to pull the lever far enough back so that the three internal blade locks engage and hold the prop in flat pitch as the engine winds down. Otherwise, the prop automatically feathers. With a feathered prop, no reverse thrust is possible until the engine finishes spooling up. During spooling, a feathered prop delivers a tiny amount of thrust. Just enough to pull an unsecured floatplane forward. Enough to resist a lineman's frantic pull with the tail line in the other direction.

Feathered prop blades lie at a sharp angle to those in flat pitch—a conspicuous difference, like wing flaps up versus down. On other occasions when the blade locks missed engagement at engine shutdown, I had noticed the obvious discrepancy and adjusted my plans for the subsequent unavailability of reverse thrust at start-up. This time, haste apparently put blinders on my face. Haste must have plugged my ears, too, because a turboprop engine spooling up with a feathered prop sounds different from one starting with the blade locks engaged. Since I often made an intentional feathered-prop shutdown when reverse thrust was not required for getting away from the dock, the feathered start this evening was familiar to the part of my brain that hears. The part that listens, though, was too absorbed in getting away from the dock to interpret that particular sound.

How could I have been so inattentive, so careless, so stupid? I, one of the company's most experienced pilots. This was the first time in my flying career that I had seriously damaged an airplane.

The evening shadows had melted into dusk when the replacement airplane landed. With N90422 securely tied down for the night, the pilot, a handful of remaining passengers (some passengers, now leery of flying, had elected to travel by ferryboat), and I climbed on board. I was a passenger now myself. Not realizing I wanted to hide in back, alone in the dark, the pilot put me in the right-front seat. I felt too humble to protest.

And so I experienced a professional pilot's worst flight.

The next day the company sent mechanics and a new propeller to Victoria Harbour, and by evening we had N90422 in our maintenance shop. Somehow I muddled through the next few weeks, writing reports and recounting the incident to everyone who asked. My mind endlessly replayed the sequence of events, modifying them with if-only wishful thinking. The first time I saw the Victoria lineman again I took him aside and apologized for initially blaming him. "It was one hundred percent my fault," I admitted.

The company decided against formal punishment, knowing that professional pride had already imposed a stiff sentence. At a routine pilots' safety meeting, I passed on the lessons: Never let pressure shortchange caution. Take your time to do things right. Use the damn checklist. No one is immune to screwups.

Many months passed before I was able to awake in the morning and realize that a whole day had passed without thinking about the incident.

Virtually every seaplane pilot occasionally was involved in minor damage to his airplane, usually while on the water. Sometimes a wingtip clipped a piling or a mast, or a float struck an unseen rock or deadhead log. Wind or current was often a factor. So too misjudgment and bad luck. One pilot, intending to run his Cessna 185 onto a ramp for overnight tie-down, used too much power, or the ramp was unusually slick; instead of stopping on the ramp, the airplane shot over the top, across the attached dock, and right into a piling. Many pilots—like me, now—had been at the controls when more serious, expensive damage occurred: capsizing in swells, making a very hard, structure-compromising landing, mismanagement of the engine that required its replacement, and so forth. Such incidents were more frequent in Alaska, but they happened in all seaplane environments.

Some pilots became superstitious about flying a certain airplane after causing damage to it, as if it were prone to problems or had a soul that sought vengeance. As one who never threw spilled salt over his shoulder, I had no qualms about flying N90422 after Victoria, but of course I took extra care in it and every airplane to avoid another incident. I had had a good record beforehand, and I wanted to rebuild it. Like a remorseful dog owner who had carelessly dropped hot coffee on his pet, I felt especially paternalistic about N90422.

The development of a vibration in an airplane is always cause for concern, because it indicates that something is amiss. Vibration that wasn't present before is like new body pain; it has a message. Ever since its overhaul and turboprop conversion, N90422 had been haunted by a mysterious vibration. The mechanics reduced it a bit before the Victoria Harbour incident by experimentally adjusting the ailerons, the flaps, the elevator, the float assembly, and other parts. Everyone hoped the new propeller installed after the damage would eliminate the remaining problem, but N90422 continued a minute trembling. We could feel it in our hands on the yoke, in our feet on the rudder pedals, and in our buttocks on the cockpit seat. It seemed present to some degree in all flight configurations, although it was most noticeable at cruise speed. Yet no passenger back in the cabin ever mentioned a vibration, and mechanics seated there on test flights to evaluate it reported nothing unusual.

The maintenance department thought the problem would not jeopardize airworthiness, so we grudgingly accepted it as inherent, unpleasant idiosyncrasy, like a coworker's persistent bad breath. Mechanics kept trying to track the vibration down during routine maintenance by fine-tuning this and that, and gradually it subsided.

It returned suddenly one chilly October morning fourteen months after the Victoria incident. I had just taken off from Lake Union for Victoria in N90422 with eight passengers, and during the climbout I felt a vibration. In any other airplane, I would have turned around immediately and returned for an inspection. Because this was N90422, I thought: darn, it's back. After leveling off at three thousand feet for cruise, I realized this vibration felt more pronounced than the previous one. It reminded me of the buzzing sensation of an electric toothbrush.

Or maybe it just seemed more pronounced because I had gotten used to its absence.

Sometimes passengers detect a serious airborne problem, such as smoke wafting from the cargo area, before the crew. I glanced at the man in the right front seat beside me. He was gazing at the scenery, apparently unaware of a vibration. In the cabin, the seven other passengers were also nonchalantly looking out the windows or reading. The several who noticed me studying them smiled, as relaxed, unworried passengers are wont to do when they catch the captain's eye. If the vibration was evident back there, it obviously hadn't caused alarm.

N90422's history of vibration tempered my initial concern and invited rationalization. This undoubtedly was just the same old gremlin acting up again, perhaps a bit more mischievously. With the gauges reading normally, the weather good, and the passengers happy, why not continue the flight; Victoria was already discernible on the southwestern tip of Vancouver Island, forty miles away. I could inspect the airplane there and call the maintenance department on the landline to discuss the situation.

But the busybody inside nagged relentlessly. It seemed to whisper: You know damn well this vibration isn't the previous one reawakened. You know it's something different, something new, a raised fist warning you. You really ought to turn around. Complacency isn't going to lessen the seriousness.

So I was dismayed but not totally surprised several minutes later when the fist struck. The airplane suddenly shook viciously for a second, and then pitched down like a roller coaster at the start of a descent. Arms flailed from the right-front seat. Instinctively I knew something on the tail had broken. Regret over not having heeded the busybody's admonishment quickly turned into fear as I realized I could not pull the nose up. The yoke seemed frozen, as if gripped in a vice. We were now over Discovery Bay, at the southeastern edge of the Strait of Juan de Fuca. The nose was pointed at the water and shorelines below.

"Noooo!" I cried aloud at the prospect of an unavoidable crash. In the same instant I yanked back the thrust lever to slow the airspeed buildup. We had been cruising at about 112 knots, and already the airspeed needle had passed the maximum allowable speed of 116 and was sweeping through 120. At what speed would the wings tear off? Painful pressure in my ears attested to a rapid descent.

By now I had both hands on the yoke. "Help me pull!" I ordered the right-seat passenger.

He did not respond; perhaps he hadn't heard. No matter; the yoke was beginning to move! Reducing power had somehow lessened the forward pressure on the yoke. Although the tug-of-war still prevented me from relaxing my grip, I was able now to take one hand off the yoke to spin the elevator trim wheel rearward. Located between the two cockpit seats, the wheel felt loose and sloppy, like a mushy spring, but what play remained removed a bit more pressure on the yoke.

At last we were stabilized, gliding toward the water, for the moment under control again. But for how long? Uncertainty over what had happened counteracted any sense of security. I pulled the boom mike on my headset down to my lips, pushed the transmission button and broadcast an announcement I had never before made. "Mayday! Mayday! Mayday! Four-Two-Two, serious control problem, making emergency landing Discovery Bay."

The dispatcher replied within seconds, asking if I wanted rescue services. We were about a fifteen-minute flight by helicopter from both the Coast Guard Air Station at Port Angeles and the Whidbey Island Naval Air Station. Although our situation was serious, a crash was no longer imminent. And I assumed that with their scanners and other sources, the media would quickly sniff out a rescue operation. I pictured news helicopters hovering over us like mythological harpies, and reporter-photographer teams hounding my passengers and company managers, and the sensationalized, grossly inaccurate news reports that inevitably follow aircraft mishaps.

"Negative on the rescue services," I answered.

A couple of other company pilots heard my mayday call and radioed that they would divert to offer help, if we needed it. I now pulled the microphone for public-address announcements off its hook and turned my head to speak to my passengers in the cabin. Most were clutching seat cushions or seat backs, their faces taut. Magazines, brochures and other contents of the seat back pockets were scattered about on the aisle floor, having been by jerked out in the sharp pitch down. In Alaska, smoking had been allowed in the airplanes, and I thought of the mess cigarette butts and ashes made when sharp turbulence emptied the ashtrays. "Sorry about that sudden drop," I said. "We had a mechanical problem of some kind. We're going to make a precautionary landing, but everything's under control now, so please relax." I realized as I spoke such words of assurance that the microphone was trembling in my hand.

Ground fog that morning had covered broad sections of western Washington, but the water below us was both clear and calm. How far could we have flown had we been over fog or trees instead of open water? When flaring for a landing on a calm surface, the challenge of depth perception normally called for extra power to make a gradual descent. This time, common sense ruled for as much status quo as possible, lest some change in power or configuration upset what might be a precarious balance; at this altitude we could not survive another plummet. I left the power at idle and gingerly pumped the flaps down just enough to prevent an abrupt deceleration when the floats contacted the water.

The airplane landed ungracefully with a thump and a bounce, but we were safely back on the water. I taxied to nearby Sequim Bay as the two company planes appeared overhead. They circled, got reassurance from me on the radio that we were okay, and proceeded on their way. Just after we tied up at the Sequim Bay State Park dock, two other planes arrived to collect my passengers and take them on to Victoria. One of those aircraft brought a mechanic.

Once we were alone, the mechanic and I turned N90422 nose out from the dock so we could check the tail. "Ah, look at that," he said, pointing to the servo tab on the right elevator. The tab deflects as the elevator is moved to help reduce control pressure on the heavy elevator. It lay at an awkward angle, broken. Apparently, the support brackets had begun to fail during or just after takeoff; consequent fluttering of the unit caused the vibration I had noticed. Then, above Discovery Bay, the tab broke at an angle that suddenly forced the elevator down and sent the airplane into the dive. Reducing power had lessened airflow over the tail, removing some downward influence.

The mechanic thought he could devise a temporary fix, so I left him to his work and went strolling along the state park's trails. Life seems especially precious after it's almost lost. I plucked a late-season salmonberry off a bush to nibble on and savored the musty, dank, smell of the woods. The raucous call of a raven sounded musical. Sunlight filtered through the forest canopy like spotlights.

After a while, I began contemplating the what-ifs: Had the servo tab panel jammed while we were at low altitude after takeoff from Seattle, we would not have had time to recover and would have dove right into the water, or a boat, or a bridge, or whatever had been beneath us. Such a fate befell a Canadian Twin Otter. After lifting off from Discovery Channel by the town of Campbell River on Vancouver Island, a sudden elevator-control malfunction sent it nose first into the water. No passengers were aboard, but both pilots died. Similarly, if I had decided to return to Seattle after realizing the vibration was unusual, the servo tab might have let go while we were preparing to land; we could have been at three hundred feet instead of three thousand.

The sudden, fatal plunges of several airliners because of failures in the tail section, both before and after the N90422 incident, suggested how fortunate we had been: United Airlines Flight 585, a Boeing 737, en route from Denver to Colorado Springs, March 3, 1991; USAir Flight 427, a Boeing 737, approaching Pittsburgh from Chicago, September 8, 1994; Alaska Airlines Flight 261, a McDonnell Douglas MD-83, off the coast of California, January 31, 2000; and American Airlines Flight 587, an Airbus A300, after departing New York for the Dominican Republic, November 12, 2001. These crashes killed all aboard, more than five hundred people (the American Airlines tragedy also killed five on the ground). Investigations resulted in both design changes and maintenance procedures to prevent reoccurrences.

And suppose I had been alone up front, with no passengers in the cabin to move the center of gravity rearward? Assuming a conservative weight of 150 pounds per passenger, the seven behind me totaled over 1,000 pounds. That weight certainly helped offset the downward force the broken servo tab imposed. Without it, raising the nose would have been much harder, perhaps impossible.

When I returned to the dock, the mechanic had patched the panel together well enough for a ferry flight back to the base. The Kenmore Air maintenance department discussed the panel failure with aeronautical engineers, federal agencies, and the developer of the Otter's turboprop-conversion kit, reaching a consensus that the servo-tab panel, designed for the original 600-horsepower piston engine, was inadequate for the additional forces the 750-horsepower turboprop engine imposed.

The remedy was a redesigned servo-tab panel, which replaced the old two-piece system with a stronger, one-piece system. More frequent inspections of tails on Turbo Otters tails were also mandated. The measures seemed to work; we had no further problems with tails on either N90422 or the half-dozen other Otters Kenmore subsequently converted to turboprops, all incorporating the servo-tab upgrade. Meanwhile, management had to deal with a lawsuit from a Canadian passenger who claimed the sudden plunge that day hurt her neck. The insurance company paid her off.

Having experienced a couple of dramatic incidents together, N90422 and I bonded in the way man and machine sometimes do. Dispatchers routinely paired us, and other pilots came to speak of N90422 as if I were the owner. "I see the line guys waxed your airplane yesterday," one might say. Official acknowledgment of N90422 and me as a team came when the company personalized select Otters with the names of senior pilots on the left cockpit door, stenciled calligraphy-like in fancy script: *"Capt. Gregg Munro;" "Capt. Tim Brooks;" "Capt. Bill Whitney."* N90422 got my name.

Chapter 17

SEAPLANES IN THE MUD

Seaplane pilots all along the Inside Passage from Seattle to Skagway, and most everywhere else, avoided mud just as pilots of ski-equipped airplanes in the far north avoided bare ground. At tide-sensitive destinations, seaplane pilots planned their arrival to coincide with sufficient water to reach the dock or beach. When pilots got stuck in mud taxiing in a saltwater marsh or estuary, they shut down till incoming water refloated the airplane. That had happened to me twice. What option was there but patience? Revving up the engine enough to blast through the mucky stuff to open water seemed potentially destructive, like repeatedly yanking a shirt snagged on a closet hanger.

Yet for one seaplane company in the Bay Area, operating in mud was as routine as dealing with boat wakes was for us. San Francisco Seaplane Tours (now called Seaplane Adventures under new management), was founded in the mid-1940s as Commodore Seaplanes on shallow Pickleweed Inlet near Sausalito. So shallow was the inlet that even at midtide, herons, egrets, and other long-legged birds could often wade far beyond the dock. At low tide, the mud extended way out to the nearest water channel, almost beyond the reach of a Tiger Woods drive. Dredging was technically possible but expensive, and it would have to be redone periodically. More significantly, in environmentally sensitive California, you might have a better chance of getting official permission to land an ultralight in the Rose Garden.

Most seaplane pilots in the Pacific Northwest had heard of San Francisco Seaplane Tours and its mud, but we dismissed the operation as an oddball, one-of-a-kind phenomenon. Unless we went to work for the company, few of us were ever likely to experience taxiing in mud.

A small percentage of seaplane pilots had dabbled in snow and ice. Mostly private pilots, they typically landed on frozen lakes for access to ice fishing or hunting. A seaplane touching down on sheer ice, of course, had the opposite problem of one taxiing in mud. Without brakes, a floatplane would slide on and on until the relative wind and the minimal friction finally slowed it. Some pilots landing on ice managed to turn the airplane 180 degrees with the rudder pedals and then, going backward, applied bursts of power.

In Alaska, a few pilots over the years had admitted privately to touching down on a snow-covered lake out of bravado, like a warrior counting coup. Usually, they kept the airplane on the step and took off again right away. On larger lakes, those with imagination managed to create S-turns, circles, spirals, figure eights, and other forms. Sometimes a pilot would eyeball the work of a previous pilot, drop down, and add an embellishment, in the way graffiti inspires contributions. From the air, such snow art suggested crude crop circles, and unenlightened passengers would point and wonder how the forms or tracks got there with no telltale entry or exit marks from lake to shore. One pilot claimed to have run down a fleeing wolf on a snowy lake, killing it with the bow of a pontoon. He shut down, stepped out, skinned the animal for the pelt, abandoned the rest of the carcass, and took off, he said.

Landing on a snow-covered lake was risky. Certain light conditions could mask snowbanks and low islets until it was too late to turn away, and a rock might lie just inches beneath the snow. One of Kenmore Air's instructors had taken a student to a snow-covered lake in the Cascades Mountains, intending to show off with a—completely unauthorized—touch-and-go. The mid-April snow was heavy and sticky, and as soon as the keels of the pontoons touched, friction slowed the little Cessna 172 to below takeoff speed; the instructor applied full power, but the airplane had become a fly on molasses. After it floundered on futilely for fifty yards or so, the instructor aborted, and the pontoons promptly sank into the mush.

Luckily, the instructor was able to radio for help, and Kenmore sent a helicopter to rescue him and the student. The 172 had to be left for a couple of weeks until the spring sun opened enough of the lake for a takeoff.

Landing on snow had long appealed to both my sense of adventure and my desire to experience a wide range of seaplane flying. I had landed on rivers, mountain lakes, the open ocean, and all types of inland saltwater bodies. Omitting snow from the list when other pilots had set an intriguing precedent was like leaving an oddball peak unsummited to a mountaineer.

On many flights in Alaska, good weather, a slow schedule, fresh powder on a frozen lake, and the absence of tattletales on board had presented a perfect opportunity. Yet as a professional pilot entrusted with an expensive floatplane, I had declined every temptation.

So a chance to get into the mud down in California at my employer's request was a serendipitous consolation. In 2002, San Francisco Seaplane Tours, which had downsized in the stricter regulatory environment after 9/11, entered into an operating agreement with Kenmore Air for the lease of aircraft and the occasional loan of a pilot. I was the third Kenmore pilot to do a stint under this arrangement.

Early on, the California pilots here removed rocks and discarded junk from the operating area. Then they discovered that taxiing indiscriminately through the mud created a maze of crisscrossing tracks, which caused an airplane to lurch and sway as it moved through intercepting, one-foot-deep tracks. To give themselves smoother lanes to follow, the pilots began restricting their taxiing, as much as possible, to a couple of routes to form uninterrupted tracks.

The main route led from the water channel to the south side of the dock and continued in a wide loop back to the channel. A pilot would taxi from the channel into those tracks to the dock, where he would shut down to let off one group of passengers and take on another. After restarting, he would taxi straight ahead in the same tracks as they swept back toward the open water.

The other, secondary route connected the channel with the north side of the dock, dead-ending there at a pullout ramp. A pilot would use this route to park the airplane on the ramp for the night or for maintenance. Because the north side faced the ramp and other structures, an airplane docked there had to be turned 180 degrees to depart. If the south side was already occupied by another airplane, a pilot could taxi in through the mud to the north side, as long as the tide would be high enough for a spin-around by the next flight; you'd need a crane to turn a stationary seaplane in mud.

An airplane could be secured for hours or overnight on the south side of the dock regardless of the tide, because the lack of obstacles there eliminated the need to be turned.

Initially, I assumed that operating in mud would be kid's play. After all, the Federal Aviation Administration required no rating for mud, so how difficult could it be? For my mud checkout Charlie Clotere, a silver-haired pilot and mechanic who had been with San Francisco Seaplane Tours for thirty years, sat in the right-front seat of the Beaver, which was aground at the dock in the main tracks. Clotere insisted that the engine be warmed before taxiing—an indication that operating in mud might be more involved than I thought. Apparently you didn't just start the engine and go, as in water.

When the temperature needles reached the green arcs, I nudged the throttle. No movement. More throttle. Nothing. Still more. Nothing. Had I forgotten to untie a line? I had the yoke all the way back in my lap now, and the 450-horsepower engine was thundering enough to enter a plowing attitude if on water. Yet we seemed to be encased in concrete.

"It takes a lot of power to get going," Clotere said with an amused smile. "Give it a burst." That broke us free from the muck and, like a recalcitrant ox yielding to increasingly stiff kicks in the butt, the Beaver finally began lumbering forward.

It accelerated more quickly than I expected. "Slow her down or we'll jump the tracks," Clotere said as the airplane starting wallowing and fishtailing as if drunk. I throttled back too much, stopping both the wallowing and the airplane.

After a few more lurching stops and starts, I found the right power setting to keep us moving with a minimum of wallowing.

I had instinctively extended the water rudders to steer, but Clotere told me to retract them. At the correct speed, he said, the floats normally followed the tracks just fine by themselves, like a locomotive on rails. No help from the water rudder was needed. Also instinctively, I held the yoke back, as I would while slogging through sloppy water. Another unnecessary procedure, Clotere said. While a nose-up attitude helped the airplane break free from a stationary position in mud, it could be counterproductive once underway because it increased the chances of jumping the tracks, especially in a crosswind.

So I left the rudder pedals and yoke alone, adjusting only the throttle to maintain the proper speed. Outside, displaced mud was spurting from beneath the floats. Occasionally a brown droplet got caught in the prop wash and splattered on the windshield. Muddy water squeezed out by the floats was also retreating in each track ahead of us in a continuous roiling stream.

As we approached the channel, deepening inlet water gradually filled the tracks. The reduced friction let me throttle back, although I could still feel the unseen mud's tug on the keels. Here and there, the Beaver careened as we moved over a ridge or through a depression in the mud.

I assumed we would keep taxiing for takeoff until the Beaver was out of the mud completely and floating, but now Clotere pointed toward San Francisco beyond the inlet to the right. "That's good enough, let's go," he said. For a moment after applying takeoff power, during the plowing stage, I could tell that the heels of the floats were dragging in the mud. Then the keels were out of the mud on the step, and we quickly became airborne.

In addition to offering sightseeing flights and charters from its Pickleweed Inlet location, San Francisco Seaplane Tours maintained a kiosk on the other side of the Golden Gate Bridge on famous Pier 39 at the downtown San Francisco waterfront. There, an employee handed out brochures and signed up tourists for a tour. Huge swells from ferries and other boats on San Francisco Bay jarred airframe and backbone on every takeoff and landing, but a perpetually strong ocean wind kept water runs to a minimum. The tours included flybys of Alcatraz Island, Angel Island (site of a major twentieth-century immigration facility, now a state park), the Golden Gate Bridge, Muir Woods, a section of coastline, and downtown. Although I was as new to the Bay Area as the passengers, I had boned up on the local history and attractions, and I managed to bluff my way through narration and questions over the headsets.

After several tours, we returned to Pickleweed Inlet and landed in the channel. The tide had since advanced almost to the dock, bringing enough water to cover and conceal the tracks but not enough to float the airplane. "This can be a little tricky," Clotere warned me.

When a pilot couldn't see the tracks while taxiing into increasingly shallow water, he had to feel his way into them. The problem was inadvertently getting one pontoon in a track and the other out. Depending on whether the tracking pontoon was in the outside or the inside track, the airplane ended up either too far from the dock to unload the passengers, or nose up against it. The solution in the first instance was to go around and try again for a proper, two-track approach. In the second, though, the airplane was stuck until the tide was high enough to maneuver it by hand. If the tide were receding, the flying might be over for the rest of the day. The inside track was desirable in dating and investing. Not here.

Why fret about getting into the darn tracks at all? Couldn't the airplane just plow its way to the dock through the mud regardless of the tracks? Clotere explained that the resulting multiple ruts would interfere with docking in the way uneven snowdrifts at curbside complicated parallel parking.

With his long experience, Clotere didn't have to see the tracks to know where they lay; he verbally guided me into them. For solo outings, when I would have to find them by myself, I tried to memorize the relative positions of the dock, pilings, boat houses, and other nearby landmarks.

"Now let me show you what a one-track approach feels like," he said, taking the controls, "so you can recognize the situation and get out of it in time." He pulled back on the yoke, stomped on the left rudder pedal, and shoved the throttle for a quick burst. The Beaver lurched with a roar and staggered for a moment, like a startled beast knocked off balance. Then it settled back into a taxi with the right wing slightly low.

"There, the right float's in the left track and the left float's out altogether," Clotere said. To get us back on track, so to speak, he repeated the process, stomping on the right pedal. "Okay, your turn.".

The Beaver was ready for me. It seemed to brace itself against my rudder stomping and throttle shoving so that it merely skidded up the sides of the tracks, then slid stubbornly right back down. We continued past the dock and back out into the inlet, where I would have space to try again.

After two additional repulses from the Beaver, I decided I should be more aggressive. Instead of a burst of power, I gave the engine a sustained blast. This time the Beaver climbed out, plowed across the target track with both floats, and was practically on the step when I yanked the throttle.

"Whoa, whoa, whoa!" Charlie yelled.

As with the taxiing, experimentation brought the right touch, and at last I coaxed the Beaver into one track and then back into two.

"If you get in trouble," Charlie said, "Putting the rudders down will help you turn, but I hate to do that 'cause it's hard on the blades. Okay, let's call it a day."

Because of the extra power needed to taxi through mud, we let the engine idle at the dock to cool before shutting down. No worry about clambering out to tie up; sitting in mud at mere idle power, the Beaver wasn't going anywhere. In fact, you don't really have to tie up in the sticky stuff at all, although everyone does, even if the next flight is right after a pit stop. Tying up is just something seaplane pilots do. Besides, you don't want to get into bad habits. The next flight might be cancelled while you're up in the office on the pit stop; you could plop into an armchair with a magazine, forgetting that the airplane is unsecured down at the dock and the tide is coming in.

On my own, I came and went for a week without incident. Tides on inbound taxis were mercifully low enough to expose the tracks or high enough to render them inconsequential. I even managed to maneuver the airplane into both unseen tracks the first time I returned from a flight to encounter a midtide.

The second time in such a condition, with a load of passengers, I thought at first I had again successfully settled into both tracks. At least, the landmarks were in the expected relative positions and the Beaver appeared to heading right for dockside. Then, when we were about forty yards out, the office manager, who had come down to greet the passengers, began to gesture frantically, as in, "Go that way, go that way!"

I realized the outside float was in the dreaded inside track; we were going to nose in. A frantic burst of power with full rudder and aft yoke was not enough; the Beaver lurched but slid back into the single track. Water rudders down. Another quick burst. Come on, come on, turn. Still in the same track. Not enough room now for another attempt. We were stuck.

The nose of the Beaver was five feet or so from the dock, facing in. I dared not risk inching closer with power lest a surge of movement carry the airplane into the dock, so after letting it cool, I shut down the engine. The office manager scrounged a board from a nearby shed and gave me one end to place on the bow of the float. Eyeing the gooey mud, the passenger stepped gingerly across the board to the dock.

"See, we make you walk the plank around here," I quipped, trying to mask my chagrin. I dutifully tied the Beaver to the dock, and then sauntered up to the hangar.

"We've all gotten stuck—every one of us," Clotere told me. "Remember, nose down to stay in the tracks, nose up to move from one track into both."

But at midtide, the pontoons moving through unseen mud, I was often unsure whether we had engaged both tracks, one, or neither. The Beaver was constantly making confusing little movements as it bore through the mud. Like a student pilot unable to differentiate between a slip and a skid in the air, I couldn't tell a wiggle from a waggle in mud unless the tracks were exposed.

I'd taxi from the channel toward the dock, the water would become shallower, and suddenly I'd feel the slimy ogre below grab the keels. Where was he placing them? Without visual feedback, I sometimes misinterpreted the cues and held the yoke against one stop when it should have been against the other.

After my passengers had to walk the plank again a week later, Clotere took me out for some remedial training. This time he stuck a flexible plastic pole deep in the mud (positioned low enough to avoid a prop strike) on either side of the main tracks about thirty yards from the dock to serve as markers.

The poles helped while I honed the seat of my pants. Over the next couple of years I returned for three more stints, one of them lasting twelve weeks. It never reached the point of child's play, but taxiing in mud became comfortable, even fun. Soon, following the tracks around the arc from the dock, I was finding time to wave at the joggers and bicyclists who paused to gawk from the sidewalk by Highway 101 near San Francisco Seaplane's facilities. Under my breath, I'd say, "Here's mud in your eye."

Chapter 18

CHASING RAINBOWS

Statistically, the driest period in the Pacific Northwest ran from late July to early August. The calendar then brimmed with weddings, picnics, and gala events such as Seattle's Seafair weekend, which featured professional hydroplane races on Lake Washington and aerobatic performances above it by the Navy's Blue Angels.

One year, though, midsummer lapsed briefly into March-like conditions. Rain fell in Seattle on July 28 for the first time since 1899, and cool temperatures during the second half of July dropped the average temperature for the entire month two and a half degrees below the normal 65.2. Along the Inside Passage in the last blustery week of the month, yachters crowded into marinas like refugees, waiting for calmer seas so they could resume their vacation outings. All that week we seaplane pilots had cinched our seat belts a little tighter against the turbulence and pulled on our rain caps before stepping from the cockpit onto the slick docks.

Now, flying back to Seattle on a Sunday evening, I was not surprised to see that a large, dark shower had moved across our route, another in a series that had been sweeping through the region all day. One of the ten passengers on board the Otter was Michael Medved, a conservative commentator who hosted a daily, nationally broadcast radio show. He also wrote essays for several major publications, including *USA Today*. Medved and his family were returning from a weekend in Victoria. While I tried to avoid favoritism among passengers, I was particularly eager to impress journalists; an enjoyable flight might bring a positive mention of the company on air or in print.

So far the air had been smooth and dry. But unpleasantness loomed in that ugly shower ahead—heavy rain for sure, possibly some turbulence. It stretched from the bottom of Hood Canal on our right across Admiralty Inlet to Whidbey Island on the left, a wall too wide to skirt. For a moment I considered cautioning the passengers about the shower over the public-address system, then decided against it as unnecessarily melodramatic. I had already made general mention of showers in the area during the preflight briefing; why generate apprehension when the shower might be relatively benign and last only a couple of minutes?

Soon scattered raindrops began striking the windshield, streaking through the air like tracer bullets as they flaked off the shower's fringe. Fortunately, the air remained smooth. I was thinking that conditions were ideal for a rainbow—the Otter between sun and rain, the sun at an angle in the early evening sky—when the first splotch of color appeared against the clouds. In a moment it grew into a brilliant arc. An announcement was merited, after all.

"Excuse me, folks, but if you haven't already noticed, there's a rainbow off the left side." As always after using the public-address system, I glanced over my shoulder around the cockpit bulkhead to make sure the passengers' expressions indicated they had heard and understood my words over the tinny cabin speaker. Medved, sitting on the forward left, and the other passengers had turned toward the rainbow. Several smiled or grinned.

Although rain was drumming steadily on the windshield now, we hadn't yet penetrated the shower deeply enough to leave the sunlight behind, and the rainbow continued to evolve, like a peacock unfolding its plumage. The heavier the rain, the brighter and fuller the rainbow. A dimmer, secondary bow now formed outside the primary one with color bands in reverse order and a shaded area—"Alexander's dark band"—between them. Then—a brilliant, spectacular near-circle, only the bottom segment blocked from view by the fuselage.

Even the familiar, standard rainbow was a universal delight, like a laughing child. But a magical circular rainbow! I had seen just fifteen or twenty in two decades of flying seaplanes. A sunset watcher glimpsing the fabled, elusive green flash wore the same smile I now had. "Ladies and gentlemen," Medved would say to his radio audience, "before we begin today's program I want to tell you about the most incredibly awesome rainbow I saw the other day. My family and I were on a floatplane. . . ." I turned around again to further bond with my passengers in this almost sacred moment.

Medved was reading. So were several other passengers. One or two were napping. Only a couple still gazed at the rainbow, which had lost none of its dazzle. One of them held a camera to her seat window. Surprise at the general lapsed interest stung me with a sort of personal indignation, as if friends had yawned at my recitation of a favorite poem. How could Medved and most of his fellow travelers content themselves with a cursory look at such a spectacle? I imagined them dismissing the Mona Lisa with a glance.

The colors began dimming as we entered the heart of the shower, and soon they faded away. Now you've lost your chance, I mumbled.

Although I noticed some of them doing it every day, passengers ignoring the scenery always surprised me. Unless fatigued or preoccupied with an aviation chore, I never tired of sightseeing, even on routes I had flown hundreds of times. Out the cockpit windows—just as out the cabin windows—the vista unfolded in endless vignettes and details that looked subtly or dramatically altered on every flight, like a vast mural an artist was continually retouching. A mountain valley's mood in sunshine yesterday was palpably different in foggy scud today. A channel wore a serene expression when calm, an agitated one in whitecaps. A reef, gnarly and brown and slimy from kelp at low tide, had disappeared when you flew by again hours later. Spot a troller here, a cruise ship there; farther on, a skiff, an oil tanker, and a yacht with billowing sails. There—a bald eagle gliding by, a deer browsing in a glen, a pod of orcas breaching.

You could be cruising under a dreary overcast when a yellow shaft suddenly punched through like a spotlight, conferring temporary importance to an ordinarily unremarkable stand of woods or patch of water. The winter rays, low in the sky, often etched the cloud tops in gold. Sometimes the sun broke the early morning stratus into puffs that gradually rose and billowed into grand cumulus columns. From above, the columns recalled a mass ascension of hot-air balloons. But descend amid them and you were weaving through a city of scruffy skyscrapers suspended beneath a brilliant blue canopy. Follow this street, turn down that alley, brush a wingtip against a wispy wall. Pegasus at play.

Like an evangelical, I automatically and unrealistically assumed all passengers shared my zeal for sightseeing. Many did, of course; often I could hear the "oohs" and "ahs" back in the cabin above the roar of the engine. When others showed little interest, I had to keep reminding myself that for many passengers—those who failed to see the light—a seaplane flight was little more than transportation.

Early morning at Kenmore Air was a busy time: groups of passengers gathering with their luggage at assigned picnic tables outside the terminal building; other passengers lined up inside to check in; aircraft engines warming up at dockside; linemen scampering about with fuel hoses and bottles of window cleaner; pilots preflighting their machines; late-arriving cars pulling into the parking area, and the occasional blaring of the public-address system, asking so-and-so to come to the reservations counter. For all but the most burned-out pilots, the bustle intensified a desire to get going, to see what the day would bring. How had the artist altered the mural from her palette of light, shadow, visibility, precipitation, wind, cloud, and other elements? What discoveries, challenges, and experiences would the new day bring?

It was this promise of a daily treasure hunt that made seaplane flying so appealing. The actual sensation of flight contributed little to the lure, at least for a professional pilot; going aloft day after day inured the senses to the thrill, just as driving seventy-five on the freeway seemed fast only the first few times. In the air, a seaplane was inherently no more exciting than a wheelplane. But a seaplane's greater versatility exposed more treasure: the world of sea as well as air. On a typical summer morning, take off from Seattle beneath a widespread blanket of stratus that restricts the airplane to five hundred feet. Weave along shorelines and islands up the Inside Passage low enough to spot seals and glance at drift-wood. By early afternoon, your rounds completed, the sun has finally burned away the clouds. Climb to seventy-five hundred feet for the long flight home. Cruise down the center of Vancouver Island, high enough to gaze at mile after mile of jagged peaks and glaciated valleys and frozen alpine ponds.

A pilot indifferent to such diversified sightseeing would be unlikely to stick with seaplane flying. Although it seemed incredible that anyone could be indifferent, I had periodic reminders that to others, some of my disinterests were just as incredible. Before satellite radio and the Internet made news universally available, I would occasionally dock at an isolated camp to be confronted by an excited passenger who would clutch my arm and ask for the score between two professional sports teams that had played during his stay. When I admitted ignorance not only of the results but even of the sport in question, his expression substituted for a comment. I saw the same expression on the face of a college-age reservationist one day after a question. I had just walked into the terminal, and the glum-looking woman told me that Kurt Cobain (lead singer and guitarist for the grunge rock band Nirvana) had killed himself two hours earlier.

"Who's Kurt Cobain?"

In the case of the frustrated sports fan, I would radio the company dispatcher or another pilot en route, get the information, and pass a note to him.

Even before a flight, a pilot could usually predict which of his passengers would be the rainbow gawkers. Some indications: those who asked questions, carried a camera, glanced around at docked airplanes, and had a gleam in their eyes. Once in a while, coincidence brought together a planeload of people who acted as if they had come straight from a motivational seminar. Strangers upon boarding, they would introduce themselves to one another before takeoff. In the air, they looked out the windows continuously, taking photos, pointing, grinning, perhaps even joining in spontaneous cheers and applause at an exciting sight, such as several orcas breaking water simultaneously. A pilot could not help appreciating their attitude and might even extend the flight a bit to circle this or that. At the destination, he might shake each passenger's hand as he stepped onto the dock, like a pastor saying good-bye to parishioners at the church doors after the service. Thanks for the dynamic chemistry. Thanks for being kindred spirits.

Passengers likely to find more interest in a paperback than the flight could also reveal themselves before takeoff.

"You got laid off from the airlines and have to fly these things now, huh?" a man in the right-front seat once asked me as we taxied out for takeoff. His assumption apparently was that a commercial pilot would fly seaplanes for a living only by default, like a baseball player signing on with a minor league team because he had gotten bumped from the majors. During the flight I pointed out some of the sights to him, hoping to inspire an epiphany, but he remained unimpressed.

On hectic, stressful days that temporarily suppressed all enthusiasm, I too questioned my presence in "these things." Out would come the old familiar self-recriminations: A few years of full-time bush flying should have been enough. Why decades? You should have made better use of your education. Nostalgia for the cockpit could have been satisfied with part-time flying. Now you're well into middle age and it's too late for a meaningful career outside the cockpit.

I was in such a funk on an overcast, blustery morning in March, heading to Victoria Harbour with five passengers. We had taken off from Lake Union in a Beaver seven or eight minutes earlier and just crossed Puget Sound, still in a climb, when a slight drop in power interrupted my musings. The change was too subtle for passengers to notice, but to a pilot it was a warning, like an unidentified noise in the night that causes you to listen intently in the darkened bedroom. In normal operation, without input from the pilot, airplane engines change power gradually, for example, as altitude increases. A sudden drop, even a slight one, signaled possible trouble.

The engine instruments showed normal indications, and the throttle felt tight and firm—no slippage. An impurity in the fuel moving through the engine would have caused just a momentary blip, not this lingering power drop. The Pratt & Whitney R-985 450-horsepower radial was not particularly susceptible to carburetor icing, especially with the heat of climb power. To double-check, I pushed the carburetor-temperature lever down to full heat, waited a moment, then pulled it back up. No ice. Had a magneto gone bad?

I glanced over my shoulder at the Seattle skyline, still visible in light rain about five miles behind us. Ahead, the weather was dreary, showery, breezy, but not a factor. Turning around for a plane change would make the passengers at least an hour late getting to Victoria, and of course, the passengers waiting there for Seattle would be equally late. Federal law and company policy required action upon any overt malfunction. But here, no overt malfunction had occurred—just an alert. Something or nothing? Get up and investigate the noise in the night or roll over and go back to sleep? It was a gray-area judgment call.

Less than a minute had elapsed since the strange little power drop, and I was still debating whether to continue when the engine suddenly faltered. Blue smoke began streaming from the cowling. The young woman in the right-front seat flinched, and from behind someone bumped my shoulder as he grabbed the top of my seat.

I pulled the throttle back to idle, and through quick experimentation found that only partial, rough power was available. Trying to return to Seattle now against a stiff headwind would be like asking a sick man to climb a mountain. I considered limping on to the marina complex at Port Ludlow, ten miles ahead, the nearest settlement with facilities and sheltered water. But to get there we would have to cross exposed portions of Hood Canal and Admiralty Inlet— and the thickening stream of smoke rendered even that distance a doubtful stretch. We had almost reached Port Gamble, the only decent water within gliding distance. Better go for the sure thing.

I turned my head and told the passengers we were going to land because of the engine problem, that everything would be okay. My radio call to the dispatcher was more dramatic: "Mayday!" I said, fearing the engine was on fire. I announced my intention to land on Port Gamble but ignored the dispatcher's follow-up questions as I concentrated on choosing some place to dock or beach. The most conspicuous spot was a small, offshore fish hatchery, about a hundred feet square with a walkway around the perimeter. I would have preferred a shoreline sanctuary, but a Beaver comes down fast with minimal power, and I had to make a hasty commitment. I decided to keep the engine running despite the fire risk. Shutting down would give us just one chance at docking, since the engine probably wouldn't restart and the wind was too strong to paddle us in. If my timing was off we would end up drifting with an engine fire.

As I banked to land into the wind, smoke wafted inside the cockpit, its acrid odor making me frantic to get the passengers and myself out. I had intended to dock at the hatchery the moment the airplane fell off the step. My landing was right on, but I underestimated the force of the wind and could not turn toward the structure with sufficient angle before forward speed carried us beyond. The wind made the 360-degree taxi back into position maddeningly wide.

As the Beaver finally neared the hatchery again, I noticed thick, rusty cables and ugly bolts protruding from the platform at waterline. Too late now to worry about possible damage to the pontoon. I nosed into the least congested section, turned off the engine, and scrambled out.

With great relief, I saw no flames. Oil was covering the pontoons, spreader bars, and lower fuselage; the smoke apparently had resulted from leaking oil contacting the hot engine. Luckily, none of the oil had splattered the windshield; it had been hard enough to see through the smoke. My concern now was securing the airplane—my feet were slipping on the slick wooden walkway as I played tug-of-war with the wind, trying to wrap the mooring line around one of the cables. I called to the passengers for help, and two Canadian teenage boys emerged. The three of us finally got the Beaver tight against the hatchery walkway.

Then I checked on the other passengers, who were already bantering with the camaraderie that arises after sharing a scary experience. All five chose to wait in the cabin, despite the lingering smoke, out of the rain and wind.

Back on the walkway, I used my cell phone to call the company and report that we were safely down. Two aircraft, the dispatcher said, would fly to us: one to pick up the passengers and take them on their way to Victoria, the other with mechanics and a couple of management supervisors. In preparation for briefing the mechanics, I checked the oil dipstick. Empty.

Free now from further immediate responsibilities, I remained outside to absorb the emotions that always follow an emergency landing. Foremost, of course, was gratitude for the altitude and geographical luck that allowed a successful outcome. We might easily have been over trees or the open, roiling Strait of Juan de Fuca, forced by weather to cruise at an altitude that would have left limited maneuvering room.

And how quickly it had all happened. One moment we were at twenty-seven hundred feet; the next, it seemed, we were on the water at the hatchery.

The dispatcher had notified emergency services after my mayday transmission. He tried to cancel the calls after hearing back from me by cell phone, but emergency-services personnel are trained to respond immediately. For the last few minutes, a couple of fire engines had been parked on a street close to the north shoreline about three hundred yards away, rotating red lights flashing, firefighters standing alongside staring at us, as if wondering how to come to our aid.

Now, even before our own support planes arrived, I heard the *whomp-whomp-whomp* of an approaching helicopter. It was an Aerospatiale HH65B from the Coast Guard air station at Port Angeles. As the orange chopper with the distinctive white stripe descended and began circling a few hundred feet above, I gave the crew a firm, prolonged thumbs-up sign. After a few moments, the chopper *whomp-whomp-whomped* away. Soon, the fire engines also left.

The sound of aircraft engines signaled the arrival of the company planes, a Beaver and an Otter. They circled a couple of times, then landed. Docking space was limited, so the Beaver came in first, on the opposite side of the hatchery. The pilot and I helped my passengers down the slippery, oil-coated steps and pontoon of the disabled Beaver onto the walkway and escorted them across to the transfer Beaver.

When that plane had taxied off, the waiting Otter docked. The two mechanics were unable to tell from a visual inspection what had happened to my Beaver, but one of them invited me to try to move the prop. I couldn't. The blade I grasped seemed to be set in concrete. Its oil supply depleted, the engine had seized once it cooled.

Meanwhile, a Coast Guard utility boat had tied up to the hatchery. I gave one of the crewmen a statement about the incident. Another boat joined us, this one an outboard belonging to a representative of the Port Gamble Reservation. The operator agreed to tow the Beaver to a tiny but more sheltered marina at the mouth of the bay. In the cockpit during the tow, I helped steer with the water rudders.

By now, my shoes and trousers were soaked from rain and oil; the warm, dry Otter cabin during the ride back to base felt like a massage after a long hike. That afternoon, the local media began reporting that one of our planes had "made a precautionary landing at Port Gamble after the pilot observed an oil leak." Well, not quite. Apparently, the media got the story from a muddled Coast Guard report. No member of the press contacted us for the facts.

But the company did hear from several government agencies concerned about oil contamination of Port Gamble. We assured each caller that most of the oil had been consumed by the exhaust system or sprayed into the air prior to landing, that the oil tank was empty at the hatchery and that the oil on the Beaver was too gooey and viscous for much to have dripped into the water. In fact, gobs of oil were still clinging to the pontoons when we flew two linemen to the Port Gamble marina with stacks of cleanup towels. We also emphasized that whatever contamination did occur resulted from an emergency situation beyond our control. Nevertheless, at least one agency, the state Department of Ecology, vowed a fine. Not one of the callers asked if anyone had been hurt in the incident.

The next day a barge the company hired brought the Beaver from Port Gamble around Foulweather Bluff, across Puget Sound, and through the locks at Seattle's Ship Canal to our base at Lake Washington. Mechanics disassembled the engine and found that bearings at the back of the engine had come apart, causing a chain reaction that included the separation of the supercharger, a crack in the rear case, and the implosion of the oil tank. The early stages of this process, the mechanics speculated, caused the slight drop in power I had noticed. It was a rare type of failure, they said, caused neither by maintenance neglect nor pilot abuse. Murphy's Law. Just one of those things.

Somehow, the incident cured me of my dispirit. Every occupation produced periods of stress and moments of levity, but few I knew of involved the extremes of flying seaplanes. Emergency landings and circular rainbows. What would tomorrow bring? I'd have to be in the cockpit to find out.

ABOUT THE AUTHOR

Gerry Bruder amassed about twenty-four thousand hours as a commercial sea-plane pilot in Southeast Alaska and the Pacific Northwest. He has also worked as a journalist for several newspapers and magazines. He has a bachelor of arts degree from Hanover College in Hanover, Indiana, and a master of arts degree from Ohio State University. His previous books include *Northern Flights* (Pruett Publishing Co.) and *Heroes of the Horizon* (Alaska Northwest Books). A native of Connecticut, Bruder now lives most of the year in southern Arizona.